The Meaning of Conservatism

Other Roger Scruton Books from St. Augustine's Press

The Aesthetic Understanding:
Essays in the Philosophy of Art and Culture

Art and Imagination:
A Study of the Philosophy of Mind

An Intelligent Person's Guide to Modern Culture

Philosopher on Dover Beach:
Essays

The Politics of Culture and Other Essays

On Hunting

Perictione in Colophon

Xanthippic Dialogues

The Meaning of Conservatism
Revised 3rd edition

Roger Scruton

St. Augustine's Press
South Bend, Indiana

2 3 4 5 6   21 20 19 18 17 16 15

Library of Congress Cataloging in Publication Data
Scruton, Roger.
The meaning of conservatism / Roger Scruton. – Rev.
3rd ed.
p. m.
Includes index.
ISBN 1-890318-40-X
1. Conservatism. I. Title.
JC573 .S27 2001
320.52 – dc21   2001002444

paperbound edition ISBN: 978-1-58731-503-9

∞ The paper used in this publication meets the minimum requirements
of the American National Standard for Information Sciences Permanence
of Paper for Printed Materials, ANSI Z39.481984.

ST. AUGUSTINE'S PRESS
www.staugustine.net

Contents

Preface to the Third Edition

The original version of this book was written twenty years ago, during the last months of a Labour administration. It was a young man's book, a response to events that are now all but forgotten. I had witnessed the student revolution in Paris, had lived through its effects in the universities where I studied and taught, and had rebelled against the prevailing ethos of rebellion. When the request came to write a book on conservatism, it was at a time when the Conservative Party was preparing to fight an election as the champion of freedom. Uppermost in my mind was the freedom that had been displayed on the barricades in Paris. The experience had convinced me, first that I was a conservative, and secondly that conservatism is not about freedom, but about authority, and that in any case freedom divorced from authority is of no use to anyone – not even to the one who possesses it. At the time my thoughts sounded harsh and uncompromising. In reworking the text from a new perspective, I have tried to retain the sense of what I wrote, while moderating the language.

My purpose was to express the root ideas of a conservative ideology, not because I hoped to convince anyone, but because it seemed to me that the conservative outlook was as much misunderstood by those who sought to defend it, as by those who imagined that it had been finally consigned to the 'dust-heap of history'. I sought to distinguish conservatism from economic liberalism and also to counter the Conservative Party's emphasis on free markets and economic growth. Conservatism, as I describe it, involves the attempt to perpetuate a social organism, through times of unprecedented change. Organisms can be cured by growth; but they can also be killed by it. And that, briefly, is what we are now witnessing, not in England only, but throughout the Western hemisphere.

A defender of the conservative position is always assumed to bear the onus of proof. Twenty years ago the argument of this book was greeted with derision by its socialist and liberal readers. In truth, however, it is not conservatives who bear the onus, since they defend the virtues of what is actual, and may, in the last analysis, point to what they mean. It is nevertheless necessary to emphasize that this work is an exercise in doctrine; it attempts not to prove a political vision, but to express it. The aim is to find the concepts and beliefs with which to articulate in modern terms an outlook that is too sober and serious to be merely modern.

Since the book was written, momentous events have changed the language of public debate. There occurred in Poland the first genuine working-class revolution in history. It was a revolution against socialism, against the planned economy, against atheism, propaganda and party government; a revolution in favour of patriotism, of a redeemed tradition and a rediscovered history, in favour of private property, autonomous institutions, religious principle, judicial independence and a rule of law. In short, it was a movement in the direction recommended at the time by conservatives.

There was the war in the South Atlantic, fought for no other reason than traditional allegiance, which nevertheless proved stronger than all the pettifogging hesitancies of diplomacy.

There was the collapse of the Soviet Empire, and the near-universal acknowledgement not merely that communism is unsustainable, but that it could be imposed only by unacceptable force.

The Polish experience showed more vividly than any argument, just how far every conceivable question of history and politics has been begged in favour of the socialist perspective; the Falklands war showed the reality, durability and efficacy of patriotism as the foundation of political unity; the collapse of communism brought with it a massive shift of attitude on the left. Instead of attacking global capitalism, the Labour Party became its most devoted defender, promoting the 'global' economy against the last vestiges of national resistance, and sneering at the reactionaries and 'Little Englanders' who were prepared to sacrifice a promise of yet more economic growth for the proven benefits of national sovereignty, local traditions and the common law.

Perhaps, in the wake of such events, this book might be read more sympathetically. Nevertheless, I have added a philosophical appendix, in which I try to show that there really is a philosophical basis for the doctrine that I offer, and that the liberal attempt to shift the onus of proof permanently on to the conservative cannot succeed. As I argue, the ultimate philosophical conflict between conservatism and liberalism resides in a clash between the point of view of the observer, and that of the agent. The substance of this book will be better understood, when it is seen that it is expressed, not from the first-person, but from the third-person perspective – the perspective of the anthropologist, concerned for the welfare of a tribe (albeit a tribe which is also his own).

In the body of the text I dealt seriously with socialist ideas, and in particular with Marxism. It should be remembered that at the time – the late Seventies – socialist and Marxist ideas were orthodoxy in our universities, and indeed that it was almost unheard of for anyone openly to dissent from them. My own college – Birkbeck College in the University of London – contained, to my knowledge, two conservatives: myself, and Nunzia (Annunziata), the Neopolitan lady who served behind the counter in the Senior Common Room, and who showed her contempt for the fellow travellers who queued there by plastering her patch of wall with photographs of the Pope. Nunzia was the only person I could really talk to in the university, and it is not surprising, therefore, if this book – my first attempt to write about politics – did not conform to the accepted standards of academic politeness.

In particular, I was deliberately disrespectful towards the ideas of human rights and democracy. My left-wing colleagues were, at the time, paying elaborate lip-service to these ideas (while offering their covert or even overt support to regimes, such as that of the Soviet Union, which defied them). It would have been wiser to join in this lip service, which operated as a kind of password to the exclusive arena of political debate. I therefore take the opportunity to suggest the true grounds of the scepticism that is expressed in the following pages.

The ideas of 'natural rights' and 'natural justice' are by no means the invention of liberal political theory. As I argue in Chapter 4, they arise naturally, out of the day-to-day commerce of rational beings, and any action which is thought to violate a law of justice costs the agent the trust and friendship of his victim. Similarly, a state whose citizens perceive its actions as unjust, sacrifices their allegiance. Hence the idea contains a vital political admonition. But what, in reality, does this admonition amount to? That people are disposed to believe in the existence of natural rights is, of course, an all-important political fact. But that there *are* natural rights, existing objectively and independently of any positive law which might otherwise be held to have created them, is a disputed thesis of philosophy. It cannot be the task of policy to settle an undecided philosophical question. Moreover, conceived in isolation, without reference to some legal tradition, the concept of a natural right is singularly indeterminate, generating now this, now that, set of intuitions about the 'inalienable' moral property of the human individual. Those philosophers (such as Aquinas, Grotius and Locke) who have attempted to build ideas of legitimacy upon a foundation of natural law have disagreed over almost every detail of the resulting political structure. And the latest attempts at the enterprise – those of Robert Nozick and John Rawls – show how far philosophers remain in disagreement, both as to the content of our 'natural rights', and as to the nature of the political system that might secure them. (A reason for this is given in the appendix.) Finally, the European Court of Human Rights issues such a string of contradictory and divisive judgements, that the credibility of this way of arguing ought by now to be in serious doubt.

More importantly, however, we must remind ourselves that a right becomes political reality only with the power that is able to enforce it. Rights without powers are political fictions. Natural rights could only be enforced by the power of civil jurisdiction, which in turn exists in order to uphold the 'positive rights' of a given system of law. The all-important political task is therefore to erect such a legal system, and to guarantee that the state will yield to it in any conflict. It is only on the assumption that we can succeed at this task that it makes sense to constrain our politics in obedience to natural law. The essential component of such a conservative legal system is judicial independence. A legal system founded in judicial precedent, operated by judges who are truly independent of all interested parties, will have a natural tendency to gravitate towards the 'natural rights' which ordinary people recognize. The true enemy of natural law, I argue, is not the judge, but the politician, and the greatest threat to just dealings between people is the attempt to remake society from above, in conformity with a conception of 'social justice'.

The idea of natural law is an instrument in the all-important battle to divide the private from the public – to mark out a sphere of individual existence, into which the state cannot intrude. Democracy also has been valued as an instrument in that battle, and to the extent that it has been effective, we must favour it. However, democracy is as contested an idea as natural justice, and in assessing our commitment to it, we should always bear in mind that it is not the business of policy to answer the questions of the philosopher – to resolve, for example, the paradoxes of collective choice, or to settle on some criterion of 'genuine democracy' that would meet the exacting requirements of a philosophical theory. Moreover, in advocating a far-ranging principle of government, such as democracy, we should be clear what we hope to achieve. It may be that we esteem democracy not as an end in itself, but as a means to other things which could in principle be achieved without it.

There are three features of conservative government that are rightly valued by the advocates of democracy: constitution, representation and legal opposition. But it is a mistake to think that democratic election is the only means to achieving these conditions, or that the democratization of every institution will always favour them. The beneficial effects of democratic election depend upon the maintenance of institutions with strong hierarchical components, and the corrosive effect of democratization threatens not only these institutions but also the democratic procedure which they sustain. We see this now, in the United Kingdom, as one by one the old constraints on democratically elected politicians are removed, and nothing stands between the Prime Minister and his latest whim except a cabinet appointed and dismissed by himself.

More importantly, we should not let our obsession with democracy blind us to its value. We seek government limited by constitution. We seek representation of the subject in the highest forum of debate. We seek legal opposition, and an active public opinion that will serve as a brake upon power. To the extent that democratic election helps to produce those benefits, we must support it. But we must also balance the benefit of democracy against its cost. It should not be thought that the cost of a system which makes an idol of ignorance and a prophet of the crowd is small.

I have made substantial alterations for this third edition; but I have not tried to indicate the various points at which I no longer agree with the argument. Nor have I removed the extended discussion in Chapters 5 and 6 of the ideas which, when the book was first written, were of such compelling intellectual importance. The text can at least claim this merit, that it does not waste words; and if I have wasted a few in this preface, it is so that the reader will not have to supply them later.

Preface to the First Edition

I have tried to present clearly and simply the fundamental conceptions which I believe to underlie the conservative view in politics and in the course of doing so to show the possibility of subscribing to them. This is not a work of philosophy, but of dogmatics (to use the theological term): it attempts to describe and defend a system of beliefs, but a system which, being directly expressed in action, assumes rather than provides the answers to philosophical questions. Nevertheless, I have drawn on the work of political philosophers, such as Hegel, Marx and Oakeshott, often without directly referring to them, trying always to use a language of my own.

I am grateful to the Rockefeller Foundation for the invitation to the Villa Serbelloni on Lake Como, where the first draft of this essay was begun, and to the friends who encouraged me while writing it. I have benefited from discussions with many people, and in particular from conversations over several years with John Casey and Maurice Cowling. A version of the text was read by William Waldegrave and Ted Honderich, and I was greatly assisted by their criticism. Many conservatives will find themselves in disagreement with what I say. Nevertheless, it satisfies the first requirement of all conservative thought: it is not original, nor does it try to be.

He that goeth about to persuade a multitude, that they are not so well governed as they ought to be, shall never want attentive and favourable hearers, because they know the manifold defects whereunto every kind of regiment is subject, but the secret lets and difficulties, which in public proceedings are innumerable and inevitable, they have not ordinarily the judgment to consider. And because such as openly reprove supposed disorders of state are taken for principal friends to the common benefit of all, and for men that carry singular freedom of mind, under this fair and plausible colour whatsoever they utter passeth for good and current. That which wanteth in the weight of their speech, is supplied by the aptness of men's minds to accept and believe it. Whereas on the other side, if we maintain things that are established, we have not only to strive with a number of heavy prejudices deeply rooted in the hearts of men, who think that herein we serve the time ... but also to bear such exceptions as minds so averted beforehand usually take against that which they are loth should be poured into them.

Hooker, *Of the Laws of Ecclesiastical Polity*, Book 1, Chapter i

There are so many plans, and so many schemes, and so many reasons why there should be neither plans nor schemes.

Disraeli, to Lady Bradford

Introduction: Philosophy, Policy and Doctrine

This is a work of dogmatics: it is an attempt to outline a system of belief, without pausing to argue the abstract questions to which that system provides no answer. The dogmatics of conservatism must be distinguished both from the philosophy upon which it rests, and from the policies which spring from it. The reality of politics is action, but action derives, however covertly, from thought, and consistent action demands consistent thought. Because there is no universal conservative policy, the illusion has arisen that there is no conservative thought, no set of beliefs or principles, no general vision of society, which motivates conservatives to act. Their action is mere reaction, their policy procrastination, their belief nostalgia.

I shall argue that the conservative attitude, and the doctrine that sustains it, are systematic and reasonable. Conservatism may rarely announce itself in maxims, formulae or aims. Its essence is inarticulate, and its expression, when compelled, sceptical. But it is capable of expression, and in times of crisis, forced either by political necessity, or by the clamour for doctrine, conservatism does its best, though not always with any confidence that the words it finds will match the instinct that required them. This lack of confidence stems not from diffidence or dismay, but from an awareness of the complexity of human things, and from an attachment to values which cannot be understood with the abstract clarity of utopian theory.[1]

It has been common for intellectuals in our time to believe that the conservative position is no longer 'available'. The twentieth century is memorable for nothing so much as its violence, and the attempt to understand this violence has brought with it the rise of political ideology. As the ignorant armies clashed in the night of Europe, the rumour spread that there were 'causes' for which they fought – causes such as 'equality', 'freedom' and 'social justice'. But no report was returned of a conservative banner and the intellectuals drew their conclusion: there is no conservative cause, and therefore no conservative dogma.

Post-war Europe was created by conscripts, for whom a creed without a cause suggests no coherent activity. But a new generation, for whom

1

the spirit of war is not the normal one, can again be attracted by the vision of the human condition in its full complexity, unsimplified by theory, or by overmastering ideals. This generation preserves the history of something greater, something for which it has begun to search. But without doctrine – in the sense of reasoned belief – it too must lose itself in the transient play of policy. The European mind seeks for a deep description of its politics, a description which reflects its real predicament, but which also remains uncontaminated by the day-to-day. Socialists and liberals have contended for this mind, each claiming to provide the system of principles with which to pass from policy to doctrine and from doctrine back to policy. Conservatives, who see value in prejudice and danger in abstract thought, have extemporized, expressing their beliefs in vague and conciliatory language. However, neither the socialist nor the liberal can be appeased. Their bigotry (and there is no greater bigotry, I shall suggest, than the bigotry of liberalism) permits no conciliation, while their statements seem clear, definite, founded in system. Until conservatives lay hold again of the principles which motivate them, they will find themselves outwitted by those who lay claim to a conviction which they may not always feel but are always ready to express. Without doctrine conservatism will lose its intellectual appeal; and (however reluctant conservatives may be to believe it), it is by intellectuals that modern politics is made.

But the alternatives to conservatism, I shall argue, are under-described. The apparent clarity of socialist and liberal thought is illusory, and their obscurity is the deeper for the ease with which it can be concealed within a gospel. By contrast, the conservative attitude is as appropriate and reasonable for the modern mind as it ever was, and, once understood, will be rejected only by those who seek in everything for an overriding purpose or a systematic plan. Such people will be distressed, not only by the conservative viewpoint, but also by the course of modern history, as it overwhelms each successive system in the flood of novelty.

Since my concern is with doctrine, I shall not consider the major issues of policy which any government must face. Nevertheless, I shall make extensive use of examples, since doctrine is useless if it does not translate immediately into practice. In addition I shall produce abstract arguments, often of a philosophical kind. But it must be remembered that argument is not the favourite pursuit of conservatives. Like all political beings, conservatives are for certain things: they are for them, not because they have arguments in their favour, but because they know them, live with them, and find their identity threatened (often they know not how) by the attempt to interfere with their operation. Their characteristic and most dangerous opponent is not the radical, who stands squarely against them, armed with myths and prejudices that match their own, but rather the reformer, who, acting always in a spirit of improvement, finds reason to change whatever he cannot find better reason to retain. It is from this spirit of improvement, the legacy of Victorian liberalism and social Darwinism, that modern socialists and modern liberals continue to derive their moral inspiration.

1
The Conservative Attitude

Conservatism is a stance that may be defined without identifying it with the policies of any party. Indeed, it may be a stance that appeals to a person for whom the whole idea of party is distasteful. In one of the first political manifestos of the English Conservative Party, appeal was explicitly made to 'that great and intelligent class of society ... which is far less interested in the contentions of party, than in the maintenance of order and the cause of good government' (Peel, *The Tamworth Manifesto*, 1834). Paradoxical though it may seem, it was from this aversion to factional politics that the Conservative Party grew. But it was an aversion rapidly overcome by another: that towards the chronic reform which only an organized party can successfully counter.[2]

In England, therefore, conservatism has sought expression through the activity (or, just as often, through the strategic inactivity) of a particular party, a party dedicated to maintaining the structure and institutions of a society threatened by mercantile enthusiasm and social unrest. In recent years, the Conservative Party has often seemed to be about to break with its tradition; it has joined in the competitive market of reform, endorsing the delegation of power, the code of economic internationalism, the 'free market economy' which it once so strenuously opposed. It has presided over the reorganization of county boundaries, and of national currency, over the entry into Europe and the consequent surrender of legal autonomy. Under the impact of New Labour it has opted for a democratic second chamber, and is, at the time of writing, fighting to survive in the face of a conversion of its old elite to the idea of a Single European Currency, notwithstanding the resulting loss of national sovereignty. It allowed during its recent eighteen years in office, the continued subjection of educational, social and legal institutions to the egalitarian ideology associated with socialist planning. In short, the Conservative Party has often acted in a way with which a conservative may find little sympathy. Most of all, it has begun to see itself as the defender of individual freedom against the encroachments of the state, concerned to return to the people their natural right of choice, and to inject into every corporate body the healing principle of democracy. These are passing fashions, well-meant, not always misguided, but by no means the ineluctable expression of the conservative point of view. Rather, they are the outcome of the party's recent attempt to provide itself with a set of policies and aims, and with the sketch of a political vision from which to derive them. Some have conceived this attempt as politically necessary. Others have wanted it for its own sake. The result has been, either transitory and unmeaning urges to reform, or else the wholesale adoption of the philosophy which I shall characterize in this book as the principal enemy of conservatism, the philosophy of liberalism, with all its attendant trappings of individual autonomy and the natural rights of man. In politics, the conservative attitude seeks above all for government, and regards no citizen as possessed of a natural right that transcends his obligation to be ruled. For what use is a right, without the law-abiding and law-enforcing power that upholds it?

Freedom and moderation

Now it is a sign of troubled times – those times when, as I have said, conservatism must feel the need to articulate itself – that advocates of 'moderation', of the sensible 'middle course' between extremes, of the demands of a reasonable (because silent) majority, should be listened to with a respect which they could not normally command. The attraction of 'moderation' to the Conservative Party has been its supposed association with the 'free' or 'open' society. And it is this free society that socialism is thought to destroy.[3] Hence 'moderation' tries to command the defence against 'Totalitarianism, whether (it is usually added) of the Left or of the Right'. During the years of Margaret Thatcher's governments, we were encouraged to see national politics, and indeed international politics, in terms of some wholly abstract conflict between 'Freedom' and 'Totalitarianism', between the 'natural' rights to speak and act one's mind, and an enforced, uneasy slavery.

Properly stated, this distinction need not be naive, and indeed, has the backing of a whole tradition in political philosophy, reaching from Locke to Robert Nozick.[4] Moreover, it represents an essential part, both of the rhetoric of American government and of the self-image of American society, so that political decisions of the highest seriousness are made in its name. This does not show, however, that the distinction can be put forward as though its clarity were immediate, as though it located definite political allegiances which could be defined in advance of the particular occasion for their declaration, or as though the whole of politics could be subsumed under the two disputing factions to which it gives a name. If it is not strange to find so many *soi-disant* conservatives identifying their position with this abstraction called 'Freedom', this is only because it is of the nature of conservatism to avoid abstractions, and to make radical mistakes when tempted by intelligent opposition to make use of them. Thus the concept of freedom – and in particular, such constitutionally derived freedoms as the freedoms of speech, assembly, and 'conscience' – this concept has until recently been the only one that has been presented by contemporary Conservatism as a contribution to the ideological battle which it has assumed to be raging. While freedom meant 'freedom from communist oppression' conservatives could advocate freedom and know that they were more or less in line with what they had always believed. But with the collapse of the Soviet Empire and the emergence of a left–liberal consensus, the old battle-cry does nothing to distinguish conservatism from its rivals.

An example

Later I shall return to this concept of freedom, and to the notion of 'human rights' with which it is associated. But let us consider, in order to make the general issues a little clearer, just one small example: the freedom of speech. It is obvious that there cannot be freedom of speech in any healthy society, if by freedom is meant the absolute untrammelled right to say what one wishes and utter one's views on anything, at any time, and anywhere. And it requires little knowledge of law to see that there is no absolute freedom of speech in the United Kingdom. Liberal thinkers have always recognized this fact. But they have seen the constraints on freedom as arising only negatively and in response to individual rights. Freedom should be qualified only by the possibility that someone might suffer through its exercise. For the conservative, constraint should be upheld, until it can be shown that society is not damaged by its removal. Thus the constraints on freedom arise through the law's attempt to embody (as for a conservative it must embody) the fundamental values of the society over which it rules. I shall argue that this vision of law is both more coherent and more true to the facts than its individualistic rival.

There is no freedom to abuse, to stir up hatred, to make or publish treasonable, libellous, obscene and blasphemous utterance. In England, as in every civilized country, there is a law which forbids the production and distribution of subversive material – the law of sedition. Now this law also makes it an offence voluntarily to stir up hatred between different sections of the community. Proper application of that law – which makes not only the manipulation of racial hatred but also that of class hatred into a criminal offence – would have made the first Race Relations Act (the Act which still required some element of *mens rea* for its statutory crimes) more or less unnecessary. It was not applied. This was not only because the symbolic gesture of a law specific to racial relations appeared immensely powerful, if not in quelling racial antipathy, at least in appeasing the middle-class conscience over its existence. It was also because the application of the law would lead at once to the curtailing, not only of what was said on the rostrum of the National Front, but also of what used to be said at every radical demonstration, and at many a Trades Union Congress.

This decline in the very idea of sedition has been brought about not by popular agitation, but by the politics of power. The fact is, not that our society believes in freedom of speech and assembly, but rather that it is afraid to announce its disbelief. This disbelief is so entrenched in English law – in the common law just as much as in statutory provisions – that it is possible to doubt that it could be eradicated without wholly overthrowing the social order which the law enshrines. But it is now principally judges and juries who respond to its demand. Politicians, and especially politicians of the 'moderate' Right, have lost their nerve.

This is not to deny the reality of some less absolute ideal of freedom, according to which it would be quite true to say that there is and has been more freedom of speech (and more freedom of every kind) in the United Kingdom than in most other countries of the world. And this Anglo-Saxon freedom is rightly valued by all of us who share its benefits, including the benefit of writing and reading the present book. But this freedom is not identifiable apart from the institutions which have fostered it. It is a freedom to do precisely what is not forbidden by law, and what is forbidden by law records a long tradition of reflection on the nature and constitution of British society. The English Common Law, which has its roots in Roman law, in canon law, and in the codes of our Saxon ancestors, is the judge's peculiar province, and has become the expression of a deep historical sense, a sense of the continuity and vitality of an existing social order.

Freedom and institutions

The argument can be generalized. The freedom that British people esteem is not, and cannot be, a special case of that freedom advocated by the American Republican Party, the freedom of pioneering dissenters struggling for community in a place without history, the freedom which is connected in some mysterious way with free enterprise and the market economy. It is a specific personal freedom, the result of a long process of social evolution, the bequest of institutions without whose protection it could not endure. Freedom in this sense (the only sense which matters) is not the precondition but the consequence of an accepted social arrangement. Freedom without institutions is blind: it embodies neither genuine social continuity nor, as I shall argue, genuine individual choice. It amounts to no more than a gesture in a moral vacuum.

The concept of freedom, therefore, cannot occupy a central place in conservative thinking, whether about national affairs, international politics or (what for the conservative is of special significance) the internal guidance of an autonomous institution. Freedom is comprehensible as a social goal only when subordinate to something else, to an organization or arrangement which defines the individual aim. Hence to aim at freedom is at the same time to aim at the constraint which is its precondition. Roughly speaking, it is the individual's responsibility to win whatever freedom of speech, conscience and assembly he may; it is the politician's responsibility to define and maintain the arrangement in which that freedom is to be pursued. One major difference between conservatism and liberalism consists, therefore, in the fact that, for the conservative, the value of individual liberty is not absolute, but stands subject to another and higher value, the authority of established government. And history could be taken to suggest that what satisfies people politically – even if they always used words like 'freedom' to articulate the first impulse towards it – is not freedom, but congenial government. Government is the primary need of people subject to the discipline of social membership, and freedom the name of at least one of their anxieties.

The political battles of our time concern, therefore, the conservation and destruction of institutions and forms of life: nothing more vividly illustrates this than the issues of education, devolution, the role of trade unions and the House of Lords, issues with which the abstract concept of 'freedom' fails to make contact. In all such issues the conflict concerns not freedom but authority, authority vested in a given office, institution or arrangement. It is through an ideal of authority that conservatives experience the political world. Their liberal opponents, whose view is likely to be ahistorical, will usually reject that notion, as an antiquated survival of monarchical ideas of government. Now Marxists (whose viewpoint I propose to take seriously, since it derives from a theory of human nature that one might actually believe) would see the dispute in quite other terms, seeking to demystify the ideal of 'authority' and to replace it with the realities of power. 'Authority', for the Marxist, is merely the ideological representation of power – power imbued with a false aura of legitimacy, made absolute and unchangeable, translated from a historical reality into a sempiternal ideal. In preferring to speak of power, the Marxist puts at the centre of politics the only true political commodity, the only thing which can actually change hands. Later I shall try to show how the Marxist's picture in all probability falsifies the realities of politics; nevertheless, it correctly locates the battleground, and for that reason, if for no other, we must take it seriously. But now let us return from our preliminary skirmish to the present task, which is to give some initial description of the conservative outlook, so that its implications as a contemporary political attitude may be explored.

The search for doctrine

As I have suggested, conservatism – as a motivating force in the political life of the citizen – is characteristically inarticulate, unwilling (and indeed usually unable) to translate itself into formulae or maxims, loath to state its purpose or declare its view. There have been articulate conservatives – Aristotle, for example, Hume, T. S. Eliot. But while they have influenced the course of politics, it has usually been indirectly, and not because of any specific political ideal with which their names have been connected. Indeed, if it is true that conservatism becomes conscious only when forced to be so, then it is inevitable that the passage from practice to theory will not be rewarded by any immediate influence from theory back to what is done. Nevertheless, intellectuals wish to hold their beliefs in conscious suspension before their minds, and will not be content, in a world flustered by faction, to stand without arguments in the midst of the fray.

The task of this book is to find the concepts with which conservatives might provide themselves with a creed, and with which they might define their own position, whether as politicians, or merely as political animals. This, let it be repeated, is not an exercise in political philosophy, but in political dogmatics. It is quite possible that the conceptions that I provide will fail to correspond exactly to the intuition which sought expression through them. A political creed, in so far as it is formulated, is partly an exercise in rhetoric, to be revised and restated whenever the times demand that the ruling intuition be given its new dressing of necessity. But we have an important question to settle: how can conservatism be an item of contemporary belief, and how in particular can it recommend itself to that peculiar species to which we all belong, the self-consciously 'modern' person?

The desire to conserve

It is a limp definition of conservatism to describe it as the desire to conserve; for although there is in every man and woman some impulse to conserve that which is safe and familiar, it is the nature of this 'familiarity' that needs to be examined. To put it briefly, conservatism arises directly from the sense that one belongs to some continuing, and pre-existing social order, and that this fact is all-important in determining what to do. The 'order' in question may be that of a club, society, class, community, church, regiment or nation – a person may feel towards all these things that institutional stance which it is the task of this book to describe and defend. In feeling it – in feeling thus engaged in the continuity of his social world – a person stands in the current of some common life. The important thing is that the life of a social arrangement may become mingled with the lives of its members. They may feel in themselves the persistence of the will that surrounds them. The conservative instinct is founded in that feeling: it is the enactment of historical vitality, the individual's sense of his society's will to live. Moreover, in so far as people love life they will love what has given them life; in so far as they desire to give life it is in order to perpetuate what they have. In that intricate entanglement of individual and society resides the 'will to live' that constitutes conservatism.

It is sometimes said (and not only by socialists) that the fabric of English society (and I shall assume for the moment that we are discussing English society) is falling apart, that the country is in decline, bereft of everything which constitutes the strength and vitality of an autonomous nation. How, then, can one be a conservative, when there is nothing to conserve but ruins? This radical scepticism may take many forms, from the apocalyptic vision of Nietzsche and Spengler, to the more homely chatter that accompanies the planning of the 'New Society', whose foundation-stone seems nevertheless always to get mislaid. But, in whatever form, it is surely of little practical interest. A society or a nation is indeed a kind of organism (and also very much more than an organism); it must therefore bear the stigma of mortality. Yet is it not absurd advice to give to a sick man that he should – in the interests of the 'new world' that waits to replace him – promptly set about the task of dying? Even at the point of death the will to live endures and desires its restoration. A society, like a person, may endure through sickness and thrive in death. If conservatives are also restorationists, this is because they live close to society, and feel in themselves the sickness which infects the common order. How, then, can they fail to direct their eyes towards that state of health from which things have declined? Revolution is now unthinkable: it is like murdering a sick mother out of impatience to snatch some rumoured infant from her womb. Of course there are conservatives who in extremity have adopted the way of revolution – conservatives like Franco in Spain and Pinochet in modern Chile. In the ensuing vacuum, however, people are disrupted, aimless, incomplete. The result is bloodshed, and only afterwards the slow work of restoration to some simulacrum of the state that was destroyed.

The desire to conserve is compatible with all manner of change, provided only that change is also continuity. It has recently been argued with some force that the process of change in political life has become 'hyperactive'.[5] Overstimulation of that shallow part of our being which constitutes the sum of our articulate views has led to a profusion throughout the public realm of a sense that anything can and should be altered, together with proposals for reform, and political strategies, mounted by those within and by those without the institutions whose life they thereby threaten. This disease is of the kind which any conservative will attend to, first by trying to recognize its nature. The world has become peculiarly 'opinionated', and in every corner of society people with neither the desire nor the ability to reflect on the social good are being urged to choose some favoured recipe for its realization. Even an institution like the Catholic Church has become afflicted with the fashion for reform, and being unable to take Christ's words to Simon Peter in their egoistic Lutheran meaning, has partially forgotten the tradition of custom, ceremony and judicious manoeuvre that enabled it to stand seemingly unshifting in the midst of worldly change, calling with a voice of immutable authority. The Church, an institution with an aim that is not of this world, but only in this world, sells itself as a 'social cause'! It is hardly surprising if the result is not only empty moralism but also ludicrous theology.

Politics and purpose

But surely, it will be said, all politics must have an aim, and in the realization of that aim, change and disruption will be inevitable? How then can conservatives both seek to guard their heritage, and not participate in the public pastime of reform? At this point, it will help to step down from the world of national politics, into the microcosm of ordinary human relations.

Some human relations presuppose a common purpose, and fall apart when that purpose is fulfilled or discontinued. (Consider, for example, a business partnership.) But not all relations are of that nature. The pursuit of a certain mechanical analogy has led to the belief (widely held but seldom stated) that an activity without an aim is merely aimless. So that if we are to consider political activity as a form of rational conduct, we should ally it to certain aims – to a social ideal that translates immediately into policy.[6] Rational politicians must therefore be able to indicate the form of society at which they are aiming, why they are aiming at it, and what means they propose for its realization.

Such a view is in fact confused. Most human activities, and most relations that are worthwhile, have no purpose. No purpose, that is, external to themselves. There is no 'end in view', and to attempt to provide one is to do violence to the arrangement. Suppose I were to approach another in the spirit of a given purpose – there is something that I have in mind in, and hope to achieve through, my relations with him. And suppose that the sole interest of my relations with the other lies in this aim. Now there is a sense in which I can still treat him (in Kant's famous terminology) not as a means only, but also as an end. For I may try to accomplish my aim by seeking his agreement. I reason with him, I try to persuade him to do what I want him to do. But, if that is my approach, then it is always possible that I shall not persuade him, or that he, in his turn, will dissuade me. A certain reciprocity arises, and the absolute authority of my aim – as the sole determining principle of what it is reasonable for me to do – must be abandoned. And there is nothing irrational in that. If my aim is abandoned in these circumstances it is because it has proved impossible or unjustifiable. In other words it has failed to become part of the fellowship upon which it was first imposed. It follows that, if I am to allow to another the degree of autonomy which his human nature demands of me, I simply cannot approach him with a clearly delimited set of aims for him, and expect the fulfilment of those aims to be the inevitable, natural, or even reasonable outcome of our dialogue. I might discover new ends, or even lapse into that state of 'aimlessness' which is the norm of healthy human relations. Indeed, if friendship has a basis it is this: that a person may desire the company of someone for whom he has no specific purpose. The continuity of the friendship will generate its own passing aims and aspirations, but no one of them can ever come to dominate the arrangement without changing it from friendship to something else.

So too in politics. Politicians may have aims and ambitions for the people whom they seek to govern. But a society is more than a speechless organism. It has personality, and will. Its history, institutions and culture are the repositories of human values – in short, it has the character of end as well as means. A politician who seeks to impose upon it a given set of purposes, and seeks no understanding of the reasons and values which the society proposes in return, acts in defiance of friendship. And yet, where else does the right to govern lie, if it is not in a politician's fellowship with a social order? The subjection of politics to determining purposes, however 'good in themselves' those purposes seem, is, on the conservative view, irrational. For it destroys the very relationship upon which government depends. This, the conservative might say, is the true source of the absurdity of communism: that it saw society entirely as a means to some future goal. Hence it was at war with the very people it had set out to govern.

It is the mark of rational intercourse that aims are not all predetermined, that some ends – perhaps the most important ends – remain to be discovered rather than imposed. And in the life of society they are discovered not by the perusal of utopian treatises, but, primarily, through participation. And that means by sharing in a form of life. (Likewise, the 'ends' of friendship are alive in its continuity, and show themselves from day to day, but have no independent existence and die with the friendship.) To participate in a social arrangement is to possess not just a set of beliefs, expectations, and feelings towards one's fellow citizens; it is to possess a way of seeing, through which the value of conduct may be recognized. That value will not be the outcome of some all-embracing principle, applied abstractly, but on the contrary, it will proceed from the immediacies of politics. One might say that, for the conservative, political ends make sense in conduct, but for the most part resist translation into recipes. Politicians cannot reasonably propose them until they have understood the social arrangement which they seek to influence, and having understood it, they may find that their ends cannot be 'proposed' in the form of a programme. To propose a recipe in advance of understanding is a sentimental gesture: it involves regarding a society as an excuse for political emotion, rather than as a proper object of it. To avoid sentimentality we must recognize that a society too has a will, and that a rational person must be open to its persuasion. This will lies, for the conservative, enshrined in history, tradition, culture and prejudice. The nations of Britain, far from being savage societies that would justify the imposition of overarching decrees, are founded in the maturest of national cultures, and contain within themselves all the principles of social life. True conservatives have their ears attuned to those principles, and try to live, as a result, in friendship with the nation of which they are a part. Their own will to live, and the nation's will to live, are simply one and the same.

Immediate objections

Is it really possible that there should be a political doctrine that recognizes no ruling purpose – no purpose beyond that of government? And is it possible that conservatism should derive from a stance of 'political friendship', when for so many people 'conservatism' denotes nothing more than old abuses and unjust decrees?

In what follows I shall provide a detailed answer to the first of those objections. I have spoken somewhat loosely of 'nation', 'society', 'government' and 'state'. Beneath those terms lies a host of distinctions which must be brought to the surface and clarified. Eventually, I hope, the metaphor of society as person will be seen to correspond to a clear and literal idea. And then it will be obvious that there can be both doctrine and policy without a ruling purpose, and that it can be as reasonable to believe in the one as it is wise to act from the other. As for the second objection, that too, I hope, will wither away. But a preliminary response is needed, if the reader is to stomach what I have to say. Conservatism presupposes the existence of a social organism. Its politics is concerned with sustaining the life of that organism, through sickness and health, change and decay. (This is not an external purpose; it is what government consists in.) There are people who, in their vociferous part, reject the politics of a 'Conservative Party'. But this does not imply that there is not some deeper part of themselves that lies embedded in the social order, motivated and consoled by the forces to which the conservative instinct is attuned. Somewhere beneath the fluster of 'opinion' lies an unspoken unity. It may have evolved, sickened, or moved since it was last identified. But clearly it never *will* be identified unless we forget the opinionated crust which covers it. Our society is confused by experiences which it has yet to comprehend. A large part of its self-conscious politics is clouded by this confusion. The doctrine of conservatism will therefore prove startling and even offensive to many whose feelings it none the less quite accurately describes.

The pursuit of power

Nevertheless, even if conservatives are committed, in this way, to the pursuit and upkeep of an underlying social unity, their relation to that unity cannot provide the sum of politics. A society has its diseased and destructive factions, and with these conservatives are at war. And although the modern politician is inevitably a somewhat 'wounded' surgeon, he must nevertheless continue to practise the healer's art. He must first seek to rule, and must therefore pursue the power that will enable him to do so. Indeed, for the conservative, power will not be able to mask itself as subordinate to some clear justifying aim – it is not the means to 'social justice', or 'equality', or 'freedom'. It is power to command and influence, and its justification must be found within itself, in an idea of legitimacy or established right. The power which the politician seeks must be, in other words, a power that is accepted. It must be regarded by the people as not just power, but authority. Every society depends upon popular self-respect, respect in the citizens for the order of which they form a part and for themselves as part of that order. This feeling, manifest in patriotism, in custom, in respect for law, in loyalty to a leader or monarch, and in the willing acceptance of the privileges of those to whom privilege is granted, can extend itself indefinitely. And it is from this feeling, which need be neither craven nor endlessly submissive, that the authority of the conservative politician derives. It will be our first concern, therefore, to describe such a feeling. Thereafter we may derive from it an account of the civil order that renders the conservative attitude both possible and reasonable.

In considering the relation between power and authority, it has to be conceded that conservatives suffer from a singular disadvantage, and this disadvantage makes it necessary for them to be stronger, more cunning, even more Machiavellian, than their usual opponents. For, lacking any obvious aim in politics, they lack any offering with which to stir up the enthusiasm of the crowd. They are concerned solely with the task of government, and their attitude defies translation into a shopping-list of social goals. They look with scepticism upon the myths of equality and social justice; they regard universal political agitation with distaste, and the clamour for 'progress' seems to them no more than a passing fad, serious only in so far as it constitutes a threat to the political order. What then can persuade the people to accept conservatives in power? It is well to say, with Burke, that the promises of revolution must be empty (since they can be understood only by presupposing precisely the social arrangement that it is intended to destroy).[7] But what other promises can the conservative provide?

The great intellectual advantage of socialism is obvious. Through its ability to align itself with ideals that everyone can recognize, socialism has been able to perpetuate the belief in its moral purity, despite crime upon crime committed in its name. That a socialist revolution may cost millions of lives, that it may involve the wilful murder of an entire class, the destruction of a culture, the elimination of learning and the desecration of art, will leave not the slightest stigma on the doctrines with which it glorifies its actions or on the people who have taken part in them. And yet those lonely restorationists who, like General Pinochet, have committed crimes in the cause of continuity, have – because they fought not for an ideal but for what they took to be a reality – often simply blemished the idea of authority which they hoped to serve. It seems, then, that in these hypocritical times conservatives will find the practice of politics as difficult as they erstwhile found its theory. But there are places where they can succeed, and Britain has been one of them.

2
Authority and Allegiance

The conservative attitude demands the persistence of a civil order. What is this order? And why should it be conserved?

We must begin by distinguishing state and society – not because they are truly separable but because they should be separately described. A society is held together by the civil bond which generates and supports institutions of government. Historians discuss the origins of the state. Often they write as though the 'state' were a modern invention – arising out of the collapse of ecclesiastical jurisdiction; or out of the eighteenth-century call for the 'rights of man' (which seemed urgently to require the invention of something against which to claim them); or (yet more parochially), out of the settling of boundaries at the Congress of Vienna. These discussions raise important issues, and I shall return to them. But for clarity's sake we must make the widest possible distinction, and allow any organization in which there is genuine government to possess two aspects, of civil society and state. Neither aspect can exist independently, and the reader must accept therefore that the conservative vision of society – which it is the purpose of this chapter to explore – will already contain strong intimations of the conservative vision of the state.

Nevertheless, conservatism originates in an attitude to civil society, and it is from a conception of civil society that its political doctrine is derived. But a political doctrine must contain a motive to action, and a source of appeal. Conservatives, unable as they are to appeal to a utopian future, or to any future that is not, as it were, already contained in the present and past, must avail themselves of conceptions which are both directly applicable to things as they are and at the same time indicative of a motivating force in people. And this force must be as great as the desire for the 'freedom' and 'social justice' offered by their rivals. There are three concepts which immediately present themselves, and whose contemporary application we must examine: the concepts of authority, allegiance and tradition.

Authority and power

It is a remarkable fact that people recognize authority in their fellows, in social arrangements, in institutions, and in the state. It is equally remarkable that this authority can command their allegiance, to such an extent that they might as willingly die for its sake as for the sake of any ideal or any religious creed. In so far as people have shown this disposition to sacrifice their lives for something greater than themselves, then, historically speaking, the nation and the social order must rival religion as the principal beneficiaries of the gesture. A cynic might say that Church and State represent the only powers able to coerce people to surrender their lives, but such cynicism is baseless. It was no state that compelled the Achaeans to assemble before the walls of Troy, but a sense of their common social identity, and of their honour and allegiance as Greeks. (The horror and the impersonality of modern warfare naturally make it difficult to sustain this attitude. Honour tends to seek expression in a kind of private grief, in the 'Greater love hath no man than this ...' of Wilfred Owen, or else in the mere 'solidarity' of those who suffer together.)

'Authority' can mean many things. In particular, it can mean either established or legitimate power. In either sense it can be granted, delegated, removed, respected, ignored, opposed. A person who has authority has it from a certain source – although it is well if he has authority in another sense, according to which it means not the legitimate or established principle of rule, but the natural gift to command obedience. For the Marxist, 'authority', and the concept of 'legitimacy' through which it dignifies itself, are simply parts of the ideology of class rule, concepts belonging to and inculcated by a ruling 'hegemony'. They belong to that immense unconscious movement whereby power has sought to entrench itself in accepted institutions, and whereby the historical nature (which is to say, the impermanence) of those institutions is masked. What is historical is presented as natural; power is represented as unchangeable power. But make no mistake, says the Marxist – the only *reality* here is power.

It is important to see that such ideas, whether true or false, may be irrelevant to the practice of politics. What distinguishes political activity from the biological grouping of the herd is that the structure of the first is determined by the concepts of those who engage in it, whereas that of the second obeys only the inexorable laws of unconscious nature. And you can try as hard as you like to undermine the 'ruling ideology' which first placed legitimacy in the centre of common consciousness, but you will not succeed in making people remove from their minds a concept which – in their actual dealings with the world – is indispensable to them. People have the idea of legitimacy, and see the world as coloured in its terms; and it is how they see the world which determines how they act on it. Now the belief in legitimacy exists and will always exist as part of common political consciousness, and a society is not happy in which people cannot see that legitimacy enacted, in which they see only state coercion, and only established power. From the Norman Conquest to the contemporary reactions to trade-union power, the concept of legitimacy has governed political practice, and whether or not there is any reality which corresponds to this concept is a question that may be put aside as of no political (although of great philosophical) significance.

The social contract

In order to understand the conservative attitude to authority, we must examine a recent and now seemingly irrepressible political idea, the idea that there can be 'no obligation on any man which arises not from some act of his own',[8] as Thomas Hobbes once put it. The most popular version of this idea sees the transition from power to legitimacy as residing in an unspoken, unknown and unknowable 'social contract'. Now no one, least of all a conservative, is likely to believe that government is possible without the propagation of myths. But this particular fiction – which at one time proved convenient in persuading people that the legitimacy of government lay elsewhere than in the divine right of kings – bears about as much relation to the facts as the view that my parents and I once surreptitiously contracted that they would nourish and educate me in return for my later care. Naturally, not every contract has to be explicit: there are implied contracts in law, brought about, for example, by an act of part performance. But even in implied contracts (except for those peculiar cases where a contract is implied by statute) there must be, somewhere, a choice, and a deliberation; a knowledge of consequences and a belief in, if not a mutual recognition of, an exchange of promises. The idea that there *must* be, at the heart of all political, and indeed all social organization, something in the nature of a contract (but a contract which, as it were, arises from social intercourse and does not – because clearly it could not – precede it), that idea stems from a singular pattern of thought which we must analyse, both here and in the chapter which follows since it bears directly on our theme.

The pattern of thought is this: human beings, as free, autonomous agents, fall under the rule of Justice. Which is to say, to put it very roughly and once again in the abstract terminology of Kant, that they must be treated as ends and not as means. To treat them as means only is to disrespect their freedom, and hence to sacrifice one's right to any similar respect from them. The fulfilment of a contract is, not the highest point, but the clearest case of just relations. A promise is made, another given, knowingly and in full knowledge of consequences. To promise in such a situation, and to rely on the other's fulfilment, while withholding any intention to reciprocate, is to treat the other as a means, to abuse his trust, and hence to act unjustly towards him. Here we can see that one person has assumed a right over another to which he is not entitled; for although the other granted that right, he did so only conditionally, only on the understanding that he acquired a similar right in return. So now we can distinguish between legitimate and illegitimate claims; the 'rights' so vociferously claimed by Mr Boffin in *Our Mutual Friend* are evidently of the latter kind. So are a vast number of those 'rights' discerned by the European Court of Human Rights, and used to transfer privilege and power to individuals and groups who have done nothing to deserve them.

The interest of contract is that it consists entirely of rights freely granted, and in that freedom (so both common sense and common law have always suggested) lies their legitimacy. To transfer the language of contract to the social sphere provides us at once, then, with a means to distinguish legitimate from illegitimate power. The criterion may be complex in its application, taking in many qualifications as society develops in response to it; but its essence is simple. Does power arise out of and express the contractual basis, or does it claim some right which transcends it? The power of the police might be seen in this light as legitimate, that of the Mafia as not.

It is difficult to be persuaded by such a view. For the very possibility of free and open contract presupposes a sufficient social order, not because it would otherwise be impossible to enforce contracts (although that too is true), but because without social order the very notion of an individual committing himself, through a promise, would not arise.

Already we have supposed shared institutions and a conception of human freedom, which could hardly have their origin in the very practice of contract which they serve to make possible. This is not to say that one cannot see society in this contractual way, in the way of contemporary American liberalism, and so construe all forms of social organization as assemblages of their members, with choice or consent as the ultimate binding principle. But for this vision to capture even the smallest part of what is recognized as the 'authority' of the state, the social arrangement must be given plausible historical antecedents (such as those of New England) with which to mystify the inquiring mind. Perhaps the most remarkable thing that has happened in American politics during this century is the recognition that the powers of the state in fact transcend their supposed contractual basis, and must therefore look for their authority elsewhere.[9]

Authority and family

But let us again step down from the political to the private realm. Consider the family. I have already suggested that it would be absurd to think of family ties as contractual, or family obligations as in any way arising from a free relinquishing of autonomy, or even from some unspoken bargain which rises into consciousness, so to speak, at some later stage. Even as a metaphor, the language of contract here fails to make contact with the facts. And it is because of this that extreme individualists – those who can see no virtue in any arrangement which does not in the end derive from conscious choice – have begun to attack the family, to fabricate an idea of its 'dispensability', to declare war on it as a form of 'patriarchal' oppression, from which women and children must be liberated if they are to enjoy a freedom and fulfilment of their own.

Were it an accident that human beings grow to love, need and depend upon one another; were it an accident that children feel bound to their parents and parents to their children in inexorable ties that circumscribe the possibilities of later pleasure and pain; were it an accident that domestic life is even now (except in the case of a minority) roughly as it has been, then the 'radical critique' might have some force. But conservatives will be sceptical. Their rare attempts to express the truth about the world are likely to be founded in observation, and to convey a disbelief in the instant changeability of human nature. Hence they will recognize that these facts are not accidental, and that the family tie is dispensable only in the way that pleasure, industry, love, grief, passion and allegiance are dispensable – that is, only in the case of the minority which can persuade itself (for whatever reason) to renounce these things.

The family, then, is a small social unit which shares with civil society the singular quality of being non-contractual, of arising (both for the children and for the parents) not out of choice but out of natural necessity. And (to turn the analogy round) it is obvious that the bond which ties the citizen to society is likewise not a voluntary but a kind of natural relation. Locke, and the other great individualists, who thought otherwise, were also constrained to think that the world contained many 'vacant places' which could be filled by those who chose to withdraw from their inherited arrangement. As we now know, every country sports the sign 'engaged'. And besides, is it not psychological naiveté to think that I, now, in middle age, rooted in my language, culture and history, could suddenly do a *volte-face* and see myself as English only by accident, free at every moment to change? If I go elsewhere I take my Englishness with me, as much as I take my attachment to family, language, life and self. I go as a colonial or as an exile, and either sink like the Tibetans or swim like the Jews.

The analogy with the family is useful if we are to understand the role of authority in politics. It is clear from the start that a child must be acted upon by its parents' power: its very love for them will accord to them that power, and parents no more escape from its exercise by being permissive than does an officer cease to command his troops by leaving them constantly at ease. A child is what it is by virtue of its parents' will, and consequently the parent has an indefeasible obligation to form and influence the child's development. In this very process is power, and it is of necessity an established power, since it resides already with the parent at the child's first coming into the world. Now there is a sense in which every child does not only need its parents to exercise that power, but will also demand that they do so, to the extent that it cherishes their protection. There can be no ministering to the love of a child, and no granting of love, that is not also, in the first instance, an exercise of established power. For how is the child to recognize, from all those beings that surround it, the object which is its parent, that is, its principal protection and its source of love? Surely, it must feel the influence of a will in its life, of a desire for its life, besides its own. It must feel the constraint of another's love for it. And it is only in recognizing the existence of an objective power over what it will do that the child is pulled out of its self-immersion into the recognition of its parent as an autonomous being, a being who not only gives love but gives it freely, and towards whom it owes love in return. The kind of personal love that we envisage as the end of family union requires, as its precondition, the sense of established power – the child's unformed recognition that, in respect of at least one other being, he is helpless – combined with the growing awareness that the power of that being is also an exercise of freedom. And it is a similar recognition of constraint, helplessness, and subjection to external will that heralds the individual's realization of his membership of society; in this recognition love of one's country is born.

Consider the other side of family loyalties. We are apt to think of children as having a responsibility towards their parents, a responsibility that in no way reflects any merely contractual right, but which is simply *due* to the parents as a recognition of the filial tie. This sense of obligation is not founded in justice – which is the sphere of free actions between beings who create their moral ties – but rather in respect, honour, or (as the Romans called it) piety.[10] To neglect my parents in old age is not an act of justice but an act of impiety. Impiety is the refusal to recognize as legitimate a demand that does not arise from consent or choice. And we see that the behaviour of children towards their parents cannot be understood unless we admit this ability to recognize a bond that is 'transcendent', that exists, as it were 'objectively', outside the sphere of individual choice. It is this ability that is transferred by the citizen from hearth and home to place, people and country. The bond of society – as conservatives see it – is just such a 'transcendent' bond, and it is inevitable that citizens will be disposed to recognize its legitimacy, will be disposed, in other words, to bestow authority upon the existing order. They will be deterred from doing so by acts of unjust or arbitrary power, or by a general 'unfriendliness' in the public order, of the kind experienced by the deprived and unfostered child.

Authority, in the sense that we have considered, is an enormous artifact. By which I mean, not that authority is intentionally constructed, but rather that it exists only in so far as we exercise, understand and submit to it. The condition of society presupposes this general connivance, and conservatives will seek to uphold all those practices and institutions – among which, of course, the family is pre-eminent – through which the habits of allegiance are acquired. As we shall see, this necessary corollary of conservative thinking is incompatible with any suggestion that the conservative is an advocate either of liberal ideals, or of the so-called 'minimal state'.[11] No serious conservative can believe that there ought to be a power greater than that of the state, a power that can, if it chooses, put itself beyond the reach of law. Conservatives believe in the power of the state as necessary to the state's authority, and will seek to establish and enforce that power in the face of every influence that opposes it. However, their desire is to see power standing not naked in the forum of politics, but clothed in constitution, operating always through an adequate system of law, so that its movement seems never barbarous or oppressive, but always controlled and inevitable, an expression of the civilized vitality through which loyalty is inspired. The constitution, therefore, and the institutions which sustain it, will always lie at the heart of conservative thinking. Conservatives place their faith in arrangements that are known and tried, and wish to imbue them with all the authority necessary to constitute an accepted and objective public realm. It is from this that their respect for tradition and custom arises, and not from any end – such as freedom – towards which these practices are seen as a means. This point is of the essence, and I shall elaborate it further.

Allegiance

It is allegiance which defines the condition of society, and which constitutes society as something greater than the 'aggregate of individuals' that the liberal mind perceives. It is proper for conservatives to be sceptical of claims made on behalf of the value of the individual, if these claims should conflict with the allegiance necessary to society, even though they may wish the state (in the sense of the apparatus of government) to stand in a fairly loose relation to the activities of individual citizens. Individuality too is an artifact, an achievement which depends upon the social life of people. And indeed, as many historians have pointed out, it is a recent venture of the human spirit for men and women to define themselves as individuals, as creatures whose nature and value are summed up in their unique individual being.[12] The condition of mankind requires that individuals, while they exist and act as autonomous beings, do so only because they can first identify themselves as something greater – as members of a society, group, class, state or nation, of some arrangement to which they may not attach a name, but which they recognize instinctively as home. Politically speaking, this bond of allegiance – which, seen from the heights of intellectual speculation as 'my station and its duties', is experienced as a peculiar certainty in day-to-day life[13] – is of a value which transcends the value of individuality. For many people, the bond of allegiance has immediate authority, while the call to individuality is unheard. It is therefore wrong to consider that a politician has some kind of duty to minister to the second of these, and to ignore the first. If the two impulses are not in conflict, as they perhaps were not, for example, in the society described by Fielding (and defended by Burke), then well and good. But if individuality threatens allegiance – as it must do in a society where individuality seeks to realize itself in opposition to the institutions and traditions from which it grows – then the civil order is threatened too. This surely is the situation that arose in Europe and America during the Sixties, and from the effects of which we are still suffering. The business of politics is to maintain the civil order, and to prevent the 'dust and powder of individuality' that Burke described as its ruin.[14]

I have sketched the formation of allegiance in the family bond, and the residue of respect or piety which grows from that, ripe for transference to whatever might present itself as a fitting social object. The primary object of allegiance is, as I argued, authority, which is to say power conceived as legitimate, and so bound by responsibility. In the family this authority and responsibility have their foundation and end in love, but from the beginning they transcend the personal love of individuals. (There is, surely, a great mystification involved in the Freudian idea of the 'family romance'. Freud was getting at something of immense importance, which is the connection – perceived also by Hegel and Wagner – between the prohibition of incest and the existence of the family as 'home'. But this surely need not persuade us that the natural bond is always and inevitably erotic. In this area the distinctions, and not the similarities, have the greatest meaning.) Authority and responsibility arise from and sustain the sense of the family as something greater than the aggregate of its members, an entity in which the members participate, so that its being and their being are intermingled. People are amplified and not diminished through their participation in such arrangements.[15] Mere individuality, relinquished first to the family, and then to the whole social organism, is finally replaced by the mature allegiance which is the only politically desirable form of 'freedom'. It is obvious that such allegiance is a matter of degree, being fervent at some times, passive or failing at others. The possibility of conservatism supposes only that it exists to some degree, and in most active people.

Patriotism – construed as the individual's sense of identity with a social order – is politically indispensable. Patriotism has had many detractors, not all of them as sentimental as the ageing Tolstoy. But it is hard to deny its power to instil a measure of generosity even into the meanest spirit, or to quieten the instinct to profit from another's helplessness or loss. If it be objected that patriotism has been a major cause of war and suffering, then the answer is, first, that it has been the single greatest obstacle to civil war, widely recognized to be the worst of human misfortunes, and secondly that, since the cause of war is the struggle for power, war can be carried on as easily in the name of an 'international' ideal as in the cause of national grandeur. (Arguably the greatest cause of war in the twentieth century has been international socialism, as propagated by the communist international.)

Suspicion of the patriotic motive arises partly because people confuse patriotism with nationalism. The latter is not a form of loyalty, but an ideology and a call to arms on behalf of it. Often nationalism results from the collapse of empire, when people previously ruled by a distant metropolitan power look for a more local form of legitimate government, a form that will correspond to the customs, language and history that tie them to each other. Almost invariably, however, this involves an act of self-assertion – either against the collapsing empire, or against rival nationalities embarking on the same project of 'self-determination'. The history of this project in our time is not a happy one; nevertheless, one part of it – which is the attempt to give political expression to a natural allegiance – commands the sympathy of conservatives. What conservatives object to is the desire to rationalize national loyalty through the myth that 'we' are somehow superior to 'them', and therefore entitled to destroy them. Patriotism is an altogether quieter view of the matter: it is, simply, the recognition that we stand or fall together, and that we therefore owe it to each other to maintain the customs and the symbols of our common membership.

There is a long-standing tradition of political thought (of which Machiavelli is by no means the first representative) that considers aggression abroad to be a condition of peace at home. If that is so, then of course patriotism becomes a necessary cement of civil society. But it is the hope of every modern person that the Machiavellian intuition contains no necessary truth, and that a habit of bargaining under international law will come to replace the previous pattern of belligerence. Nevertheless, it has to be recognized that patriotism is not simply a stance towards the international world. It is in the first instance a condition of private life, and occupies a unique place in the deliberations of the citizen. To understand it we must refer again to two axioms of conservative thought. I call them axioms, although they are implicit and unspoken in the instincts of *homo conservans*.

The national focus

The first axiom is the simple principle that, lacking an overmastering ideal (in the sense explained in Chapter 1), conservatism must necessarily take many forms. Solon, asked what is the best form of government, replied 'For whom? And at what time?' It is a country, a particular history, a particular form of life that commands the respect and energy of conservatives, and while they may have an imaginative grasp of other real or ideal arrangements, they are not immersed in them as they are immersed in the society that is their own. No utopian vision will have force for them compared to the force of present practice, for while the former is abstract and incomplete, the latter is concrete, qualified by familiar complexities that may be understood without describing them. To the extent that there are arrangements that have been proven in social life, and which have power to command the loyalty of their participants, to that extent is there variety among the forms of conservative politics. Moral scruples may turn conservatives from condoning everything that conservatives think and do elsewhere; but their preferred form of political life will not be a deduction from abstract principles sufficient in themselves to forbid what they find distasteful.

The priority of appearance

The second axiom is more difficult, although equally fundamental to the conservative creed. This is that the political activity of citizens is determined by their own conception of their social nature. The reality of politics is not to be found outside the motives of those who engage in it, and whatever Marxists may say about the relation between base and superstructure, or about the economic causation of social behaviour, its truth does not bear on the political understanding of humanity. (This is a point to which I shall return in Chapter 5.)

The argument may be illustrated by an analogy from the science of linguistics. Suppose that a linguist presented a law of English speech, which told us when someone will say 'The house is white', and when he will say 'Something is white'. Given sufficient theory, this law would provide a complete account of the relation between those sentences, since it would tell us all the facts about their utterance: when, where and why. But in another sense it would be incomplete. For there is a connection between those sentences that may have nothing to do with causality, and yet which is of the first importance, a connection of meaning. It is this connection which is grasped by the person who understands them, who may have a complete understanding of them while being ignorant of the linguist's laws. And conversely, the linguist may have a full knowledge of causal laws, and yet lack the native speaker's understanding of what is said. For his laws may not issue in a dictionary.

Similarly, whatever the economic, social and biological determinants of a person's behaviour, that behaviour is understood by him and his fellows in another way: in terms of its meaning. To describe this meaning one would have to use the concepts available to the agent, and not the specialized classifications of a predictive science. Moreover, a person's intentions and acts derive from his own conception of the world; there can be no 'impartial observer' of human behaviour, if that means an observer who has no imaginative understanding of the concepts which determine agency. To engage in political activity is to understand, and in varying degrees to share, the common way of seeing things. This may require an act of imaginative identification; but it does not involve (and indeed is largely incompatible with) the application of any neutral 'science of man'.

What is this 'surface' of social affairs, this thing that is understood in participation but which may resist translation into words? In the first instance, to put the matter very simply, one may refer to the 'culture' of a society or nation. By 'culture' I mean all those activities which endow the world with meaning, so that it bears the mark of appropriate action and appropriate response. It is this which constitutes the individual's understanding of his social nature. Such understanding is given not through choice, but rather through concepts and perceptions embodied in the social organism, practices (such as that of marriage) which it does not make sense to think of as the products of individual will, or the outcome of some 'social contract' the terms of which no one can state or remember. A practice belongs to culture whenever it leads its participants to perceive the value of what they do. This perception may not be fully available to an outsider, but it may be essential to the intention which underlies a social act.

There is, to put it bluntly, something deeply self-deceived in the idea of a fulfilled human being whose style of life is entirely of his own devising. The cult of 'authenticity' – emphasizing the truth that the individual self is in some sense an artifact – espouses the self-contradictory position that it is by himself that he is made. This myth of self as *causa sui* is one to which few people now subscribe. Clearly the artifact of self is not of my making; it was cast first in the mould of a social arrangement and lives with that shape stamped permanently upon it, more or less distorted or embellished by later acts of choice. I shall argue that, once we have rejected the cult of 'authenticity', we shall be forced to reject along with it the entire apparatus of radical dissent. In particular, we shall have to abandon the attempt to erode whatever is 'established', whatever has a vested power to overcome opposition, which is the first principle of liberal as of socialist thought. Which is not to say that we must accept all that is established; but we will be forced to acknowledge that, whatever we postulate by way of an ideal, the ideal itself may have little life outside the social arrangement which provided the concepts and the perceptions of those who pursue it. And once it is clear that a major and perhaps central part of those concepts and perceptions is inherited, then custom, tradition and common culture become ruling conceptions in politics. If these provide ordinary citizens with a sense of the value of their acts, then self-identity and allegiance to public forms are ultimately one and the same.

Patriotism

We now begin to see the relevance of our second conservative axiom – the axiom that politics deals with the surface of social consciousness. A full understanding of the idea of allegiance will require in its turn an understanding of tradition, custom and ceremony – of the totality of practices through which citizens are able to perceive their allegiance as an end. For the liberal, allegiance to society is a means: 'stick to this arrangement and on the whole you'll be left to yourself'. But the conservative cannot see it as a means to an end, since there is no description of the end in question that does not refer back to the values – and hence to the customs, institutions and allegiances – of those who pursue it. It follows that while the forms of patriotism will be many and varied, they will seek always to express themselves in symbolic acts, acts which resist translation as 'means to an end'. Consider the loyalty to the Crown, as English people envisage it. Monarchy is an institution, with a complex constitutional background, that elevates the person of the monarch above the realm of individual character and endows him or her with the dignity and, so to speak, the objectivity of office. It is not the personal qualities of the Queen that draw the English to her nor is it any considered knowledge of the function and history of the Crown. It is rather a sense of the monarch as a symbol of nationhood, as an incarnation of the historical entity of which the English are a part. Their loyalty to the monarch requires ceremonial enactment, customary usage, an established code of deference: for this is the style of all symbolic gestures in which society and individual are merged.

Now conservatives are likely to value the institution of monarchy, and the kind of patriotism that it engenders. For the legitimacy of monarchical rule arises 'transcendentally', in the manner of the duties and obligations of family life. The monarch is not chosen for her personal attributes, nor does she have obligations and expectations which are the subject-matter of any 'social contract'. She is simply the representation of sovereignty, and its ceremonial presence. Her will as monarch is not her individual will, but the will of the state. The monarch forms part of that surface of concepts and symbols whereby citizens can perceive their social identity, and perceive society not as a means to an end, but as an end in itself. Attachment to the monarch is therefore patriotism in a pure form, a form that could not be translated into a policy, or a choice of means.

As a matter of fact, even when the titular head of state is 'chosen' – where there is an elected president, say, who offers 'promises' to the voters – the choice is not in fact a choice of policy. The aims of politics, as they arise from day to day, are beyond the voters' competence, the ideals of social policy largely beyond their care. Usually, therefore, the president is chosen not as a means to an end, but as a peculiar kind of end in himself – as a 'statesman'. Once again, he is a symbol. In a world of mass communication this means that a president will be chosen for his 'style', where style carries an implication of inward identity between president and nation, an identity that derives from no common end to which they might both be moving. This attachment to style represents an attempt to escape from the burden of democratic election, to escape from the 'contractual' element of the choice, to escape most of all from the sense of the state as constantly remade at each election, like a machine that has become outclassed. It is an expression of the conservative instinct, the instinct to make a future in the image of the past.

But just as the past constrains the future, so does the future commandeer the past. The past as understood by the citizen is the past directed to the future. Continuity is a selective aim; it looks both backwards and forwards with a measure of distrust. But we must remember the distinctive place of the past in our practical understanding: unlike the future, the past is known. How then should it enter our political calculations?

Tradition

That question brings us to the final concept that will be necessary in giving articulate voice to the conservative instinct towards society, the concept of tradition. Under this concept I include all manner of custom, ceremony, and participation in institutional life, where what is done is done, not mechanically, but for a reason, and where the reason lies, not in what will be, but in what has been. It does not matter if the reason cannot be voiced by the person who obeys it: traditions are enacted and not designed, and none the less conscious for the lack of speech.

The power of tradition is twofold. First, it makes history into reason, and therefore the past into a present aim (as the whole history of the nation is enacted in the ceremony of coronation). Second, tradition arises from every organization in society, and is no mere trapping of the exercise of power. Traditions arise and command respect wherever individuals seek to relate themselves to something transcendent. They arise in clubs and societies, in local life, in religion and family custom, in education, and in every institution where people are brought into contact with their kind. Later, in considering questions of politics, we must show how the state can bring authority, allegiance, and tradition together, in order to define the citizen as subject.

I am aware that any reference to tradition will cause scepticism among those who believe themselves free from its charm. And there is no doubt that, while the concept may be essential to conservative doctrine, it will also (like the 'equality', 'freedom' and 'social justice' which rival it) have to bear more weight of political argument than any single conception can sustain. But we must do our best for it. Whatever difficulties may attend the enterprise of defending tradition, the fight concerns no fiction but a genuine reality.

Modern liberals tend to scoff at the idea of tradition. All traditions, they tell us, are 'invented', implying that they can therefore be undone.[16] This looks plausible only if you take the trivial examples – Scottish country dancing, Highland dress, the Coronation ceremony, Christmas cards, and whatever else comes with a 'heritage' label. A real tradition is not an invention; it is the unintended *by-product* of invention, which also makes invention possible. Our musical tradition is one astounding example of this. No single person created it. Each contributor built on previous achievements, discovering problems and solving them through the steady expansion of the common syntax. Notation developed side by side with harmony and counterpoint. No single person could ever have discovered the knowledge of the human ear and the human heart which these practices contain, any more than a single person could discover a language. The example shows what a tradition really is: not a custom or a ritual but a form of social knowledge.

By social knowledge I mean the kind of knowledge embodied in the common law, in parliamentary procedures, in manners, costume and social convention, and also in morality. Such knowledge arises 'by an invisible hand' from the open-ended business of society, from problems which have been confronted and solved, from agreements which have been perpetuated by custom, from conventions which coordinate our otherwise conflicting passions, and from the unending process of negotiation and compromise whereby we quieten the dogs of war.

It was such knowledge that Burke had in mind when he attacked the a priori thinking of the French revolutionaries. 'We are afraid to put men to live and trade on their own private stock of reason,' he wrote, 'because we suspect that this stock in each man is small, and that individuals would do better to avail themselves of the general bank and capital of nations, and of ages'. Burke's imagery is in one respect misleading. Social knowledge does not accumulate as money does, nor does it grow in the manner of scientific knowledge, which can be stored in books. It exists only in and through its repeated exercise: it is social, implicit and practical, and can never be captured in a formula or plan. The best way to understand it, indeed, is through the failures of the planned economy.

The Austrian economists argued, plausibly enough, that prices in a market contain information that is indispensable to economic life.[17] This information exists only in the free exchange of goods and services; it is information about the real pressure of human needs. Hence the attempt to encompass economic life in a rational plan, with prices controlled from the centre, will destroy the information on which the plan must draw. Rationalism in economics is irrational.

The Austrian theory parallels Oakeshott's attack on rationalism in politics.[18] It can also be applied in other spheres where social knowledge is the foundation of rational conduct, as Hayek has shown.[19] The common law, for example, contains information that could not be contained in a legislative programme – information about conflicts and their resolution, about the sense of justice in action, and about human expectations, which is dispersed through the open-ended record of the law, and which is never available when legislation is the sole legal authority. Hence the attempt to remake the legal order, through a legislative code which embodies all permissible solutions, is profoundly irrational. Such a code will destroy the source of legal knowledge, which is the judgement of impartial judges, as they confront the unforeseeable course of human conflict.

Social knowledge arises from the search over time for agreement. Even the common law, which leans on coercion, involves the attempt to find socially agreed solutions. Hence the outcome of a case in common law is always clear: rights and liabilities are determined. But the principle – the *ratio decidendi* – may not be clear at all, and may emerge only later, in the tradition of judicial reasoning.

The example of the common law gives the lie to the liberal scoffing at tradition. Equally important, however, is the example of art, which is in a curious way nearer to the conservative sense of the value of tradition than either the law or the traditions of parliamentary government. Both art and politics are imbued with significance and purposefulness, and yet neither (on the conservative view) has any real external purpose. Art shows in microcosm the great architectural problem of politics as we are beginning to envisage it. And the comparison enables us to see why we should consider again the complaint that conservatism holds no prospect for the 'modern man': that it is far from being the impulse of life in death, but rather the will for death in life. For in art too we have felt the cravings, the disorientation, the overwhelming estrangement of 'modern' man, and in art too it has seemed necessary to present as self-conscious what was previously felt as nature, instinct and life.

But in the very sphere where the embattled consciousness of modern man has most displayed itself, so too has the conservative principle been repeatedly affirmed. By this I do not mean that the artists who brought about the major aesthetic achievements of the twentieth century were, politically, of a conservative cast. If this is true, then it is only an instance of a more general truth – swallowed with some difficulty by critics of the New Left – that significant artists can be, and very often are, that way. (It is interesting to note the frequency with which it has been assumed, since the Romantic movement, that art must necessarily be a revolutionary force, simply because it has revolutionized itself. The assumption looks very odd when set beside the varieties of social conservatism expressed and advocated by James, Conrad, Yeats, Pound, Eliot, Joyce, Waugh and Lawrence – to name only the greatest of those who created our modern literature.)

What does it mean, then, to say that the conservative principle has been repeatedly reaffirmed in contemporary art? Partly this: that for most significant artists – for Eliot, Pound and Joyce, for Schoenberg and Stravinsky, for Matisse and Moore – the problem of giving articulate voice to the modern consciousness was conceived as the problem of making that consciousness part of a tradition of artistic expression, and so bringing it back, by whatever complicated route, to the point where it might be understood. For Schoenberg the tradition of German music was what principally mattered: the problem was to re-create it, through self-conscious understanding of its inner life. The 'live tradition' that Pound hoped to 'gather from the air' was conceived in equally self-conscious terms. Eliot went so far as to represent tradition as an individual artifact: to belong to a tradition is also to make that tradition;

to be part of history is to have created history.[20] However, this process, which begins in loss and in conscious exploration, ends too in genuine discovery, the discovery that 'History is now and England'. In that discovery is a restoration of the whole of things.

It would be interesting to digress further into the transformation of the idea of tradition in the modern mind. But let us simply draw the obvious conclusion from our parallel. Just as tradition circumscribes the possibilities of artistic expression, and so must be constantly re-created in artistic change, so too does it lay down the forms of political life, and must be re-created in every conscious political act. Now it is both difficult and yet (it seems) at the same time necessary for the modern consciousness to create tradition, setting itself in the centre of tradition as it sets tradition in the centre of itself. It may require an act of imagination, insight and will for politicians, in the midst of confusion, to reassert the identity of the society that they seek to govern, even when nothing less than that is required by the people. The route back to the place from which we started will not find the place unchanged, and the way will be hard and uncertain. Politicians will need exceptional qualities – the qualities of a De Gaulle or a Disraeli – if they are to reaffirm as statesmen the reality which they know as people. Yet, if they have the will to live, and the will to govern, nothing short of that can satisfy them. As one writer has suggested,[21] there is no general explanation of how people re-create and accept traditions. Nor is it easy to draw the line between genuine re-creation and the establishment of new and divergent social forms. But in all attempts to restore, re-create and assimilate tradition, the feature of continuity remains. When someone acts from tradition he sees what he now does as belonging to a pattern that transcends the focus of his present interest, binding it to what has previously been done, and done successfully. Naturally there are rival traditions, and it would be vain to pretend that there is reason to belong to all of them: there are traditions of torture, crime and revolution. The traditions which conservatives uphold have the weight of a successful history – which is to say that they are the palpable remainder of something that has flourished, and not the latest in a series of abortive starts. Secondly, they engage the loyalty of their participants, in the deep sense of moulding their idea of what they are and should be. (Contrast the traditions of family life with those of torture.) Finally, they point to something durable, something which survives and gives meaning to the acts that emerge from it.

But what does this tradition concretely amount to? No simple answer to this question can prove satisfactory: the task of doctrine is to bridge the gap between philosophy and practice, and it is only in practice that the sum of our traditions can be understood. Nevertheless, it still belongs to doctrine to delineate the *kind* of thing that is intended, and to present some partial exposition of its instances. Tradition, then, must include all those practices which serve to define the individual's 'being in society'. It constitutes his image of himself as a fragment of the greater social organism, and at the same time as the whole of that organism implicit in this individual part. The institution of the family, as it has variously developed, provides a clear example. Those who participate in that institution cannot remain unaffected in their conception of themselves. They can no longer regard the fact of fatherhood, for example, as a biological accident. In seeing yourself as father you find yourself entangled in a bond of responsibility. And the reason for this bond and for the actions which express it, lies in the fact that this is how things are. Moreover, they are like this because they have been like this. The idea of 'family', through which your responsibilities, aims and preoccupations are from day to day defined, is one inherited without thought from your own participation in the arrangement which it designates. This is what is 'given'. Had you not conceived your activities as exemplifying the historical pattern contained in that concept, then you would nevertheless have needed some adequate replacement, some rival conception in terms of which to define your ends. And if this conception does not belong to tradition it will make way for the dangerous thought: 'Perhaps I do this, not for its own sake, not for what it is, but as a means to an end. Where then is the end? Where is the profit?' This thought signifies the emergence of the individual from social life, and the first glimpse of the empty solipsism that waits outside. Tradition restores the individual to the present act: it shows the reason in the act, and stills the desire for a justifying aim.

The family is of course an obvious example, as is the common law. But there are others, such as the customs which surround the momentous occasions of birth, coupling and death, the customs of hospitality, rivalry and class allegiance, of manners, dress and common courtesy. There are also the institutions of religion, in which the desire for an identity greater than human nature provides reaches out of history altogether, to what is outside time and change. Only some of these institutions, it might be thought, are truly political. But to take such a view is to take too narrow a view of politics. Every tradition of any importance in the life of the citizen will tend to become part of the establishment of a state. This principle – which we might call the law of establishment and which I shall illustrate in Chapter 8 – is part of the natural history of politics, and shows the continuing necessity for political action to extend beyond the bounds of economic management. It is illustrated not only by the explicit establishment of the Church and, through the operation of law, of the family and private property, but by the more recent establishment of the traditions of organized labour in the trade-union movement, and by the extension of law (less automatic in America than in England, but manifest even there) to protect every aspect of social life, just as soon as it seems to be of more than individual concern.

A note of scepticism

What of the conservative attitude to social transformation? What 'tradition' has force, in comparison with the violence of industrial expansion and of over-population, with the spread of irreligion, and the growth of the urban underclass? Is there not an element of make-believe in the view that allegiance, authority and custom might have survived these historical convulsions, so as still to provide the bond from which politics derives its inspiration and appeal?

If this scepticism is the prelude to a rival politics, then it calls for only one reply: what other bond are you imagining? And how will you bring it about? But usually it takes a more unsettling form, the form, as one might put it, of the 'broad historical perspective'. It makes no recommendations, espouses no policies, and stands above the particular beliefs of the communities which it seeks to observe. The historical perspective looks down on the world of human beings from a height where their activity is seen only as the movement of impersonal forces, which propel the politician precisely when he most believes that he is guiding them. Withdrawing to this height, it may for the moment seem as though the task of discovering and asserting continuity is a hopeless one, that all things have changed utterly, and that in nothing is there a lasting principle of government.

I shall try to answer certain common forms of this historian's doubt. But two things should be said at once in reply to it. First, some of the items of doctrine that I have considered have a philosophical basis which places them beyond the reach of historical criticism. The view of society as requiring forms of allegiance, and a recognition of authority, both of which transcend the operation of any contractual agreement, is a view not of this or that community, but of the essence of civil life. It is this transcendent bond that constitutes society, and which is misrepresented by the liberal theories of contract and consent. Moreover, one particular tradition, which both embodies a transcendent bond, and also reinforces social allegiance, has survived the upheavals of recent history and is only now beginning to crumble. This is the tradition of family life. Even a 'revolutionary state' will find itself dependent upon it, and placed under the necessity to create (usually through the old expedient of belligerent foreign policy) the corresponding bond of social unity. And when, as is now happening, the family begins to disintegrate, people do not look on the result as a liberation, but rather as an enormous social threat, against which they seek to defend themselves.

Secondly, it may be true that particular bonds of allegiance have decayed or fallen apart. But if some people think (in their vociferous part) that the bond of citizenship has been loosened or undone, this does not show that their thought corresponds either to reality or to the true political sentiments which guide them. Much is disturbed; old loyalties have gone under and new ones risen in their place. But through all this, I shall argue, conservatives can find and uphold a genuine continuity. And their reason for doing so will be apparent in the attempt.

Concluding remarks

I have surveyed the great 'datum' of civil society. What, then, are the doctrines to which that survey gives support? There are two principles so basic as to constitute axioms of conservative thinking. First, the principle that there is no general politics of conservatism. The forms of conservatism will be as varied as the forms of social order. Second, the principle that conservatism engages with the surface of things, with the motives, reasons, traditions and values of the society from which it draws its life. There are further ideas, abstract in their origin, but specific in their implications: society exists through authority, and the recognition of this authority constitutes a bond that is not contractual but transcendent, in the manner of the family tie. Such a bond requires tradition and custom through which to realize itself as a public fact. But tradition is no static thing. It is the active achievement of continuity; it can be restored, rescued and amended as grace and opportunity allow.

It is to the political implications of social life, and the constitution of the order in which it is lived, that we now must turn.

3
Constitution and the State

Burckhardt wrote of the 'great modern fallacy that a constitution can be *made'*.[22] It would be equally true to speak of the greater modern fallacy that a constitution can be endlessly and in every particular reformed. The customs, allegiances and traditions to which I have referred form the life of a civil society: they do not yet amount to the constitution of a state. And yet clearly they owe their continuance to a presiding power, and that power (which is the power of the state) must contain in itself the authority of something 'given' if it is to protect and enshrine loyalties and obligations that arise from no individual choice.

The making of a constitution

Liberalism, which sees the state as a means to the end of individual freedom, is bound to consider civil society to be absolutely separate from the state, and to require of the latter only the minimum of interference in the life of society which the aim of freedom requires. It therefore must naturally tend to the view that a constitution can be made (for if it is no more than a means to an end, it suffices to understand the end in order to calculate the most effective means to it). Liberals often point to the example of the American constitution as proof of this contention. And constitutional reforms proposed by the government of Mr Blair seem to be based on the American model. But the example is a bad one. It ignores the American inheritance, and the peculiar circumstances that led to drawing up a document designed both to secure the unity and to safeguard the eccentricities of the original participant states. It ignores all that language and custom had already established – in particular the tradition of English common law which both preceded and survived the break with the Crown. It ignores the unique social position of the Founding Fathers, educated gentlemen who could propagate the myth of a 'new constitution' while enjoying the privileges of an established order which already defined their social goal. (Madison was able to say in Federal Convention in 1787: 'our government ought to secure the permanent interests of the country against innovation'; it is part of the genius of such men as Madison and Jefferson that they were able to fulfil that aim.) It ignores the conflicts which were suppressed in the final ratification, which still persist and which generated the bloodiest civil war yet to have been seen. It ignores the already constituted rights and liberties which made the conscious adoption of a 'constitution' into a coherent gesture. It ignores the logic of common-law jurisdiction, which entails that the American Constitution is not contained in a single document but in four hundred volumes of intricate case law. In short, it ignores the fact that the written constitution of the United States – like any written constitution – is an abstract formula, of no more concrete significance than the *Déclaration des Droits de l'Homme et du Citoyen*. It is true even now that the very meaning of this slender document is something that can be decided only by judicial process.[23] And judicial interpretation takes account – whether consciously or unconsciously – of issues that determine the fabric of civil life. It is history and not the written word which reveals the constitution of America, and that part of it which is usually identified as the whole is no more than a delicate superstructure, resting on an unfathomable base.

State and civil society

Now it is clear that, while conservatives may require a loose connection between the state and civil society (looser, say, than that which exists in communist China), they will see the state as end and not as means, just as they see civil society. The state as means (as administrative machine, or business enterprise, or welfare officer, or whatever) – such a state is not one to which citizens can belong in the way that they belong to a family, a marriage, a regiment or a club. Nor are the ends which the state is supposed to serve really capable of independent description. This is certainly true of the liberal end of freedom. Naturally, one's neighbours may interfere with one, to a greater or lesser extent, but until we are given some concrete description of the social and political arrangement, it is impossible to say whether more or less of this interference is desirable. The 'interference' proper to a rural community in Zululand is greater than anything once experienced in a Soviet city. Yet it would be sadly misguided to call it a loss of freedom, when subjection to this kind of interference is precisely what it is to *be* a Zulu. And as soon as there is interference, there is a form of rule, and therefore a state, however loosely constituted. Without some move in this direction, towards constituted power, a person is neither free nor unfree but lives like the nomads of the anarchistic commune, in a perpetual hallucination of freedom that can be translated only into solipsistic acts.

To treat the state as end and not as means is to see the aims of the state as arising internally, out of its own life and self-interaction. It is wholly natural to see institutions in some such way. Consider a football team, an institution to which some people belong and to which others attach their loyalty. It commands this loyalty not as a means but as an end: it is *this* group, acting in this way that matters. It is not a means to the end of scoring goals (an activity which, outside the institution of football, would make no sense). Nor is it a means to the pleasure of those observing it. It is, rather, something to which one may belong, in a variety of ways, and the benefit of which resides precisely in the tie of membership.

Conservatives are recognizable as political animals partly by their respect for constitution (for the state as 'given'), and by their reluctance to effect any complete separation – either in theory or in practice – between state and civil society. It is (as I remarked) a fundamental tenet of liberal thought that this separation exists in theory, and ought also to exist in fact. One modern writer has compared fascism and communism in our times by saying that, whereas the former elevates the functions of civil society to the level of state, the latter allows the state to swallow the functions of society.[24] But such rhetorical juggling misrepresents the nature of the relation. There are not two entities here, but rather one entity seen under separate aspects. Similarly a human being is not two entities – soul and body – but one entity which can be seen in both a material and a personal way. Liberalism is like a political survival of the Cartesian theory of mind, an attempt to represent the mind of society as functioning in accidental relation to its body. And in order to verify this image to itself, the massive conscience of liberalism has laboured to sunder the life of society from its spiritual 'form', and contemplated with increasing amazement the result, which is not the life but the death of the 'body politic'.

Conservatives see the constitution as the inherited principle of the life of the state, and the state in its turn not just as the guardian but also as the expression of a social entity. They are not concerned with 'alternatives' – for to speak of alternatives suggests that we are considering rival means to some universal end. For conservatives end and means are the same: the life of the body politic. Moreover it is as deep an instinct in a conservative as it is in a socialist to resist the champions of 'minimal' government, and to recognize the essence of politics in established power. Where they differ is in their idea of legitimacy, which, for conservatives, stems not from results but from origins. The reasons that conservatives acknowledge refer not to any hypothetical or abstract future, but to a real and concrete past. It is in the past, and the past as it makes itself present, that they will find their reasons for the pursuit of power. And that pursuit will again be seen not as means but as end, as an expression of their political identity. The pursuit of power by politicians is simply a part, and a necessary part, of the life of the state, and the true statesman is the one whose personal ambition and personal success coincide with the enduring forces of civil order.

Human rights

How is this attitude to the state to be translated into doctrine? I shall approach this difficult question negatively. First, conservatives will be loath to found their political enterprise upon any idea of 'universal' or 'natural' rights. In the conflict with communism the conception of 'human rights' played a major part, partly because it provided a simple way to envisage the evident fact – that the communist governments imposed on Europe by the Soviet Union had no legitimacy, and were, in the last analysis, masks for a destructive empire. As the example reminds us, there are good states and bad states, tyrannies and peaceful communities; and conservatives must judge between them. And they do not deny themselves the use of such epithets as 'just' and 'unjust' in the process. But to think that the whole difference can be summed up in terms of a simple body of abstract rights, which can be specified for all human beings, independently of their origin and allegiance, is neither feasible politics nor plausible doctrine. There are only rights where there are obligations; and whose is the obligation to provide? No doubt the United Nations Charter of Human Rights contains many moral truths; but what social arrangement, what community of common interests, what mutual understanding between people, gives rise to the political obligation to comply with it?

The British people are the fortunate inheritors of a long tradition of social life and established power; their rights have been granted and won through a process in which the nature and identity of the nation was seldom at risk (and was never more at risk than when the doctrine of the rights of man gained sudden ascendancy). Naturally their rights, embodied in the common law, grant to them a measure of freedom, and an expectation of just treatment, that other people have not achieved, and maybe have never desired. This is surely not the best language in which to pass judgement on the tyrannies of the modern world, whose deficiencies arise less from their failure to acknowledge the 'universal' rights enshrined in Western democracy, than in their destruction of all procedures whereby the citizens can defend themselves against the arbitrary use of political power.

Rights and privileges

The notion of 'rights' has achieved an unnatural predominance in the language of politics. Conservatives have tended to conceive the power of the state as an embodiment of privilege, rather than as a source of gifts. A privilege is part of the apparatus of government, and not separate from the exercise of political authority. (Thus the title 'Duke' is a privilege only if it represents some form of social or political precedence, otherwise, as Huckleberry Finn discovered, a Duke is a very ornery kind of thing.) A gift, on the other hand, is a benefit that is freely bestowed. It requires neither service to, nor position in, nor even membership of the state. Welfare, for example, is a gift, which consequently confers on the recipient no political status; while it is often claimed as a 'right', it cannot possibly be so conceived by someone who takes the conservative view of politics. Moreover, such gifts involve a transference of power without any transference of authority (in this they differ markedly from political privilege). Indeed, this illustrates one of the channels through which authority flows away from the heart of politics, and transforms itself into the mere power of the underdog, who has nothing political but his 'rights', and no reciprocal obligations which would establish a genuine title to them.

Now conservatives are not opposed to charity, and, as I shall later argue, they will be constrained to accept some version of the welfare state. Nevertheless they may be reluctant to subscribe to the universal transfer of charity to the offices of the state, and for reasons which the example demonstrates. In fostering the illusion of a 'natural' right to home, health, wealth and comfort, the state erodes both the individual's will and its own authority. The state becomes a kind of machine, a centre of distribution, an alien object which sometimes grants, and sometimes withholds, what is thought of as an independent right. For the conservative the state is not a machine, but an organism – more, a person. Its laws are those of life and death, sickness and regeneration. It contains reason, will and friendship. Not all its citizens lie at an equal remove from it; some enjoy privileges that others may not have. For its substance is power, and its form authority. There is no equal distribution of the first of these, that does not dissipate the second. In Chapter 8 I shall ask the question how, and for what reason, might power become authority, and what are the privileges that emerge, or ought to emerge, when it does so.

The state as person

The last two sections have given covert content to the metaphor which lies at the heart of conservative thinking. People are organisms: they are born, they flourish, they sicken and die. Our attitudes are conditioned by mortality: it constitutes our impetus and limitation. But we are not mere animals, we are also rational beings It is not that we are two beings, joined by some Cartesian knot, but that our organic forces are subject to a peculiar living principle, and the proper functioning of this principle constitutes our happiness. We have the capacity to argue, to persuade and to be persuaded. We can form ties and obligations, recognize rights and duties. We have consciousness of self and other, and a system of values which stems from that. Our world is imbued with will, directed from past to future. Reason informs our organic life, lifting it from the immersion in present appetite, and casting it in the dramatic roles of self-conscious reflection. Hence, just as reason depends upon organic life, so does life's continuity come to depend upon the exercise of reason.

Likewise the organism of society is shaped by a reasoned intellect. This intellect is the 'constitution' through which the self-image of society is formed. Such a constitution, like the rational principle in people, will recognize ties, obligations, privileges and duties. It has arguments; it persuades or is persuaded. (Hence there is a distinctly political process, which is not the process of revolution, nor the mere pursuit of power.) Constitution endows the life of society with continuity and will. It creates history in the place of succession. But the state depends upon its organic base: its will and self-image require the continuity of the social organism, just as the organism comes to depend upon the forms of constituted power. State and civil society permeate each other; in their sundering lies the death of both. It is hardly surprising therefore that, in a healthy body politic, the constitution remains tacit, general and inexplicit. To suppose otherwise is like supposing a rational being to control himself from outside, in accordance with a programme of instructions that remain unchanged by the appetites and passions of his body. Just as reason permeates the life of man, so does constitution permeate the movement of society. If we speak of a 'bond' that joins society and state, this is only because their peculiar mutuality exists in varying degrees. In the primitive tribe society barely translates itself into political forms: all is instinct, organism, outside history and change. In the authoritarian state, society marches rigidly, bound in the fetters of a constitution that hampers its movements and deadens its life. It is the body of a puritan marching in the chains of his conscience. The ideal of relaxed personhood, in which reason and passion flourish together, is reached differently at different times. In the political sphere, it is reached when social life and constitutional forms exist in harmony. But of course it never is reached; only approached, in manners which exhibit no universal pattern and no external aim. We must therefore look to the ways in which our society has come near to its ideal, and the ways in which it falls away from it.

I hope that enough has been made of our metaphor to give it cogency. The arguments for its truth are deep and difficult. I shall hint at them, and sometimes bring them forward. My purpose in doing so will be not to prove the underlying philosophy, but to articulate and give support to crucial items of conservative thinking.[25] But here we see why we must reject the language of the 'rights of man'. No more than any other person can a state represent the privileges which it confers as 'natural'. A state's relations with its citizens reflect the same principle that is embodied in the citizens' relations among themselves: the principle that to claim a right is also to confer one. The doctrine of 'natural' rights is an attempt to avoid the penalty which all true rights impose. Hence its immediate appeal. And hence its political vacuity.

Essence and identity

To reject the language of 'natural' rights is to take a steptowards Burke's idea of a national 'essence': the idea that there is a core of political life which generates the activities of the state. This essence will be the true 'constitution' of the state. A constitution, whether written or unwritten, is not a body of rules. What rules there are can be interpreted only in terms of a background of custom, habit, convention and a certain 'style' which shows how things are done. This is evident in the conduct of the British Parliament, where it is impossible to separate rule from custom without doing violence to both. (It is customary for the sovereign to ask the leader of the party which commands a majority in the

Commons to be her minister. This is not a rule, nor is it a habit: but it is presupposed in the entire practice of government. The flexibility of the sovereign power in this respect can be immediately verified in the exercise of George V's prerogative in the matter of the National Government of 1931.)

If the constitution is not just a body of rules, how are we to identify it, and how are we to separate it, if at all, from the customs which constitute civil society? The answer, to put it briefly, is that the constitution consists in those rules and customs through which people engage in the exercise of power: it is what guides, limits and authorizes power, and thus manifests itself primarily through law, through the 'style' of law, and through the position of the citizen as defined by law. It may change and develop in accordance with its own inner logic – the logic of precedent, practice and judicial abstraction.[26] The conservative instinct is not to prevent that change – since it is the vital motion of the state but to guard the essence which survives it, and which enables us to say that its various stages are stages in the life of one body politic. And the constitutional essence guards in its turn the social essence. Here then, is the conservative cause in politics. Civil society, once destroyed, can seldom be revived. Yet this living thing is vulnerable. It demands protection and fulfilment in the constituted state. And one business of the conservative politician is to fight the contagions which oppress the state, and uphold the institutions which nourish it. I shall describe some of the contagions, and then later attempt to show the constitutional essence which has so far survived them. This is not the place for either optimism or pessimism; to borrow the image which was once used to such effect by an Indian chieftain: men drink the water of life from many cups, and ours is not broken.[27]

Democracy

De Tocqueville wrote of democracy that it 'not only makes each man forget his forefathers, but it conceals from him his descendants and separates him from his contemporaries; it ceaselessly throws him back on himself alone and threatens finally to confine him entirely in the solitude of his own heart'.[28] That is a strong way of putting it, and one that reflects the bitterness spread by the French Revolution in the feelings of all its descendants. But it contains a truth. The great difficulty lies in finding the language with which to persuade people to acknowledge de Tocqueville's meaning. The social fragmentation presaged by de Tocqueville is as elusive as it is virulent, while the supposed legitimacy of the democratic process is a conception of permanent and vivid appeal. Should politicians wish to criticize the democratic process they must represent themselves as opposed, not to democracy, but to some local or specialized form of it – proportional representation, say, or the single-chamber parliament, or the plebiscite. But these specialized forms exemplify the same principle that they must also claim to be defending, the principle that, in matters of government, it is the opinion of the governed that confers legitimacy upon what is done. It might be possible to argue against the use of a referendum, on the grounds that twenty million people ought not to be asked to make a momentous decision concerning a matter about which almost all of them know nothing (for example, whether to join or not to join the European Monetary Union). It might be possible to argue against proportional representation, on the grounds that it will generate a parliament that is weak, irresolute and peppered with crackpots. But all such arguments rely on a principle that denies the basis of democracy. For they assert that popular opinion is a legitimate guide only in so far as it is authorized by a constitution that limits its excesses. Hence the legitimacy of government cannot be conferred merely by democratic choice.

It is for some such reason that, when Burke first tried, in his great essay on the French Revolution, to locate the principle of constitution, he could not see total franchise as a necessary part of it, or as having anything to do with the legitimacy of rule. And it is quite possible that even now the constitutional essence of our country would remain unaffected were the franchise to be confined to people of position, education, wealth or power – to those, in other words, with a self-conscious interest in the fortunes of the nation. When Disraeli suddenly snatched from the Liberals the banner of electoral reform, it was certainly not because he had regarded universal suffrage as a Tory principle. The gesture was strategic and opportune. It also satisfied his sense that conservatives reside as much at the bottom as at the top of the social scale, and that it is in the middle class, with its contempt for the prejudice of others, that liberalism finds its natural home.

The extent of the ensuing commitment to democracy should not, however, be underrated. It survives in the doctrine (given increasing rhetorical impetus at every general election) of the 'mandate', according to which a party programme is a kind of promise to the people, and election success tantamount to a contractual undertaking to honour it. (If the programme contains more than one such 'promise', then a party may obtain a majority from an electorate all of whom had voted in a minority on the issue which most concerned them. To whom, then, is it fulfilling its obligation? This is no curious exception, but in all probability wholly normal. The view of electoral success as creating a quasi-contractual obligation is therefore nonsense.)

The commitment to democracy can be seen too in the recent decision by the Labour Government of Mr Blair to reform the House of Lords, in which it is taken for granted that the Upper House stands in need of reform simply because of the undemocratic process whereby it has been filled. This argument, taken seriously, would lead to the subversion of any institution (such as school, hospital, college, monastery) which depended for its health on a privilege to govern arising independently of the 'mandate' of its members. The underlying idea is again the profoundly anti-conservative one, that legitimacy can reside only in contractual or quasi-contractual agreement, and not in established usage. Hence, it is thought, the only legitimate government, or procedure, is one that has been 'chosen' or consented to by its subjects. Yet as soon as one considers the highly artificial circumstances of democratic choice, one must see that this 'choice' presupposes in its turn that the citizens should recognize some prior legitimacy in that which they do not and cannot choose – namely the procedures which make choice available, and the people and offices which guard them.

There is, however, a deeper reason for conservative suspicion of the democratic process, which is that, however fair and free, it will always give precedence to the needs and desires of those who are choosing now, regardless of the needs and desires of those who are not yet with us or those who are already dead. The very same theoretical weakness which afflicts the social contract, afflicts democratic choice – namely, that it privileges the living and their immediate interests over past and future generations. Hence it threatens to become a solvent of the long-term community and of the long-term perspective required by national survival.

Burke made the point in something like those terms in his great polemic against the French Revolution. But it is worth setting it in a more modern context, since it bears upon the most important questions that now confront us. Burke argued that we can view society as a contract (as the French Revolutionaries, following Rousseau, proposed) only if we recognize that the contract includes not the living only but also the unborn and the dead. Mention of the dead seems quaint to modern ears: after all, they are no longer with us, and therefore, you might suppose, have no interests which are affected by what we do. That is not how Burke saw the matter, however. The dead, he believed, have an enduring interest in our respect for them. Moreover, this is recognized by the law, which obliges us to carry out the will of a testator, whether or not it is in anyone else's interest.

But there is a much deeper reason to include the dead and their wishes in our calculations. From the beginning of time, it is respect for the dead that has formed the basis of institution-building. Schools, universities, hospitals, orphanages, clubs, libraries, churches and institutes began life as private foundations, dependent on property given or bequeathed by people no longer alive. The present holders of that property were, morally speaking, the temporary trustees. Respect for the dead forbad the arbitrary use of their bequests, and compelled the trustees to further the purposes which the founders and donors would approve. By honouring the dead, the living trustees were safeguarding the interests of their successors. Respect for the dead is the foundation of the attitude of trusteeship upon which future generations depend for their inheritance. Remove the dead from the equation, and you remove the unborn. And that, not to put too fine a point on it, is the real danger of unmoderated democracy.

Procedural limitations on democracy must therefore be designed to ensure that the voices of the dead and the unborn are heard in the political process. But not *any* dead and unborn: only those who belong to the first-person plural over which the sovereign power presides – the community-through-time which in modern terms is usually seen as a nation, the term 'nation' being etymologically connected with the idea of birth and descent without which the long-term perspective is seemingly impossible to grasp as a part of politics.

Monarchy

If democratic choice is to be rational, therefore, it must take place in the context of institutions and procedures that give a voice to absent generations. These institutions and procedures would, in effect, urge on the representatives an attitude of trusteeship, whereby the immediate demands of the living could be moderated or deflected in the interests of the long-term future of society. One such institution is the monarchy, as traditionally conceived. Not being elected by popular vote, the monarch cannot be understood merely as representing the interests of the present generation. He or she is born into the position, and also passes it on to a legally defined successor. If the monarch has a voice at all, it is understood precisely in the cross-generational way that is required by the political process. Monarchs are, in a very real sense, the voice of history, and the very accidental way in which they gain office emphasizes the grounds of their legitimacy, in the history of a people, a place and a culture. This is not to say that monarchs cannot be mad, irrational, self-interested or unwise. It is to say, rather, that they owe their authority and their influence precisely to the fact that they speak for something *other* than the present desires of present voters, something vital to the continuity and community which the act of voting assumes. Hence, if they are heard at all, they are heard as limiting the democratic process, in just the way that it must be limited if it is to issue in reasonable legislation.

The House of Lords

We in Britain have enjoyed another and more interesting incursion of the hereditary principle into the political process, through the existence of a hereditary second chamber in Parliament. This chamber has now been destroyed. But the arguments which prevailed against it are so weak and confused that it is worth saying something here about the virtues of the institution, lest it disappear unmourned from the political landscape.

The most important feature of the hereditary peerage, as traditionally understood, was that political office went hand in hand with enhanced social status, and with a title attached directly or indirectly to a piece of national territory. People coveted peerages, not for the wealth attached to them – for they were in fact expensive to maintain in the style expected, and were sometimes refused (as by Winston Churchill) for that very reason – but for the romance and dignity of the title. As traditionally conceived, the title was awarded not to an individual but to a family: it was passed from father to son, and constituted a permanent endorsement of a family's social status, while crowning it with real political power.

The result was that the upper chamber of Parliament consisted largely of people whose interests were not the short-term interests of a living human being, but the long-term interests of a family. And first among such interests is a deep-seated desire for social and political continuity. A privilege enjoyed by inheritance can be safeguarded only if the social and political arrangements which confer it are maintained. Inevitably, therefore, a hereditary upper house will see itself as guardian or trustee of a social and political legacy, and to that extent a brake on the democratic process. If we think that the democratic process needs just such a brake, then this is a strong argument in favour of the hereditary upper house.

Heredity is not sufficient in itself to generate aristocrats who are worthy of the privilege. We need further conditions, if a competent political class is to emerge from the inheritance of office, just as we need further conditions, if a competent political elite is to emerge from majority voting. Nevertheless, 'the hereditary principle', as Burke called it, is one of the few proven ways to place the long-term point of view at the heart of politics.

I admit that this is no answer to the question – virtually the only question currently debated – why should the accident of birth confer a right to legislate? But then there *is* no answer to that question. Nor is there an answer to this question: why should democratic election confer a right to legislate? For there *is* no right to legislate. Legislation is not a right but a privilege, conferred differently under different political systems. It is, of course, a privilege that can be abused, and which has been repeatedly abused, under both aristocratic and democratic dispensations. The unuttered wisdom that until recently prevailed in our country, was that abuse could be minimized by balancing aristocratic and democratic chambers against each other, each having the power to correct the excesses of the other.

In order to understand the defects of untramelled democracy, we need to compare it with some alternative. My argument has been tending towards the traditional alternative of aristocracy. But let us be clear what we mean by this. The term comes from the Greek, and literally means 'rule by the best'. But this is not what it has meant in our history, and not what it could mean as a political prescription. There is no known method for securing 'rule by the best'. Many methods for gaining and bestowing political power have been tried in the course of human history, and all of them have, at some time, produced 'rule by the worst' – and that is true of democracy too, as we know from the case of Germany. What is valuable in democracy, is that such mistakes can be corrected. The discovery that we have voted for the wrong people leads eventually to their ejection from office. And this is the strongest argument in favour of democracy, and the reason for retaining democratic procedures at the heart of politics: namely, that they enable us to get rid of our rulers.

It is fair to say that, for the most part, the hereditary aristocrats have not enjoyed sovereignty in Europe, forming rather a privileged cast between the ruler and the ruled. Nevertheless, aristocracy in the normal sense of the term carries with it a particular conception of public office and public duty, and also a culture which emphasizes distinction rather than equality. Even if the nobles themselves have little to recommend them as people or as rulers, it is essential to their hereditary status that they should think in terms of public office, its rights and responsibilities, and that they should cultivate distinction in all its forms. Conservatives tend to believe that this facilitates the transmission of both public spirit and high culture, while endowing the country with a political class that can be called upon at any time, and will have leisure enough to offer its services. The existence of this class endows the public sphere with the charm and dignity of something permanent, and at the same time marks out taste, cultivation and knowledge as legitimate attributes of the one who aspires to office – attributes which allow their bearer, to however small an extent, to measure himself against the titled and the great. The aristocrat is hungry for legitimacy; he needs to shore up the privileges which come to him as a destiny, but which others fight for and earn. Hence the aristocrat has much to gain from the perpetuation of a culture of excellence.

Of course, the old aristocratic society has vanished. But the vision of culture and public spirit survived for a while the society that engendered it. This vision animated our universities and schools, was imparted through the BBC, and retained its hold on our national life until very recently. It was – to use a much abused word – 'elitist'. That is to say, it was concerned to safeguard difficult and exclusive attainments, and to ensure that they were not diluted by cheap substitutes and outright fakes. It was founded on critical judgement, taste and social distinction; and it supported educational and cultural institutions which had the generation of elites as their natural outcome. Nobody can deny that this vision of the national culture rapidly became offensive to democratic ways of thinking, or that curriculum reforms and educational philosophies sprang up which expressly repudiated the 'elitist' ideal. The result has been a serious loss of knowledge, and a decline in standards throughout the media of communication. It may be too late to arrest this decline; nevertheless, the attempt to do so defines a goal of conservative policy, and one that is more popular than its critics suppose.

To return, however, to the subject of the Upper House. If there is an institution which confers offices and responsibility, and which requires only some gift of inheritance in order to qualify for it, how can this be condemned outright as inimical to the well-being of the state? To say that the hereditary principle (even when refined as it is by the constant creation of peers) is 'anachronistic' is to say nothing; it needs but a glance at the state of international politics to see that the same is true of democracy. And to argue that the hereditary principle confers office and responsibility at random, and without consideration to the fitness of the person who receives them, is to repeat an objection to every mode of preferment. Is it to be supposed that the ability to fascinate an electorate (as Hitler did) has some connection with the fitness for public office? It is odd, indeed, listening to the present debates in the House of Commons, to reflect on the fact that the author of *Troilus and Criseyde* once belonged to it. But the fact ceases to surprise, when one remembers the activities which are now needed to arrive there.

An upper house that derives its membership from those whose social and political dignity is inviolable has one remarkable quality which will always be absent from an assemblage of elected members – the quality of leisure. Leisure transforms argument into conversation. In our Upper House views and interests have been consulted which, being useless to the demagogue, must be passed over in the scramble for power. Moreover, peers such as the Law Lords, whose office is consequent upon their learning, have had the great benefit which conversation confers and argument removes: they have carried the day on all issues which they alone have been competent to decide. It is the Law Lords, indeed, speaking not to a body of agitators, but to a gathering of listeners, who have stood in the way of much muddled or vindictive legislation. Their presence in the Upper House increases their authority in the affairs of state, and, as I shall argue, it is essential to conservative thinking that their authority should prevail.

In recent years the Conservative Party has responded to the aggressive tactics of its opponents with gestures of reform and amendment which have seemed more like appeasement than a preparation for war. There are reasons for this, the chief among them being that conservative politics does, in the end, require a consensus of feeling that transcends party loyalty. Nevertheless, policy apart (and policy here is vast and delicate), it is important to see that the issue is of the essence, and that conservatives ought to take a stand. Reform of the Lords must be calculated both to strengthen its powers and to conserve its detachment. Bagehot, in his spirited defence of the Upper House, regarded two reforms as imperative, not in order to reduce its power, privilege or dignity, but in order to restore them.[29] (These two reforms – abolition of the proxy vote, and the creation of life peers – have since been calmly effected.) The reforms currently proposed by the New Labour Party of Mr Blair seem designed to achieve the opposite effect – to remake the Lords as a kind of TV chat show, in which dignities are discarded and opinions assessed for their 'political correctness' rather than their truth.

The illusion of democracy

It has been the conservative hope that our hierarchical institutions will accommodate the principle of democratic election, without according to party the power that belongs to the state. Some politicians have seen the House of Commons as the debating chamber of the nation, the guarantee of liberties, the defender of the people against the powers that be. This pearl, grown around the sand of popular opinion, has often, it is true, rendered that opinion harmless to the social organism. But it is a cultivated pearl. It is there because the constitution placed it there, and it has no rights which the constitution has not bestowed on it. In a series of cancerous growths it has begun to swamp the shell which harbours it, and so transform the institution of government into an excrescence upon the political process, which it distorts and constrains. The principal cancer has been the cabinet – an inner circle of ministers appointed entirely by the Prime Minister, which decides all questions in secret, and which pretends to be answerable both to Parliament and to the monarch while in fact being answerable to no one, not even (as recent ludicrous volumes of memoirs by its former members illustrate) to itself. No outside observer can fail to despise this system of government, and all conservatives ought to be by instinct opposed to it. For it enables politicians to exploit what is bad in democracy – the appeal to majority opinion, the indifference to constitutional constraints, and the promotion of comfortable falsehoods over uncomfortable truths – while avoiding what is good, namely answerability, consultation and the sovereignty of Parliament.

The problem consists in a loss of organic balance. Our parliamentary institutions evolved from the need to reconcile competing powers, to resolve, in a manner compatible with social continuity, the complex vectors of new and established interests. Democracy has been seen as the most effective means to this. Unfortunately democracy is the name of an ideal which power itself does not recognize: power seeks to coerce and rule. Too much of the democratic principle unsettles the balance of parliament, giving rise to the 'professional' politician, the opportunist who wishes to advance as far and as quickly as possible in an institution which maintains sufficient outward dignity to make the pursuit worthwhile. But the real powers in the nation remain indifferent to this display of glamour and pursue their purposes relentlessly, often outside the reach of parliamentary control. So long as politics is regarded as a profession, where people scramble for office with the assiduity and insolence of salesmen, then the House of Commons must remain a battleground, whose best quality lies in its power to exhaust its members. It is possible even now to envisage a kind of politics which is not one of 'career', a politics nearer to the pursuit of learning or office than to the bargaining of the market-place. But to aim at such a politics is to subdue the presentation of politics.

Judicial independence

How do conservatives envisage the constitution, and how, and for what reason, will they set about its defence? It is not possible to describe the entire constitution of the United Kingdom, which is in any case now barely intelligible, following a spate of uncalled-for reforms. I propose instead to consider one small part of it, in order to show how the conservative attitude might display itself in the intricacies of power. I shall consider the issue of judicial independence. Parliamentary battles are often fought over this issue, but always fruitlessly, since no politician has yet thought of a way of undoing this constitutional knot. Nevertheless judicial independence has proved an obstacle to the policies of the Left. Indeed, there is a fashionable argument that since judicial decision is founded in the ideology of a 'middle class' it must automatically stand in the way of legislation which seeks to damage the self-interest of that class. In China, where such arguments do lead to re-commendations, almost nothing of the judicial process remains – simply peremptory trials conducted by local dignitaries. The Compendium of the Laws and Regulations of the People's Republic of China originally consisted of one medium-sized volume published every year. By the late Fifties it had become very slim; publication ceased in 1964. By then law had become entirely a matter of party directive and local custom. For, as every good Leninist knows, the withering away of the state involves the withering away of law.

Now the state, for the socialist, is what it is for the liberal – a means; the end being 'social justice', an expression which, in so far as it stands for anything, describes a society that we do not have, and may equally not desire. Naturally the Old Labour Party hesitated to identify itself with that view, since it was far from representing an exclusively socialist, or even anti-conservative, attitude. There has been a residual respect for the British constitution which reflects both the citizen's own respect for law, and also the urgent desire of the new interest groups – trade unions, local government apparatchiks, and the 'quangocracy' – to become part of the political establishment. Hence the rise of New Labour, as a party dedicated not to social justice, but to the advancement of the class which uses 'social justice' as its corporate logo.

For conservatives, the matter is simple. They regard the axioms of egalitarianism as conveying no concrete idea of future reality; by contrast, the constitution displays an order in which we live from day to day. The maintenance of that order is an intelligible goal; 'social justice' is not.

Judicial independence is an intricate phenomenon, rooted in an ambiguous area of politics where fact and fiction conspire. It has the history and the myth proper to every rooted constitutional device. In reality it can be neither absolute, nor self-sustaining. It is customary, following Montesquieu,[30] to divide the powers of state into three: the executive, the legislature and the judiciary. Although the instinct is a sound one, there is no clear theory to sustain it. It is of course neither necessary nor desirable that the process of administration, the making of law and the execution of justice should all lie in the hands of a single body. But the three functions cannot be disentangled, and, in some sense, the will behind each of them is one and the same. The British Cabinet, for example, could not govern if it attempted to separate its legislative and its executive powers. Moreover, a law-making body is powerless unless it can compel the judges to apply its laws. The titular head of the judiciary must therefore be answerable to the legislative power. Thus our Lord Chancellor is answerable to the Crown, and to the will of the Crown as this is enacted through Parliament. Here we see one of the advantages which spring from the myths of monarchy: that a power may be both one (as for government's sake it must be) and at the same time many (as civil obedience demands). But how, then, do we describe the constitutional fact of judicial independence?

What we call judicial independence is a relative thing. In the United Kingdom it has three main causes, the first being that legal reasoning and procedure remain autonomous. Indeed, the ascendancy of Equity in Scottish and English law (brought about, paradoxically enough, by James 1, in his attempt to bring the judiciary to heel) entails that no parliamentary edict could in fact control the mode of judicial argument. This element of judicial independence exists in every country where legal decisions are arrived at through the application of abstract principles of evidence and natural justice, principles which all people (even politicians) must accept in their daily undertakings.

In the second place, judicial decisions cannot be reversed by Parliament, but only by due process of law. There is (in normal circumstances) no retroactive legislation. However, we must remind ourselves that the highest court of appeal in the land – the House of Lords – is also a parliamentary body, and it is only a constitutional convention that prevents peers who do not hold judicial office from casting judgement there.

Finally our law is not (or not yet) codified. It is based in a system of precedent, or common law, expanded, restricted and amended by statute. The law has therefore evolved often through judicial, and not political reflection, and when suddenly it may seem as though Parliament has advanced, simplified or clarified matters – as in the formulation of the Property Acts, the Theft Act, or the exemplary Occupier's Liability Act of 1957 – this may be because an order has been seen in, and extracted from, the judicial reasoning that already existed. The judicial mind has been applied directly to the facts of our society, and in that process it has incorporated into the law of the land a lasting image of the nation, an image that was often provokingly invoked by Lord Denning in his snubs to Parliament.

A barbaric state is one in which it is impossible to distinguish the 'due process of law' (the will of the state) from the will of a party or an individual. In such a state the law has no independent authority, only delegated power. The constitution of the United Kingdom defends us from such barbarism partly because of the three principles of judicial independence. There are qualifications. In times of war judicial procedures may be peremptory, and legislation may be retroactive (again as a result of war). But these are abnormalities. What is of far greater concern to conservatives is the move to subordinate our common-law jurisdiction to the Napoleonic and Roman-law codes that prevail on the continent, and which identify abstract principles rather than concrete cases as the source of legal authority. This is the real origin of the conservative resistance to European unification – not that it will destroy the sovereignty of Parliament (since that has already been done by the system of Cabinet government) but that it will override the most important source of authority in the United Kingdom, which is the common law.

The ascendancy of statute

There is a perfectly normal method through which the activity of the judiciary may be controlled; and while it is a method which appears constitutional, the appearance is misleading. There is no constitutional rule which governs the matter; but in so far as the motive of the practice arises independently of the governing principle of the United Kingdom, it is, to that extent, not unconstitutional, but against constitution, expressive of the ethos of the state as means. I refer to the attempt to remake the nation through statute, and to substitute statute wherever possible for common law, even in defiance of natural justice. When this happens, it is to statute that the judge must bow.

But in a constitution adapted to the real world, obedience becomes a complex and creative thing, by no means to be understood as a punctilious servitude to rule. It has often been noticed that the judicial mind has been given to seek, not the letter, but the spirit of the law, and (for all its necessary protestations of obedience) it will not regard the spirit of the law as vested in Parliament alone. Parliament is therefore part of the apparatus of the state, but not the state itself; the consequences of this for the British people are enormous. Judges have been able to reinterpret harsh, absolute or confused legislation in the light of their own existing principles. It is natural for a judge to look for some means to hold people to their freely chosen bargains, or to infer an obligation when someone has been deliberately encouraged to act to his detriment. Legislation designed to overcome such judicial foibles has to be draconian, and drafted with an exactness which, in times of hyperactivity, is naturally somewhat rare. Manifestly unjust laws – laws such as the 1968 Rent Act, which have the intention of rewriting contracts to the consistent detriment of one of the parties, bills of expropriation and nationalization, statutes which attempt to eliminate *mens rea* from offences which may nevertheless be severely punished – all such laws have to be most carefully set out, in order not to die the death of judicial qualification.

Now this procedure depends upon a balance between judicial and parliamentary power, and conservatives are likely to add their weight to the first. For judicial reflection is governed by no ruling purpose other than the pursuit of justice within the framework of a given social order, while parliamentary reflection, being purposeful, contains a potential threat to that social order. The balance can be turned by an exaggerated quantity of statute law, and the associated attempt to restrict the law-making capacity of the judges. Naturally it is not possible to dispense with statute; all administration depends upon it. But in England statute has normally been a deliberative affair, constrained as much by judicial precedent as by 'reasons of state'. Now, with a European bureaucracy dedicated to the production of 'directives' which must be incorporated as law in every subordinate jurisdiction, statute is finally killing off the common law.

Socialists welcome this result, as does the New Class of welfare bureaucrats. Politicians given to the pursuit of 'social justice' are apt to be impatient with those who prefer the more 'natural' kind. They therefore seek statutes that are immune from judicial qualification. And they must come in fast succession, forbidding time to the community in which to take stock of change. (Consider the attempts to enforce comprehensive education, in the face of which judges continued to dispense remedies wherever they were able.) Inevitably, in the fever of fomented change, the judiciary must act as a conservative force. For judges seek to align the decrees of parliament with an established legal system, and hence (indirectly) with institutions that find protection under the existing body of law. A politician who sought to destroy those institutions would therefore desire to remove law-making capacity from the judges and vest it entirely in Parliament, specifically, in the House of Commons, where the judiciary is neither directly represented, nor overtly influential.

Those who suspect the judiciary, under common-law jurisdictions, of being a conservative force, are surely right. A judge acting under the disciplines of English law can do no other than respect the social arrangement that is expressed in law. In doing justice he removes resentment and so indirectly restores some part of the *status quo*. The ethic of 'social justice' might demand that whole classes of society be punished on account of their privileges, success, talent, intellectual or material superiority. Neither the constitution, nor the ethic of natural justice, can be made to recognize such a law. Hence, indirectly, the law-making capacity of the judges has impeded the formation of the egalitarian state.

Government and party

There is a further danger to judicial independence, as to all matters which lie balanced within the constitution by deephistorical forces. This lies in the constitutional irreverence that must naturally accompany political activism. Politicians whose aim is to change the established order cannot regard their aim as open to qualification from the existing constitution. They will respect the constitution only in so far as it serves their purpose; otherwise they will seek to ignore it or to cast it aside. It is for this reason that politicians are increasingly making light of the distinction between government and party. Now the judiciary is answerable to Parliament, and, through Parliament, to the Crown. Certain parliamentary officers – such as the Attorney-General, and the Lord Chancellor – have the function of mediating the relations between those who make, and those who administer, the law. But such officers are officers of the Crown, answerable through the Crown to the interests of state. Democratic politics requires (although this is no more than a constitutional convention) that those officers be appointed through the dominant party; but they are not directly answerable to that party. It is important to see, therefore, that a constitutional threat is already present when these officers are compelled to act in response to party pressure, as is increasingly the case with the Lord Chancellor. It is necessary for conservatives to challenge assailants of judicial independence into speaking not with the authority of the state, but only with the influence of a party. They will find themselves far more confused as to their meaning.

This brings us to an aspect of the constitution which is, and must be, of the greatest concern to conservatives: the nature of Parliament, and the role of party politics in determining its affairs. Now it was Burke, a conservative whose factional association was with the Rockingham Whigs, who first urged his parliamentary friends, in the face of the threat of constitutional reform, to organize themselves into a party. Some might suppose that this division into parties is both alien to conservatism and destructive of the constitutional balance. But I doubt that this is so. Burke was surely right in his intuition that party politics is a bastion against the fragmentation of political life which might otherwise ensue under the process of democracy. Through the influence of party, votes are cast not as an expression of individual wish (for this or that feature of national life), but largely as a gesture of allegiance to a style of government; and the continuity of the party is felt as the nearest substitute for the continuity of the nation. But the corollary of this is that party politics must be taken seriously: a conservative party constantly faced by drastic measures of needless reform, must, when in office, wield as much power as its opponents in order to undo those measures; not because such to-ing and fro-ing of domestic policy is a healthy thing, but because this is the only way to bring it to an end. It is a means of forcing the parties to recognize a common cause, so that they become once again not 'movements' but factions, equally committed to the national interest and to the constitutional authority, conflicting in this or that attitude over matters of state, but over nothing so much as their common desire for power. The composite image which they will come to form must contain large conservative fragments. In order to achieve this it is important to keep government and party separate, to vest as much power in the former as is assumed by the latter, and in particular to vest power in those aspects of government that do not lie within parliamentary jurisdiction.

Civil society and the state

In order to understand what is at stake in the constitutional issues I have raised, we must return again to our earlier reflections and discuss the nature of civil society, and its proximity to the state. It is basic to a conservative view of things (I suggested) that individuals should seek and find their completion in society, and that they should find themselves part of an order that is greater than themselves, in the sense of transcending anything that could have been brought about through their own voluntary agreement. They must see themselves as the inheritors, not the creators, of the order in which they participate, so that they may derive from it (from the picture of its 'objectivity') the conceptions and values which determine self-identity. They will see their extension in time from birth to death as taking on significance from civil stability: their world was not born with them, nor does it die when they depart from it.

It is natural to conclude that a constitution adapted to the realization of a conservative outlook will make room for, and certainly find nothing . wrong with, principles of hereditary entitlement. Inheritance reinforces the connection between family and property which, being part of human nature, is also part of the 'natural' politics that conservatives propose. Here we see an aspect of constitution (hereditary privilege) reflected, first, in a feature of civil society, and, second, in a demand of fiscal policy. It is impossible here to separate 'matters of state' from all the sustaining features of civil life with which they are associated. To see the precise way in which conservatives might formulate belief in the hereditary principle (or in any other aspect of the constitution) we shall always have to discuss matters far more serious and more elusive than immediate policy. We live in a nation so constituted that state and society move together, pointing to the common end of national sovereignty. To envisage a political future for our nation is to aim at both its outer continuity in politics, and its inner cohesion in social life. As the example of hereditary government indicates, and as I earlier argued, it will be impossible to separate the two. However, in certain matters of government, it has been liberal policy to enforce a separation between state and society.

Consider, for example, the issue of devolution. This has now been partially effected by Mr Blair's Government, with incalculable consequences. A political organism must necessarily have a centre and a periphery, and unless the periphery is governed with the same strength and resolution as the centre, the nation falls apart. In our new 'English' kingdom, founded on the hegemony of North London, what is to prevent the dissatisfied Northumbrians from asserting their native right to independence? What will deter the oil-rich town of Yarmouth from self-government? Who will rule over the republic of Brixton when its customs, manners and language seem to provide so little application to the laws of distant Westminster? And who will be motivated to defy the rebellion led by the Napoleon of Notting Hill?

Moreover, a state that is sure of its boundaries, requires government within those boundaries, and autonomous decisions that can be identified by the people as in some way stemming from themselves and expressing their collective life. From the constitutional point of view this means legislative autonomy. It is certainly hard for a conservative to accept the strange and voluntary renunciation of sovereignty which has argued that British law is better made in Brussels than at home. Now European law, being of commercial intention, has largely benefited companies engaged in international trade. Indeed it has grown out of the kind of thinking which imagines that economic well-being is the whole of politics and the true aim of law, and which identifies the well-being of people with the profits of multi-national corporations. As the decisions emanating from Europe begin to reflect more nearly the ideology of its members, many things will be imposed on Britons of a kind that they do not like, but which they will be powerless to reject except through the total rupture of treaties under which the economic life of the nation is being rapidly subsumed. While conservatism is founded in a universal philosophy of human nature, and hence a generalized view of social well-being, it recognizes no single 'international' politics, no unique constitution or body of laws which can be imposed irrespective of the traditions of the society which is to be governed by them. As a political position 'Euro-conservatism' is therefore nonsense – unless, of course, it means the maintenance of close alliances and commercial ties, or perhaps something more wild, like the restoration of the Holy Roman Empire, and the sovereignty of the Church.

The issues just discussed are constitutional, but they reflect a view of the civil order. Conversely there are issues which arise out of popular sentiment and yet which seek expression in decisions of a constitutional kind. This is true of all those sentiments which compose the inarticulate idea of nationhood, and which impose upon the government the necessity to lay down, as constitutional fiat, a legal determination of citizenship. The law has been formulated comparatively recently, under the pressure of universal migration. Many Britons, who have never heard of the Nationality Acts and the laws on immigration, feel strongly about something which was once called 'the alien wedge'. And surely it cannot be doubted, even by those who profess allegiance to the 'multicultural society', that our society, unlike America, is not of that kind, and therefore that immigration cannot be an object of merely passive contemplation on the part of the present citizenship. There is perhaps no greater sign of the strength of liberalism (a strength which issues, not from popular consensus, but from the political power of the liberal elite) than that it has made it impossible for any but the circumlocutory to argue that the English, the Scots and the Welsh have a prior claim to the benefits of the civilization that their ancestors created, which entitles them to reserve its benefits for themselves.[31] But while it is a long-standing principle of British law that the fomentation of hatred (and hence of racial hatred) is a serious criminal offence, it is not clear that illiberal sentiments have to be forms of hatred, nor that they should be treated in the high-handed way that is calculated to make them become so. On the contrary, they are sentiments which seem to arise inevitably from social consciousness: they involve natural prejudice, common culture, and a desire for the company of one's kind. That is hardly sufficient ground to condemn them as 'racist' – an accusation which has no definition in law, and against which there is now no defence. To be accused of racism is to be guilty of it: this is the great achievement of liberal thinking about nationality. One of the most important conservative causes in our time must surely be the attempt to undo the apparatus of censorship and intimidation, which has effectively silenced the appeal to national identity.

In all the issues which I have mentioned it has been the business of liberalism to prise state and society apart. The conservative idea of the constitution as something generalized and tacit can be put into practice only by holding the two together. The reason why such matters as devolution, legislative autonomy, immigration and so on are of the first concern to conservatives is that they indicate battles which could be won. The magnetic pull of civil society is here at its strongest; it is only necessary to place the constitution within its field.

Pessimae republicae plurimae leges. The words of Tacitus are beginning to apply even to England, of which Joseph de Maistre wrote that 'the true English Constitution is that admirable public spirit ... which leads and saves everything, whereas that which is written down is nothing'.[32]

But, as I have tried to show, de Maistre's ideal, modified as it inevitably has been by the passage of time, and by the complexity of modern administration, is still at work in the United Kingdom. It suffices to know the points at which the 'deep' unspoken constitution still reveals itself. For they are the places where conservatives must fight.

Concluding remarks

A constitution is not a book of rules, nor can it be cast as one. It permeates the body of society, just as a person's self-image permeates his organic nature. It is not founded in a 'natural' right, for it grants rights as it grants privileges, so as to demand obedience in return.

The unity between state and society demands no democratic process; indeed, at present, democratization is in many respects a threat to this unity. But there is a greater menace in the liberal desire to remake the constitution, so that it matches no particular social order, and answers to no particular historical identity. In resisting that attempt, I have argued, conservatives must seek to vest the power of the state outside the forum of speculative change, in particular, outside the opinion-ridden turmoil of the Commons. Hence they must uphold the judiciary, the House of Lords, and every autonomous institution through which the political process finds tacit and faction-free enactment. For a conservative the movement of the constitution must express the movement of social feeling, and not the opportunistic aims of the small class of professional politicians. But if conservatives belong to that class, then they must fight boldly and warily, taking a stand at every point where the bond of society lends support to them, and allowing no party to usurp the loyalty which, because it stems from the social order, belongs not to any party but to the state. But we must now consider, not the state as such, but the will of the state, which is law.

4
Law and Liberty

If we were to remain on the level of 'party politics', we should discuss the process whereby the Conservative Party came to regard itself during the Seventies as the party of 'law and order'. But 'law and order' is simply the business of government, and no political party which spoke or acted as though it were not concerned to uphold them could ever be elected – as the Labour Party discovered to its cost. The truth was given by Machiavelli, in one sharp sentence which everybody recognizes to be true the moment he feels the reluctance to believe it: 'The Prince must use first law, which is natural to man, but must be prepared to use violence, which is bestial, in order that the rule of law be maintained.' The issues that will concern us are those of the nature of law, its scope, and its 'image' in conservative thinking. The rest is a matter of tactics. Theoretically speaking 'law and order' can be left to look after itself.

The sphere of law

What can, and what cannot, be subject to law? And to what extent may the law define and limit the activities of the citizen? Again conservatives are unlikely to be content with a single and absolute answer, framed for the use of every nation and every institution, regardless of its history and character. Nevertheless, they have still to contend with their liberal opponents and, in the sphere of law, liberalism is all-powerful, being, so to speak, the first thought that comes to mind. Since the Enlightenment, it has seemed quite natural to suppose that the cause of 'individual liberty' is what is at issue in every question of law, and while this is not how the law *is*, it is how it has been theorized. Should we remove the liberty of *this* person, to protect the liberty of *that* person? Such a philosophy sees the law as legitimate only to the extent that it protects individuals from harm; and the law must allow the maximum of individual freedom compatible with that aim. Clearly, it would be impossible to dismiss the liberal view out of hand: it has a respectable intellectual history, and a perennial intellectual appeal. But it is important to see that conservatives are in no way forced to accept it.

As I have already suggested, the liberal view is individualistic. It sees individuals as potentially complete in themselves, and possessed of reason, which they can use either well or ill. To use it well is to use it freely – to live one's life according to the precepts of 'autonomous' (or even 'authentic') choice. It is from the exercise of this autonomous choice, argued Kant,[33] that all the good of human nature derives, and the single most important degradation of that nature lies in the 'heteronomy of the will' – action according to precepts that are not self-commanded. It is easy to see in this philosophy ancestor of Sartrean existentialism, and the quintessence of the Enlightenment concept of man – a ground for the view that our well-being lies in freedom, and that all government is valid only as a means to that end. One does not have to go so far as Dostoevsky's Grand Inquisitor in pointing to its defects. Kant thought that he could derive from the overriding principle of autonomy certain subsidiary laws of action, the moral laws, which each person would be constrained by reason to accept. But these laws remained, as Kant recognized, purely 'formal', and his own attempt to derive from them specific rules of conduct was not only somewhat strained, but also remarkably apolitical in conception, giving no indication of the kind of social organization that would best serve the moral ends of mankind. Indeed, the operation of the moral law seemed to require that we conceive ourselves as belonging, not to this, but to some other world, ideal members of the 'kingdom of ends'.

It seems to me that the liberal conception of politics is no more nor less plausible than the Kantian idea of the free, autonomous being. The conservative view begins from a conflicting premise, which is that the abstract ideal of autonomy, however admirable, is radically incomplete. People have free will: they make choices, act on reasons, are guided in everything by a conception of what they are, and what they wish to be. But the 'form' of freedom requires a content. Freedom is of no use to a being who lacks the concepts with which to value things, who lives in a solipsistic vacuum, idly willing now this and now that, but with no conception of an objective order that would be affected by his choice. We cannot derive the ends of conduct from the idea of choice alone. We must show how the agent values what he intends to do. Through what concepts, and through what perceptions, does he represent his end as desirable? To recognize something as desirable, is to view it as an achievement. This means seeing it as conferring merit, dignity, respectability – in short, as conferring social recognition. (I speak of the normal case, not of the hyper-sophisticated examples, such as you and me, who must be defined by extrapolation.) This sense of the merit of something is not as a rule to be translated into words: it suffices that it be real and vivid. Without this kind of ready perception of the value of things, there can be no autonomy, and the perception cannot be acquired through an act of choice. It is brought about, not by freedom, but by striving for freedom, not through self-obsession but through knowledge of others. In short, value requires the perception of the self as other, and only from that perception can freedom begin. There is no autonomy that does not presuppose the sense of a social order, and if the order may be ideal, this is only because it was once experienced as real. The autonomous individual is the product of practices which designate him as social. The individual person is the person who recognizes that he is no mere individual. Anarchy (which is freedom from the constraints of a public realm) is not the gain of individuality, but its loss. Individual freedom is the great social artifact which, in trying to represent itself as nature alone, generates the myth of liberalism.

The consenting adult

The meaning of the last paragraph will be clearer in the application. What I have said stands opposed not only to liberalism, but to the more pragmatic conception of law, which sees it simply as the power of government to constrain the wicked and uphold the good. It is the exercise of that power without which the life of man is, in the famous words of Hobbes, 'solitary, poor, nasty, brutish and short'. But such a view might still have its liberal expression. It could be said that the legitimate function of law had been fulfilled as soon as it possessed the power and the machinery whereby to restrain individuals from interfering with one another's 'rights' – for example, the right to life, peace, privacy and property. (And no doubt, the view would find some natural, universal, basis, in an implied contract, or in some Kantian version of the 'natural law'.) It follows that the function of law is largely protective, and, having given its protection, it cannot legitimately infringe the 'natural' right of citizens to do as they please, provided they also please those 'consenting adults' who do it along with them.

Everyone feels the attraction of such a view, for everyone, in some small portion of his psyche, is a 'consenting adult in private', anxious to retire from the surveillance of the state into a sovereign sphere of his own. Like the great Athenians, we seek to be, 'Free and tolerant in our private lives; in public affairs obedient to the law'.[34] And no modern state can flourish without a careful attitude towards this hyper-civilized yearning for privacy, even when its principal manifestation lies in the freedom of the Sunday newspapers to provide vignettes of privacy to those who have never achieved it.Nevertheless, the view cannot stand alone as definitive of the new social order, or indeed of any social order at all.

The right of property

To take one small example: the right of property. On one extreme liberal view, there can be no legitimate interference with a person's right to dispose as he thinks fit with that which is legally and morally recognized as his. (Let us assume, for a moment, that there are no complications introduced by the division of legal from beneficial ownership.) But it is absurd to think that a merchant has some indefeasible right to throw his grain into the sea, or even to withhold it from the market in time of famine (whether or not the motive of this act be profit). Naturally, no one doubts that his behaviour is immoral; but surely a state that refused to make it also illegal would be refraining from exercising the very power vested in its constitution, the power to ensure the continuity of a human society. Perhaps, it will be said, the example is an extreme one, and that there should be something like a 'rebuttable presumption' that a person may deal freely with his own. But that too is questionable. What, for the ordinary person, is his own? Let us consider his house, since that is closest to him psychologically, and the locus of all that is 'private'. Whether he holds it as tenant or as freeholder is irrelevant, since these are both property rights in English law, representable as exchange values. For a long time it has been recognized that a person may not deal freely with his house, and not merely because some ways of dealing with it directly 'harm' his neighbours. He may not demolish it, alter it, even (on occasion) redecorate it, without the consent of legally authorized bodies. And the reasons for this might be entirely aesthetic, matters of 'local character', 'traditional appearance', in short a public expectation as to how the property should look. Nor should it be imagined that this legal respect for aesthetic principles is a modern thing, a protection against the suddenly mobile market in real estate. In sixteenth-century Venice the very pattern on the prow of a gondola was determined by law. The ascendancy of the aesthetic in matters of planning is of immense significance. For it shows the law expressing a will for visual continuity that can have no other legitimate origin than in the vested power of the state, conceived not as means to individual freedom, but as the guardian of an established social order, and of a culture that is the common inheritance of everyone. Such a law can be understood as legitimate only if we abandon the individualistic picture of human nature.

Morality and law

What, then, is the legitimate sphere of law? The law is the will of the state, and the domestic expression of its power. And since state and civil society are interdependent, the legitimate sphere of the law includes all that matters to social continuity, all that can be taken as standing in need of state protection. The law must cover all activity through which the bonds of trust and allegiance are cemented or broken. Obvious instances – the upholding of contract, the outlawing of gratuitous violence, the common essence of civil and criminal law – follow from this view as from any view. But so too do more controversial instances, concerning matters in which the dominance of liberal ideology is likely to be the cause, not of freedom, but of licence.

Consider the case of public decency, and the massive propaganda issued (partly through the medium of 'sex education') on behalf of an experimental approach to sexual relations. These are difficult matters to write about: for one thing, people will dispute that there is any connection (or at least that there ought to be any connection) between the issues of public decency and private morality. For another thing, this is an area which, because it concerns the quality and not the quantity of something (the quality, namely, of the erotic tie) does not yield itself to statistical investigation. As a result, the bureaucratic mind, which can imagine that it has some grasp of issues like television violence, is apt to think that there is here no decidable issue, and therefore no issue at all. In fact, as everyone feels instinctively, there is an issue. Moreover, in none of these matters do statistics have any serious relevance. Suppose statistics were to show that, in societies which periodically arrange spectacles involving the martyrdom of consenting Christians in public, before wild beasts or knife artists, incidents of public violence are fewer than in other arrangements, where these healthy, cathartic practices do not occur. Does that prove anything? Naturally not; for the evil lay, not in the results of the thing, but in the thing itself. And not, primarily, in the suffering of the victims (who may well have desired and gloried in what was given to them), but in the mental degradation of the crowd. That is clearly what matters also in questions of public decency. It is irrelevant that more or fewer people do or do not go away after watching pornographic films and engage in this or that practice. That is not the primary, the social fact. The primary fact is that they watch them.

Now in all these issues it seems that the opinions of a minority have commanded more attention than the inarticulate feelings of the ordinary citizen. Those feelings, which grow from the constraints of the family, and the abstinence necessary to an ordinary, responsible life, deserve not contempt but civil protection. It is only an exaggeratedly liberal view of politics that can refuse to see that matters of private morality and public decency are connected, and that both are of urgent political concern. It was a source of surprise to some that juries have recently been able to return verdicts not only of obscenity but also of blasphemy. But it would cause no surprise to anyone who has observed, either in himself or in another, the strength of the feelings which find their fulfilment in family life, and the fear with which ordinary people, whose lives as citizens begin with the family, must contemplate their dissipation. This may seem a small matter, but surely it is far from small. For it is through the channelling of libidinal impulse that the bond of society is formed. Conservatives are unlikely to be persuaded by that particular brand of German–American sentimentalism which imagines the free expression of sexual impulse and the true harmony of social intercourse to be deeply compatible, and which sees the ills of society as stemming from some single experience of 'repression'. That is surely just wishful thinking, false to human nature and also self-deceived. Repression, as caricatured by Marcuse and Fromm, is simply another name for moral discipline.

Let us put to one side for a moment the vexed problem of sexual conduct, and concentrate on that of public decency. It is surely difficult to contemplate with ease the free marketing of sex as a spectacle, and the consequent transference of erotic passion from personal commitment to abstract titillation. To borrow a Marxist concept: this fetishism of the sexual commodity is also a source of sexual alienation. It places a barrier between people and their fulfilment, turning the sexual act into a caricature of itself: not an existential choice, but the gratification of an appetite. This kind of 'fetishism' is the enemy of the human spirit: it is the hallucination of freedom, meted out by the vacillation of the sexual market. It marks the obsession of man with his animal nature, and the theft of his social essence. It has been objected repeatedly since the trial of *Madame Bovary* that censorship threatens art and culture. But one must distinguish the individual work from the culture which engenders it. And having done so, why not be sceptical? There was no civilized period previous to ours that lacked effective censorship, and few periods so seemingly devoid of artistic inspiration, so driven – in the pursuit of a cut-price originality – to fanatical desecration in the name of art.

Consider now the question of sexual mores. Surely, it will be said, these at least are not within the sphere of law? But we know that they are, and that law moves in a slow and complicated way in obedience to what one can only call the convulsions of civil society over these matters, matters where the animal and the rational natures of man are sometimes in direct and irreconcilable conflict. Consider the legal fiction of 'consent'. It is a crime to make love to a willing, but under-age, schoolgirl, a crime which grows in seriousness as a man discovers the ease of committing it. And yet, says the law, the girl has not consented. Behind that legal fiction lies a moral fiction, and one which is vital to the self-image of society. It is the fiction, the myth, or (from the political point of view these are all the same) the value, of 'innocence'. It is through a conception of innocence that sexual relations are experienced and understood – understood, that is, as something other than a merely animal performance. It is this conception (and the corresponding idea of personal maturity) that makes possible the representation of sexual love as the consummation of something; as the end of courtship. The existence of this law can therefore be seen as legitimated by an indispensable moral idea. The idea may in fact correspond only very approximately to the way people behave; but most normal people wish to see their behaviour in this way, and to see their values enshrined in law. This is the kind of law which liberals find difficult to accept. The proponents of 'sex education' might even consider the whole concept of 'innocence' to be profoundly unhygienic.

The example is a minor one. But it is important. For it shows how a conservative stance towards civil society might begin to translate itself, without violence to its sense of the legitimate activity of the state, into laws which seriously restrict what some would call the 'freedom' of the citizen. And these laws make no reference to 'harmful' consequences; or if they do it is only because 'harm' is being redefined in the process. You cannot say that the doctrine of an 'age of consent' corresponds to a prior conception of what is 'harmful' to the young. People extend their idea of 'harm' to cover such difficult conceptions as those of innocence and maturity only by imbuing the idea with a moral meaning. Not:

premature sexual experiment is wrong because it is harmful but: premature sexual experiment is harmful because it is wrong.

Freedom and harm

That last thought brings us into direct confrontation with the liberal view of law, as stated and defended by Mill and his successors. The issue has been discussed many times, not only in the great controversies of the Victorian era,[36] but even now, many years after Utilitarianism has fallen into disrepute. Its most recent outbreak – precipitated by Lord Devlin's *The Enforcement of Morals* – led not only to fervent protestations of liberal faith throughout the intellectual world, but also to the Wolfenden Report, and to the subsequent measures designed to remove from our legal system every imprint of sexual intolerance. Since the Sexual Offences Act 1967 many of the issues must appear parochial. But this testimony to the vitality of liberal thinking cannot be ignored. A perusal of the issue reveals two fundamental principles at work in the liberal mind. The first constitutes its premise: that the criminal law should be concerned solely with the protection of the citizen from harm. The second constitutes its method, which is that in all questions of law and morality there is room for debate, and that the onus of proof lies upon the person who would retain some precept rather than upon the one who would have it abolished. The liberal is the one to ask 'why?' of every institution, never the one to doubt the premise from which the possibility of such a question springs, the premise of unbelief. The ground of morality, as of the law which embodies it, remains obscure and inaccessible. The liberal, who knows no more than anyone just why it is wrong to rape, to steal, to make public display of obscene or gory spectacles, delights in tricking his opponent into inconsistencies over matters which – because they lie at the limit of human understanding – must breed either inconsistency or naiveté whenever they are the subject not of prejudice but of speculation. What is meant, when it is said that a given practice does no 'harm' to its participants, is that it can be viewed (from some position of secure and emancipated detachment) with no more than the vestiges of moral sentiment. What else is the invocation of harm capable of signifying? The idea is clear enough in its physical application: we know what it is to damage or destroy a human body. But physical injury is not the normal accompaniment of rape, a crime which must therefore be condemned largely on account of the 'psychological', 'spiritual', or 'moral' harm which stems from it. But am I harmed by something purely because I do not consent to it? If that is the criterion, then we must change the fiscal, educational and environmental laws of the country. Am I harmed by the spectacle of a public execution? How do we find a serious answer that does not stretch the concept of 'harm' to embody the finest shade of moral disapprobation? Again, am I harmed by the destruction of a beautiful building or a work of art? The only answer that will generate the law which most liberals would wish to see is that I *am* harmed, and in a way that quite transcends the minor grievance of the property developer made bankrupt by the enforcement of the law. Finally, am I harmed by the opportunity to engage (in private) in practices against which (unknown to myself) my whole moral nature may at some later stage revolt? Clearly no sensible answer to any of these questions is forthcoming, until we begin to embody in the concept of 'harm' precisely the moral and social sentiment which liberals wish to remove from it. The whole dispute, represented as that between dark intolerance and enlightened reason, is nothing more than a clash of prejudices. And while one side frankly admits that the feelings it brings to this dispute are moral, the other hides its bigotry behind a mask of reason, serenely expecting to carry the day.

This is not to deny that there could be such a thing as a genuine liberal consensus. The invocation of that consensus would give grounds for a corresponding shift in the law. And it may be true that the liberal morality is less and less the property of an elite, and more and more the common currency of popular opinion. How could one know? The answer is not to be found by argument, but by the test that has always been used – by the response of magistrates and juries. As moral feeling recedes so too does the desire to convict or to subject to punishment. Thus it became necessary to invent the offence of Causing Death by Dangerous Driving; for what jury, seeing another accused of an act which they themselves barely avoid each day, will find for a verdict of manslaughter, and a possible ten years' imprisonment? Likewise, it could be that popular feeling about the age of consent is changing, and beginning to show itself in court.

To advocate this traditional test is not to preach the doctrine of *vox populi, vox Dei*. It is simply to keep the law within the sight and understanding of those who are governed by it, to refuse to assume a consensus before it is proven in the only forum where people are forced to be truly serious. To suffer the opinion of the majority is the natural penalty of an education which condemns majority values; and the sense of a common moral order is the greatest force which reconciles that majority to eccentricities that it can neither understand nor emulate.

Constitutional rights

It is worth pausing to mention another liberal manoeuvre in the face of the problem posed by popular morality. This is to argue that the law is a distributor of constitutional rights. And if the constitution involves a commitment to 'moral pluralism', then the citizen will have no legitimate expectation that the law may enforce his moral code against another's, even when the rival code is postulated merely for the sake of argument. On this view, however strong the consensus, law is public, morality private. Moreover, the purpose of law relates to one thing alone – the constitution which confers the rights contended for in open court. It is in this way that American jurists tend to see their law; and while one may naturally concur in the view that the rights conferred by law are constitutional, one may doubt that the commitment to 'moral pluralism', even when set against the accepted theory of the American judicial process, is a coherent one. The theory here is the old one of the social contract: how could any American bind himself to a morality that is not his own?[36] From which it follows that those incapable of joining the social contract cannot benefit from the protection of the law. A foetus, for example, is in just that position, as was definitively proven in the American case of *Roe v. Wade*. Not being a 'person', said Mr Justice Blackmun, the foetus can naturally claim no benefit from a law which, while conceding nothing to morality, concedes everything to the contract on which the state is founded. For liberalism to have advanced to such a position from its initial premise is astonishing. But conservatives would prefer to go back to that premise, so as to see 'moral pluralism' for what it is: a devious form of the Kantian Moral Law – a way of imposing moral uniformity around a liberal social agenda. 'So natural to mankind', after all, 'is intolerance in whatever they really care about' (Mill, *On Liberty*).

Law and society

The authority of the law, however filtered through the apparatus of the state, depends upon the sense of social cohesion. And no law which tries to transcend that sense will ever have the firm allegiance of the citizens. Likewise any area of social life which is vital either to the strength of the social bond, or to the social image of its participants, will be one into which the law may legitimately intrude. Thus, it is inescapable that there should be family law, planning laws, laws which regulate the days and times of work and recreation, even laws which control the nature of permitted intoxicants. (Just as Islamic law recognizes the conflict between the outlook which it expresses and the consumption of wine, so does our law recognize a conflict between the foetid banter of the public house – generally assumed to promote the right kind of bonding – and the menacing gentleness of the drug culture, generally assumed to be the first step towards solipsism.) It is a great merit in the conservative view of law that it can explain these things and make them intelligible. On the liberal view, it seems to me, almost the entire legal system of our country, outside a small central core of criminal and civil law, becomes indefensible.

One could go further: *how* far is a matter of the actual politics of the day, the full details of which must lie outside the scope of this book. It is a very difficult matter to adjust the workings of the law to the movement of society, and to attempt to follow only that movement which proceeds from the life of society rather than that which foreshadows its demise. On the whole, it seems to me that judges have been better equipped to make this adjustment than Parliament; consider the fine shades of obligation that have been introduced recently into the relations between man and mistress, using purely judicial concepts (such as that of the constructive trust) in order to accommodate difficult cases without disturbing the fundamentals of family law.[37] And should the enthusiasm of the judge overstep itself, judicial adjustment is still possible, without the need to unravel the complex knot of law, and weave some other conception of the family.

Liberalism, which is the creed of an elite, and an impossible substitute for the pieties of ordinary existence, has been the guiding force in the many bodies devoted to legal reform. Their overriding aim has been to loosen the relation between law and civil life – extending the sphere of choice into those realms where traditionally people have sought not permission but constraint. Liberalism seeks to remove from the law the image of a particular social arrangement. For conservatives this is simply to deprive the law of its authority, to remake it as a system of formal and avoidable rules. Just as private individuals need to find themselves reflected in the social order, so as to recognize externally the value of what they do, so must that order find its image in the law. Civil society cannot provide its own self-image, any more than an individual can rise to self-consciousness by staring in a glass. The civil society is confirmed in the institutions of the state; law, as the will of the state, is therefore the concrete reality of civil life. To the extent that, one by one, customs, manners, morals, education, labour and rest are 'liberated' from its jurisdiction, so too does the sense of their social validity suffer a decline, as citizens find the gulf widening between their customs and their form of life, and the law which supposedly protects them.

Punishment

Having adopted the conception of law that I have outlined, one will find little difficulty in accepting punishment as an essential part of it. Intellectual confusion over the problem of free will has led among criminologists to a conception of the law as an instrument, not of enforcement, but of cure and reform. I do not propose to debate these issues, which are of great complexity. I shall simply make a suggestion, which is that any philosophy which purports to eliminate from the understanding of human affairs either punishment or blame must also dispense with reward and praise, with anger, resentment, indifference, respect and admiration – in short, with all those attitudes which constitute the web of moral relations between people. Such a philosophy must finish by clearing from the world the elaborate superstructure of human values, leaving in its place a behaviouristic desertland, where soulless computers may thrive, but people never. To take that philosophy as a basis for moral life and for political activity is to remove the significance from both.

The question to consider is not that of law and order, but that of how the law and its infringement are conceived. And we must recognize a fundamental opposition between those who see the conflict between crime and law as a conflict of will, and those who see it in terms of the 'adjustment' or 'maladjustment' of the individual (or of society). The first view is common to both conservatives and subversives, who each conceive criminals as acting deliberately, and for their own ends, in defiance of society. It may not be their purpose to oppose the 'General Will' (in Rousseau's phrase) – unless, like Genet, they attempt to find their self-image in just that way, turning the garment of society inside out so as to dress up in its seamy side. Nevertheless the criminal purpose is antagonistic to society, and since society is expressed in the state, and since the criminal too is a subject of that state, so does he bestow on the state the right and the duty to punish him. The reason for his punishment lies in what he does. The effects of it are irrelevant. It is unimportant that he be reformed, cured, or subdued into acquiescence: it suffices that he acted as he did. It follows that the motive of punishment – being essentially backward-looking – is founded in some respect for the established order, and for the system of authority of which the crime constituted a violation. Punishment does not seek to redress a wrong (for that is the province of civil and not of criminal law), but to express and propitiate the general outrage. Thus while there may be forgiveness of a civil wrong, for a crime there can be only mercy. The healthiest form of punishment will be immediate intelligible, conceived by the citizen as a natural retaliation, which takes away the sting of resentment and removes the necessity for private revenge. The institution of punishment simply transfers to the law the authority that is invoked in every act of retaliation.

Now such a motive is perfectly intelligible, not only to the political observer, but also to the citizen, since it is nothing but his own motive rewritten in the larger characters of the state. To conceive punishment in such a way is to uphold the ideal of the state as person, as will and as end in itself: and that is the ideal of conservatism. Its intelligibility and coherence are the mark of its political common sense; and the fact that it can generate a clear and humane canon of punishment is a mark of its reasonableness – for the way is now open to the suggestion that the mode and severity of punishment should be directly determined by the nature and seriousness of the crime.

Let us now consider the view – which it would be not unfair to regard as one of the premises of modern 'penal reform' – that the true reason for punishment is to be found, not in its antecedents, but in its effects. On this view, it is legitimate to punish just so long as the criminal, or the public, in some tangible way benefit from the act, so that the true nature of punishment must lie in the protection of society, or the reform of the individual. It becomes at once extremely difficult to explain why we should not reserve the death penalty for minor motoring offences (a move that would eliminate them for ever), and punish murder by a course in sociology at the University of Essex (a punishment which, for such private, domestic crimes, must prove at least as reformatory as prison). Nor is this kind of absurdity the only defect in the 'forward-looking' approach to the institution of punishment. There is the more serious defect that it makes the institution unintelligible. For it removes from the description of punishment any reference to the evil of what has been done, presenting the crime in neutral terms as a kind of biological accident, generated by a disorderly organism which it is now our sole concern to 'cure'. That attitude (described in *A Clockwork Orange*) represents the crime and its penalty as not inhuman but unhuman acts, removed from the sphere of common understanding, motiveless, aimless, valueless. It constitutes a surrender of the indispensable concept of freedom to a vulgar misconception, dressed up as the 'objective', 'scientific' view of man.

As the established power of government has become adulterated by the expert and the careerist, this woolly-minded humanitarianism has begun to replace the natural sanctions which are the intelligible opposite to crime. Humanitarianism is in fact a sign of an unwillingness to take full responsibility for the offices of the state, while nevertheless enjoying the advantages which stem from them. It may represent itself as 'conscience', with all the associated trappings of 'sincerity', although in considerations of such importance, one cannot but feel tempted by the opinion of Oscar Wilde, that it is style and not sincerity that counts. For ordinary people punishment is simply a moral necessity, which has nothing to do with any humanitarian aim. It is a retribution, an institutionalized revenge, the desert of the criminal as much as the right of his victim. To replace punishment by 'reform' is to separate the law from its moral foundation; it is also to assume a right of forgiveness which lies with the victim of crime alone. This unreal forgiveness reinforces the sense, either that crime is 'subjective', so that acts are criminal only by convention, or else that the objectivity of crime goes unnoticed by the state. The first of those thoughts spells the decline in the standards of common conduct, while the second fosters the desire for personal, rather than institutional revenge.

What form, it might be asked, should this 'illiberal' system of punishment take? The answer cannot be abstractly determined. But there is no doubt that one vital feature of punishment – which is the vivid sense that there is human agency and not unhuman mechanism at its source – must be restored if the institution is to have the place in social arrangements that conservatives would accord to it. Modern writers, from Kafka to Genet, have sufficiently described the plight and the degradation of man in a world without agency: such a world is a world beyond morality, and beyond politics, a world which it would be irremediable folly to bring into being. Now consider the institution of prison. Is it obvious that this is the best way of conveying either to the criminal or to the public an adequate sense of punishment as a response to crime; in the way that a human action may constitute a response? The answer is by no means certain. The demoralizing effect of long sentences, the natural tendency of prison to create a criminal society with values and traditions of its own, the corrupting and disturbing effect of a social life without the benefit of home, all conspire to render prison both cruel and dangerous. Moreover, its nature as deterrent and retribution is rendered nugatory by its inscrutable exterior, and to retain prison as the only form of punishment is to give rise to an absurd mathematics of crime, according to which it seems that the robbery of a mail train is roughly four times as bad as premeditated murder – a result which is deeply repugnant to the normal conscience.

The natural law

A criticism of some significance is always made against conservatism, which is that, to direct one's political aspirations towards an established order removes the means of social criticism, and requires one to uphold whatever arbitrary despotism might have achieved or usurped the power of the state. The idea of the good state simply slips away as irrelevant. The challenge of such a question can be met, but the conservative answer, unlike that of the reformist, is not easy to formulate. Conservatives cannot criticize the existing order because it is an inefficient means to some end that they designate as the sole aim of politics. They must find, within the operation of law itself, the criterion of its validity.

A state is not despotic just so long as the law represents a power that bears authority. The unwritten constitution of the United Kingdom, which vests the making of law in institutions many of which are only indirectly answerable to the sources of power, makes despotism unlikely. For the important part of English criminal law stems not from parliamentary enactment but from what I shall call (to use an old and much misused label) 'natural' justice. By natural justice I mean a process of reflection recognized (but not always obeyed) by everyone in their mutual dealings, a process without which no human intercourse could be conceived in the spirit of friendship. I previously criticized the concept of 'human rights' with which politicians wage so many wars of words, not because there is no intelligible notion which attaches to that label, but because it is thought to sum up the entire legitimacy of government, and to generate, as a principle of universal politics, the parochial preconceptions of Western democracy. The notion merely obscures the major issues of foreign policy in connection with which it is used.

Nevertheless, there are natural rights, to the extent that there are natural obligations – to the extent, that is, that a concept of 'just dealing' arises naturally between people. In using the word 'natural' I do not mean that the authority of these rights can be exercised independently of the protection afforded by a political order. But they can be independently understood, and they are in some sense 'nearer' to the citizens than those rights and obligations which define their membership of a specific society.

In administrative law, certain formal or procedural principles are given the name 'principles of natural justice' – the right of representation, the obligation not to be judge in one's own cause, and so on. But apart from this residue of principles derived from canon law, the distinction between the 'natural' and the artificial is made only indirectly, through the distinction between equity and law. Nevertheless, the distinction is intuitively obvious. It is undeniable that the very process of development from child to adult, from animal to rational being, involves people in relations with their fellows which, were they not mediated by an instinctive conception of what is just, would be without the benefit of friendship, benevolence and love. It is unjust to strike someone who has given you no cause, unjust to appropriate another person's property without consent, unjust to force another to submit to sexual desire ... and so on. The list is long, and even in the application of laws which derive only from the political constitution, an independent judiciary will follow principles of reasoning which have their intellectual basis, as those elementary principles have their basis, in a conception of justice that is presupposed in every social arrangement, and which cannot be conceived as the mere creation of the sovereign power. The question of the origin and justification of this sense of justice is philosophical: is it a reflection of that fundamental principle of practical reasoning which Kant derived from the idea of autonomy (the principle that one must treat all rational beings as ends and not as means)? Or is it, perhaps, simply part of the natural history of friendship? The answer is of no concern to us; for what is important, politically speaking, is that the sense of justice is immediate, part of the surface of social life. It cannot be eradicated from human feeling by any political power, nor by any process of 're-education'. The best a despot can do is to prevent its expression. And just as natural justice is an essential ingredient in friendship between people, so must the laws of a state embody it if that state is to command the friendship of its citizens and be honoured as end and not as means.

Social justice

It is here that we must recognize, however, that 'natural' justice has an unnatural enemy: the 'social' justice of the egalitarian reformer. To illustrate their conflict it is best to consider a specific example. I shall consider the law of property.

The principal application of 'natural justice' is to human actions, and, by extension, to the characters from which those actions spring. It has no application to a state of affairs as such, judged independently of the agency which produced it. The sense of justice, being founded in and expressive of our reciprocal dealings, arises only because we can see the justice of individual actions, and feel drawn towards the will from which they spring. If, at some later stage, we come to extend the idea, and speak of the justice or injustice of social and political realities, we mean to refer, not to their nature, but to their cause. It is not unjust that one woman is born better looking, or more intelligent than another. Indeed, conservatives would say that our understanding of this idea of a 'just state of affairs' is so uncertain that we could not say that it is unjust that one person is born richer than another, or that such and such a proportion of citizens holds such and such a proportion of the national wealth. These things happen, but they are unjust only if they are brought about through injustice. If they are to be criticized then it must be in other terms, and terms which, unless they make reference to human agency, will be more aesthetic than moral.

In order to employ this concept of 'justice' in political debate, therefore, the advocate of 'social justice' creates a peculiar unconscious fiction: the fiction that really all wealth, and perhaps all advantage, belongs to a single owner (society), which (in some inexplicable way) has the duty to ensure its 'distribution'. And, given a sufficiently bare and unhistorical description of the facts, it might seem that it would be unjust to distribute wealth unequally among people who are all equal in their right to claim a portion of it (equal, simply in the fact of being citizens); just as it is 'unfair' to divide the sweets unequally at a children's party. But this fiction of 'distribution' is so often in conflict with the immediate perception of what is just that one can come to believe it only through repeatedly and ritualistically rehearsing its desirable implications: namely, that it succours the poor and casts down the rich.

To illustrate the conflict between social and natural justice, I shall consider an example that has been of great political importance in our times: the 1968 Rent Act, which provided statutory protection to most classes of private tenant. I choose this example, not because it is an easy one to discuss, but because it illustrates the depth at which the fight between natural and social justice occurs. The Rent Acts conferred powers to interfere in contractual bargaining, and so grant rights in law which transcend the rights contracted for. Now, it is not alien to the spirit of natural justice to refuse to uphold a contract, or to impose conditions that were not contained in it. It has always been recognized that the freedom with which a promise is made is a relative thing, and that a person may contract away his life, like Antonio, under the pressure of necessity. Part of the exercise of natural justice might involve undoing, or rewriting, contracts, in order to remove whatever element of oppressive usage might otherwise be sanctioned by them. And it is clear that, since it is necessary to people to have a home, it is unlikely that the law will stand aside from contracts concerning residential (or, for that matter, industrial) property. From the earliest feudal times the law has offered 'rights' – even to squatters – without which relations between landlord and tenant could have become despotic, as they were in Russia (and as they remained under the communist system). It follows that, since contracts for the use of land are and have been subject to close judicial and statutory control, it will be very difficult to provide a formula which defines the uniquely just arrangement. Nevertheless, it can hardly be considered just that a certain kind of contract must *always* and *inevitably* be rewritten in the interest of one of the parties, and in such a way as to effect a transfer of ownership to someone who was contracting only for a right of use. Suppose that a statute existed which declared that anyone who freely contracted to hire a car could at once rewrite the contract so as to claim the use of the car for life (and for the life of some chosen dependant), at a reduced rent, and with all obligation of repair still resting with the hirer. Natural justice would be outraged, and common sense would bring such contracts to an end.

Now the sense of justice is bewildered by the more complex case of land, for reasons I have mentioned. Clearly, a person's attachment to home and to the place which surrounds it; the difficulties of moving house, of finding another place to live compatible with retaining a job, and so on – all these put a tenant at the mercy of a landlord who chooses to raise the rent, or terminate the tenancy. Nevertheless, the difficulty of steering the sense of justice through this complex web of free and unfree bargaining should not give grounds for a complete adoption of the ethic of 'social justice', and the consequent attempt (manifest in the Rent Acts) simply to redistribute property, so that tenants acquire the property rights that were previously vested in their landlords. (Just as, in my example, ownership of a car is effectively transferred under the name of an 'agreement to hire'.) The example has been very important; for having led to the demise of private letting agreements, except under very special circumstances, it caused whole tracts of our inner cities to become first empty, then vandalized, and finally sealed off from the civilized world. It has been the major cause of that 'flight to the suburbs' which modern governments and planners helplessly deplore.

It is clear that the statute in question can be understood as an exercise of 'social justice', since, other things being equal, it will effect a transfer of wealth from rich to poor. But it is also clear that its provisions are so strict in the favouring of the 'weaker' party that they constitute a direct violation of natural justice. Consider the following case, which was not uncommon. A widow, being left with nothing more than the matrimonial home, and a little money, buys for herself a small apartment, hoping to live from the rents provided by her house. This house was purchased over many years, at considerable sacrifice, and is the principal fruit of her and her husband's labour. Having installed tenants, the widow finds that she cannot move them, and has little control over them. The house can no longer be sold. Moreover, the widow cannot raise the rents to keep pace with inflation, and her statutory obligation to repair the house encumbers her with expenses that she is unable to meet. The result is not merely hardship, but destitution. It is of course not the hardship that is in question: to appeal to that is simply to invoke the very concept of 'social justice' that led to this iniquity. What is wrong is the natural injustice of the law.

The example, as I said, is a complex one, because it deals with that area of law where historical and contractual rights intermingle, and where each is constrained by necessities that cannot be subject to the vagaries of individual choice. As I shall argue in the next chapter, 'freedom of contract' is at best an ideal, and subject to constraints that make it impossible for conservatives to rest their case in this concept alone. Social complexities will always force us away from the paradigm of just relations. But it is precisely in examples of the kind I have discussed, where these complexities modify and inform the operation of 'natural' justice, that the conflict between 'natural' and 'social' justice can be seen to be both genuine and deep. If this is so, then the adoption of the ethic of 'social justice' in the practice of government will already cause an unnatural strain in the social bond (the bond which is founded in friendly relations between citizen and citizen, and between citizen and state). Moreover, its effects are never more than temporary; consisting in the transfer of wealth to the ineffective. Social justice cannot, in the nature of things, root out those deep inequalities of skill, industry and talent which will once again cause some to rise and others to fall. The recent history of Russia perfectly illustrates this point.

It is in the concept of natural justice, therefore, that conservatives will find one answer to the sceptic, and a partial criterion of the social good. And natural justice, far from being an external aim of politics, will be inextricable from legal procedure, qualifying and varying the very laws and customs that constitute the state.

The broad historical perspective

A familiar ghost now comes to trouble us. I have avoided philosophical argument, and presented the conception of 'natural' justice through a single instance. Doctrine requires concreteness. But to talk of what is concrete is to enter the purview of history. What, it will be asked, does this 'natural justice' amount to, when surveyed from the uncommitted standpoint of the historian? The answer may seem disconcerting. Natural justice has its antecedents in the *jus gentium* of Roman law. This remnant of law applied, not to citizens, but to the mass of conquered peoples from whose customary procedures it provided a convenient appeal – convenient because, in representing Rome as the final arbiter of justice, it also confirmed Rome as the final ruling power. The *jus gentium* (rationalized as *jus naturale*) passed into canon law, to be upheld as the 'natural law' of the medieval jurists and theologians. But what did that transmission amount to, historically, if not the attempt of the Church to constitute a court of appeal from the local laws of European sovereigns, and so to cling to the ascendancy of Rome? And why again did the *Code napoléon* lean so heavily on the rhetoric of natural law, if not to bolster the political hegemony which sought expression through its counsels? Let us take a more recent example. The Northern Rhodesian Order in Council of 1924, providing for the administration of that protectorate, enacted that in civil cases courts must be guided (where possible) by native law, provided that law should not be 'repugnant to natural justice'. Again, the constraint of natural justice is the constraint of a ruling power. The singular failure of Grotius to extract a coherent 'international law' from the remnants of ecclesiastical jurisdiction at the Reformation only serves to confirm the 'historical' view.'Natural justice' is the slave of a ruling class. Where there is no such class (as in the matters arising between nation states), then there is no natural justice to apply.

It is impossible to consider all the issues of fact, diplomacy and legal theory that our historian raises. Let us rather stand him on his head. Why, let us ask, was anyone (not already a member of some ruling class) taken in by the doctrine of a 'natural' law? Not (as honest historians will admit) because of an attachment to the 'rights of man'. It is plausible to suggest, therefore, that the doctrine arises, as it claims to arise, quite 'naturally' – which is to say, from the exigencies of human nature. And that is why it is in the interest of a ruling class to uphold it, as it is in the interest of a ruling class to confirm and consolidate every natural sentiment of its subject people. The feeling of injustice which attaches to gratuitous violence, to rape, theft and fraud, to imprisonment without trial – this feeling is an inescapable outcome of the experience of society. Why that should be so is a question not for the historian but for the philosopher; that it is so is given. And that is how we could begin to *explain* the power and durability of Rome, of the Church, and of the *Code napoléon*. Far from being besmirched by its proximity to political power, natural justice constitutes one of the justifications of power, since power has been necessary to make justice possible.

But there is also power without justice. In modern history, one might say, it is 'social justice', and not 'natural justice', that has done most to sustain that possibility. The first represents a political aim (the aim of social equality); the second merely translates into law a vital principle of society. And, as my example was designed to show, at some point the conflict between the two will be inevitable and open.

Natural justice exists not absolutely, however, but in varying degrees. One cannot suppose that the rapacity of human nature could be so overcome that justice alone would serve to govern us. So we must return, after all, to the remark of Machiavelli's with which this chapter began. While the authority of the state prevails, then the allegiance of the citizens has a guarantee, and they may struggle for whatever liberties and benefits may seem desirable without threatening either the social order or their own fulfilment within it. In such a state, natural justice may be at the heart of every constitutional device and inhabit every judicial decision. But it is too much to hope of human nature that the authority of the state will go unchallenged, or that civil society will not contain elements which regard established institutions not as expressions of authority but as mere instruments of power. In every legal system, therefore, there must be provision against sedition, laws which enable the state to reassert itself against antagonists, and these laws may stand wholly outside the rule of natural justice, being determined by the principle of necessity alone. This truth is so evident that no political doctrine can dispense with some soothing rhetoric that will serve to make it palatable. It is unquestionable that, if the power of the state is threatened, so too is its authority, and with it the structure of civil society. To sacrifice power for the sake of justice, is to make the exercise of justice impossible. It cannot, therefore, be an insuperable defect in a law of sedition that it provides for imprisonment without trial, a reduced judicial process, or summary execution. What matters is the extent to which such laws must be invoked. If this invocation constitutes – as in Communist Russia – a major portion of the judicial process, then clearly the state has no real authority and the whole arrangement stands on the brink of illegitimacy.

Here we see what might be called the dialectic of justice and allegiance in the state. The exercise of justice is only possible within the framework of established institutions which command respect. To command respect it is not sufficient to make just pronouncements: it is necessary also to have the power to put them into practice. And that power must be seen to be embodied in judicial decisions, so that a single power translates itself into executive commands, the enforcement of law, and the resolution of private quarrels. A general acquiescence towards the established order is required for the exercise of this power, and hence for the just dealings which the citizen expects from it. In return for this expectation of justice, the state expects the allegiance of its citizens; they are constrained in conscience to sanction the most violent and even 'unnatural' methods in the suppression of rebellion, provided the aim is as rapid a return as possible to the condition where just dealings become the norm. This is surely what should be said in defence of those, like Chile's General Pinochet, who have had to make the choice between violently establishing an order in which natural justice has a chance, and acquiescing in the ongoing violence and degradation of a society devoted to 'social justice'. Only those who have no experience of communism will be without sympathy for the General in this dilemma – which is not to say that he ever experienced it as one.

The conservative view of law will therefore pay special attention to the constitutional artifact known as the 'rule of law'. The rule of law is the sign of a successful constitution – for it is a sign that all exercise of power can be described and criticized in legal terms. Hence it enables the citizen to make a prompt distinction between the authority of the state and the power of some rebellious body. It is an essential feature of the conservative state that this 'rule of law' should prevail, not because law has an authority greater than the power of the state, but because the power of the state and the authority of the law should be ultimately one and the same. The state achieves its full mantle of authority only when clothed in law. As we shall see, political dispute is always represented by conservatives in legal terms. In industrial relations, in habits of assembly, in the control of monopoly and the curtailing of individual power, even in the sphere of international relations where the state of nature still prevails, it is through law that they seek a solution rather than through the confrontation of subject powers.

Concluding remarks

The conservative view of law is, I have suggested, clear, consistent, and, through being in harmony with normal feelings, at variance with received ideas. As the will of the state, the law must express the will of society. The idea of 'individual freedom' cannot suffice to generate laws that will be either acceptable to the normal conscience or compatible with normal administrative needs. Nor is it cogent to claim that law derive its legitimacy solely through preserving the individual from 'harm'. Legitimacy arises from the bond between citizens, and the law must be thought of in the same way – as the common law is thought to arise from the primary experience of society. Such an attitude to law necessitates a corresponding attitude to punishment. This attitude, which may seem harsh when initially stated, is in reality as humane as its liberal competitors.

I considered the possibility that there might be general principles of justice, which carry an authority greater than the authority of a particular constitution. I claimed that there are such principles, that they are in deep and inevitable conflict with the goal of 'social justice', and that they cannot be viewed merely as the instruments of power. Their generality stems from the general condition of the social order. Hence, even the conservative view of law, which gives special weight to existing social arrangements, can generate a criterion of validity that applies beyond the *status quo*. In virtue of that, it is possible for conservatives to deny that each and every arrangement deserves to be conserved. Whatever merits conservation, however, must endure within the framework of a rule of law, in which adjustments and changes are mediated by the courts.

5
Property

It may seem surprising that I have advanced so far in describing the conservative attitude without mentioning what some take to be its principal fetish. But the reader will begin to see that there is a world of difference between the political outlook that I have described, and the view which sees all politics as a question of ownership, and of the creation and distribution of wealth. Nevertheless, a political doctrine that said nothing about these things would be hard enough to believe, and even if it be fashionable to over-emphasize matters of wealth and ownership, that only constitutes a yet stronger reason for taking them seriously. We must, in particular, examine the nature of private property, and determine how and to what extent conservatives are committed to its safeguard.

Wealth and management

Economics is the major preoccupation of practising politicians. Moreover, in so far as there is a consistent popular image of the machinery of the state, it is that of a corporation, with a 'management' directed towards 'economic growth'.[38] This image is fostered by the media. It is also fostered by politicians themselves. But to what extent is it a true picture of the political process?

If the question of ownership is central to conservatism, then this is not because that is how conservatism is defined. There is no logical identity between conservatism and capitalism, for example. The connection arises because the need for private property stems automatically from the basic attitude of conservatism as I have already described it. It may still be no part of conservatism to be associated with any particular economic policy, or even to align itself with the pursuit of wealth.

Property

Perhaps the most simple-minded case for something called 'conservatism' consists in the argument that a 'free market' economy is a guarantee of national wealth, and the best way to maintain or raise the 'standard of living', by ensuring that each person, through pursuing his own material well-being, has the incentive to pursue the well-being of the whole. And if that is so, then the true enemy of 'conservatism' – now identified as 'socialism' or 'public ownership' – must necessarily deprive the citizens of the material incentive upon which we all depend for our prosperity.

Such arguments – while they may provide the content of electioneering slogans – present us with a vision of politics that is desultory indeed, as though the sole aim of social existence were the accumulation of wealth and the sole concern of politics the discovery of the most effective means to it. No doubt there is truth in the contention that public ownership destroys incentive; and no doubt the attempt to erode the institutions of private property is incompatible with the highest economic objectives. But it is not clear that these objectives are the sum of politics. Socialists, for example, are more interested in the distribution of wealth than in its accumulation. And they commanded popular support on that basis alone. There was a time, indeed, when the English Tory party stood against the 'market' economy, not in the interests of national wealth, but in the interests of a social order which it felt quite rightly to be threatened by it.

One cannot ignore the question of national wealth, which must inevitably bear on every issue of domestic and foreign policy. But there exists no persuasive theory of politics or of human nature which shows wealth to be an unmitigated good, or poverty an unmitigated evil, and it is perhaps only the desire to reduce all human goods to something measurable that would represent things in such a way. Nobody is likely to consider that the wealth enjoyed by the Eskimo through his labour in the fish-canning factory means anything when set beside the impoverished existence that he once enjoyed in fellowship with his kind. Naturally, material wealth is important in international politics and in national security. But the vast wealth of America counted for little in the Vietnam war, no more than the amassed resources of England,

Holland and the Empire did against the resolution of the French who followed Louis XIV. It has been argued, too, that wealth is the great precondition of domestic order and of national culture: do not Venice, Holland and Florence give proof of it? But then one must forget Greece, and ancient Japan, forget the destitute world of Piers Plowman, forget most of all that every nation in the West possesses wealth far in excess of what was conceivable in Renaissance Italy, while not one of them can produce an artist to match the least among the hundred who briefly flourished in the tiny town of Florence. The fact is that the relation of wealth to social and political well-being is a mystery, and to cast all politics in economic terms is to surrender the known facts of human life to the flimsiest speculation.

This is not to say that the production of wealth has no part to play in political deliberations. It is, rather, to insist on the ascendancy of policy over production, where policy means the directing of activity towards the maintenance of social life. So conceived, the creation of wealth is not a sufficient policy. If it is thought to be so, this is partly because the creation of wealth is believed to be a necessary guarantee of economic stability. The emphasis on the 'standard of living' in politics – while it is a natural effect of the democratic process – has its most important explanation in the experience of uncontrolled inflation, economic depression, rapidly fluctuating and changing material circumstances, as these have affected Western society in the present century. And these sudden reversals have been accompanied by 'social, political, and moral disasters which the general framework – the patterns of behaviour, habits, outlook, language, that is, the "ideological superstructure" of the victims – could not sustain'.[39] It is the truth encapsulated in that remark of Berlin's that has led politicians to seek for some understanding of these things, and to attempt at all costs to avert the drastic fluctuations experienced in the inter-war years. The allegiance of the people requires fixed expectations, a settled idea of their own and others' material status, and a sense that they are not the victims of uncontrollable forces that might at any moment plunge them into destitution or raise others to incomprehensible wealth. In so far as that sense is integral to the authority of the state, then it becomes part of the responsibility of the state to settle and uphold the common currency and all the material expectations that are associated with it. But, as conservatives have until recently always realized, this argues not for a free market but for something like its opposite. Indeed, it has at times led to the acceptance by the Conservative Party of economic theories – such as that of Keynes

– which regard the interference of the state in the market process as a social and economic necessity.

The ascendancy of economics

Before considering the institution of private property, however, it is important to reflect on the ascendancy of economics in matters of policy. Some might consider this to be a sign of the wholesale adoption of the Marxist view, the view that 'the mode of production of material life determines the social, political and intellectual process ...', and that one should always distinguish 'the material transformation of the economic conditions of production, which can be determined with the precision of a natural science', from the 'legal, political, religious, aesthetic or philosophic – in short, ideological – forms in which men become conscious of this conflict and fight it out'.[40] In other words it might seem to be tantamount to the theory that the true understanding of the facts of social life is to be found in the 'science' of economics. Politics is nothing more than the unruly attempt of consciousness to express and control a reality which in fact proceeds in obedience to laws which no merely political conception can grasp.

In fact, matters are worse than that. For Marx's high-spirited attempt to subvert the deliverances of political common sense was redeemed by a theory which restored, at the so-called 'economic' level, all those features of human self-consciousness which it seemed to invalidate at the level of surface politics. The 'labour theory of value' is less a theory of economics than a theory of political exploitation. 'Labour' is a concept integral to the self-consciousness of humanity, and in describing it as the economic reality Marx was at the same time describing the thoughts and feelings through which social life is experienced.[41] Until recently the 'economic advisers' who surrounded our politicians were possessed, as a rule, of theories which both claimed to be more scientific than Marx's, and also remained wholly divested of any reference to the moral life. Citizenship was reduced to consumption, and the triumph of economics co-existed quite happily with the downfall of political understanding. Other less managerially minded politicians fell victim to those economists who – while preserving the appearance of scientific expertise – disguised as economic theorems the political prejudices which could not be deduced from them. It came to seem as though a Galbraith, a Hayek or a Friedman could speak about political matters with the authority of a scientist, when in fact his political doctrine remained as a rule detachable from his economic theory, the theory itself being as questionable as its competitors. As a result of all this, one response to the ascendancy of economics has been scepticism, scepticism most of all about its scientific pretensions, about its predictions, concepts and results, many of which, in the hands of established 'advisers', seem to derive directly from the antecedent policies of a political party, and not from the axioms of an impartial science. (The point is evident in the 'neo-classical' theories of the market; it is only slightly less evident in the recent American attacks on 'oligarchical business'.[42])

Nevertheless, scepticism is premature. The acceptance by our major parties during the Seventies of similar economic policies (partly under pressure from the International Monetary Fund), and the subsequent triumph of free-market thinking under Margaret Thatcher and the influence of the Institute for Economic Affairs, suggest a minimum of received wisdom in economic matters. Wisdom which triumphs even over Labour Party ideology might well encapsulate the basic truths of some budding science. But now, suppose that there is this science, and that it has all the power to predict and explain which Marx and others have claimed for it. Should not politicians avail themselves of its results, and will they not thereby enhance their political understanding?

In answer to that question it is necessary to remind ourselves that no natural science of man could replace or subvert the mode of understanding that we call political. We can of course imagine a neutral, predictive science of social behaviour; but the result may make human action not more intelligible, but less, since it may have to eliminate from its account of things all reference to how action is conceived. Economics stands to politics in much the same relation as neurology stands to personal affection. While I could, in principle, regard my friend as an organism activated by a complex system of nerves, and base all my knowledge of him and all my anticipations of his behaviour in that description, I certainly would not thereby understand him as I understand him instinctively through friendship. He would have become, for me, a mechanized corpse, towards which love and hatred, liking and anger, admiration and contempt, indeed all emotion that is distinctively human, would be more or less impossible. I would be forced to turn away from him as something alien and unintelligible.[43] In just such a way the purely scientific economist might have to see civil society as a corpse, moving in obedience to scientific laws which can be formulated without reference to the conceptions, values and feelings through which people understand themselves as political beings. The only result of that scientific enterprise would be to render politics incomprehensible, to retreat from direct involvement in it, and to cease to want either to belong or not to belong to the social arrangement by which one is surrounded. Some such objection, I shall later argue, applies to all 'deterministic' economic models, and in particular to the Marxist theory of history, which seeks to replace political understanding with a 'value-free' predictive science.

The right of property

None of this is to dismiss the importance of economics, or to suggest that there is no room for a genuine 'political economy', tempered by the priorities of politics in much the way that domestic economy is tempered by the needs of family life. But, before laying emphasis on this unborn 'science', we must study the principles from which the politics of property will spring. Conservatives are not concerned merely with the creation of wealth. Will they then turn their attention, as socialists do, to its distribution? The answer is that they will, but only indirectly, and only because of a certain view about private property. This view is difficult to state, for the simple reason that the intuition from which it derives lies in the very centre of social consciousness. It is only by ignoring this intuition that it has been possible for the opponents of conservatism to regard political issues as concerned with 'control of the means of production', and to set up a simple-minded dichotomy between socialism and capitalism as containing the whole of contemporary politics. For conservatives that dichotomy is naive, for it simplifies beyond recognition the principle of their outlook, which is the absolute and ineradicable need of private property.

Ownership is the primary relation through which man and nature come together. It is therefore the first stage in the socializing of objects, and the condition of all higher institutions. It is not necessarily a product of greed or exploitation, but it is necessarily a part of the process whereby people free themselves from the power of things, transforming resistant nature into compliant image. Through property man imbues his world with will, and begins therein to discover himself as a social being.

Those high-flown sentiments belong to Hegel;[44] they demand translation into the plain talk of government. And the task is not easy. But a first step is made when we see how near is the idea of private property to the notions that I put forward in Chapter 2. For consider what people are without the institution of property. They cannot identify in the world any object as their own; hence they cannot freely avail themselves of objects and expect others to accord the use of them. Everything they desire they see as the object only of desire, and not of right. Nor can they see any part of the world as connected (except by some accident of strength or interest) with anyone else. A person who wields power over woods and fields has no more authority to dispose of them than does his neighbour. The concepts of 'right', and 'possession' fail to inform their common understanding of a world which, in consequence, remains alien to each of them, and a battleground for both. Nor can the battle be terminated by a gift, since gift supposes property. Objects can therefore play no part in establishing or reinforcing social relations. Instead they stand wholly apart from the world of people, an inanimate, inhuman scenario to their unformed transactions.

If people are to awaken from this state into true self-consciousness – consciousness of themselves as agents – then they must see the world in different terms, terms of right, responsibility and freedom. The institution of property enables them to do this. Through property an object ceases to be a mere inanimate thing, and becomes instead the focus of rights and obligations. These rights and obligations need not be (in the first place) contractual. Indeed the question how they arise is of little immediate importance. The point is rather that, until they arise, until property passes from 'effective control' (to use the Marxist expression) to institutional right, it contains no contribution to human society. Through property, and the rights associated with it, the object is lifted out of mere 'thinghood' and rendered up to humanity. It bears now the imprint of human social relations, and reflects back to its owner a picture of himself as a social being. By instilling the world with the rights of ownership man remakes the world as an image of his true – his social – self. He is now at home where before he was merely let loose.

It is for this reason that a person's principal proprietary attitude is towards his immediate surroundings – house, room, furniture – towards those things with which he is, so to speak, mingled. It is the home, therefore, that is the principal sphere of property, and the principal locus of the gift. (Hospitality is the only form of gift that imposes itself as an obligation: for it arises when another has been invited into the sphere that defines one's own.)

There is, then, a deep connection between private property and self-realization. If this has been doubted it is partly on account of a common confusion between possession and consumption. The activity of consumption does not presuppose ownership, and takes place even in that 'state of nature' where philosophers locate their primeval human beings. In the civilized state, however, consumption is also an exercise of right, and implies ownership of the things consumed. Nevertheless consumption is only a part of property, and not the part which reveals its social essence. The important aspect of property is its stable aspect, in which ownership is conceived as permanent or semi-permanent. For the full fruition of the sense of property there must be permanent objects of possession. It is this which explains the enduring place of land in the psychology of ownership. The true gift is not the thing that is consumed (and which does honour only in the process of hospitality), but the thing that is kept beyond foreseeable consumption. This thing is the embodiment of a right of use. The right may be exclusive or qualified, permanent or semi-permanent, absolute or defeasible: there are many distinctions here, and they are distinctions which must necessarily be passed over in economic theory. (It was 'obvious' to Keynes that 'consumption is the sole end and object of all economic activity',[45] obvious only because Keynes's economic theory could not distinguish the various kinds of property, and the various modes of holding it.) Similar considerations explain why the sense of property tends to transform itself into the pursuit of aesthetic value, and why beautiful objects are consecrated to God. A paradigm of the personal gift is the ornamented, decorated object, which retains its worth beyond the life of any owner. Among such things the important examples are the house, its furniture, and all those assorted oddments that used to come in a decorated *cassone* from bride to groom.

Property and household

Home is the place where private property accumulates, and so overreaches itself, becoming transformed into something shared. There is no contract of distribution: sharing is simply the essence of family life. Here everything important is 'ours'. Private property is added to, and reinforces, the primary social relation. It is for some such reason that conservatives have seen the family and private property as institutions which stand or fall together. The family has its life in the home, and the home demands property for its establishment. Whatever abstract arguments might be offered against that connection, it has a savour of irrebuttable common sense. And so far as I can see, the abstract argument is very feeble, representing the connection between 'family' and 'property' as an accident, peculiar to something called the 'bourgeois' family, the imminent demise of which it seeks to foretell. This attack is rooted in the shallowest of observations. For where do we find the 'non-bourgeois' family, in which the connections between kinship, household and property are supposedly loosened or undone? Here radical critics usually choose to refer to some hypothetical future, of which neither they nor anyone else has a concrete understanding. If they attend to history it is usually in order to misdescribe it.[46] For consider some typical 'non-bourgeois' families. The Homeric *oikos* (from which word our own 'economy' is derived) referred not merely to a social unit but also to a household, endowed with property, and standing under rights of ownership and obligations of hospitality. (Nestor, exhorting the Achaeans beside their ships, cries: 'Friends, be courageous, and consider the shame of other men, and remember, each of you, children, and wife, possessions and parents ...' (11. xv, 11. 661–3). And lest it should be thought that Homer spoke only for the ruling class, see also Hesiod, *Works and Days* (1. 405f.), and the comments in the pseudo-Aristotelean *Oeconomica* (Book I).) The modern proletarian family is similarly constituted, as was the extended aristocratic family of the Renaissance. In studying such social units one will see how deeply intertwined is the private aspect of social life with the institution of property, and how much of a distortion it must be to prise the two apart. Those who imagine that the proletarian family somehow escapes from the attachment to property, simply because it cannot afford, or does not require, the purchase of a house, are surely confused. Property does not consist in the accumulation of proximate objects: it is a particular form of *right*. A right of way is property; so is a right to use a common lawnmower, a right to shut a door against another person. Even the occupancy of a council flat is a property right, defeasible at law, but in practice no more defeasible than a private lease, and carrying with it as fierce a sense of territory as pertains to any country house. The difference that exists is of course important: it enables the proletarian family to accumulate moveable goods and gadgetry (cars, televisions, washing-machines) in a manner which changes the aspect of the home. And it may be that these goods, and the specific appetites towards them, point to political considerations that condemn the whole arrangement – as the opponents of the consumer society believe. But to discuss that complication will only obscure the present issue; the essential connection between household and family is undeniable. It follows that conservatives must be concerned with the distribution of property, and not only with its accumulation. Given their belief in the political importance of the family, and their reliance on family loyalties in forming respect towards an established political order, they must desire the distribution of property through all classes of society, in accordance with whatever conception of household might be generic to each of them. How, and in what measure, is this distribution to be effected? And to what extent is it the concern of the state to further it?

Distribution and the market

It is, I think, an inescapable consequence of the existence of property, and of the active nature of people, that there should be exchange and accumulation. There are philosophies that envisage the institutions of private property as existing without these consequences. We are asked to imagine a society of people endowed with such plenty that they have only to reach out a hand to satisfy their needs, and possessed of natures so lassitudinous that the desire to overcome and dominate is unknown to them. The literature is full of such visions, and nothing that Aristotle, Hobbes or Nietzsche have said will prevent them from being produced and pondered. But let us be realistic: people seek domestic peace and security; they seek fame and applause; they seek power and influence; they seek friendship and love. Of all those, only love cannot be acquired through property, and love without security is tragic. Moreover, the other aims are not only furthered by property: they require property, since they require the ability to assert a massive right against intrusion. The desire for property will therefore be mingled with the desires for security, status and power. All these ends are furthered by exchange (since no one can produce everything that he requires), and equally by accumulation (which brings security and power). Since talent, ability, energy – indeed the sheer attachment to life – are unequally distributed, so too therefore will be property, a fact which can be called 'unfair' only by invoking that concept of 'social justice' which we have already seen reason to reject. Thus the very process whereby man first humanizes the world and renders it intelligible as an object of his social will, also creates the divisions which, on one view, set people against one another. Socialists, who seek for the redistribution of wealth (believing that only in a condition of equality will social conflict be brought to an end) have devised methods for achieving this aim, and I shall later consider three – taxation, nationalization and expropriation – since their place in the activities of the state is so fundamental that no political doctrine can ignore them.

'Distribution' can be considered both from the political and from the economic viewpoint. One may consider the justice of a particular form of taxation, or the political wisdom of expropriation, or the relation between the distribution of property and the quality of social life. These are political questions; they depend upon the conceptions – justice, friendship, and community – through which the social organism is understood by those who compose it. One might also consider the economic benefits of progressive taxation, or the effect of taxation on investment income, or the fiscal benefit consequent on a general ownership of moveable goods. These are economic questions, which must be answered through an adequate theory. The answers to them will contain no recommendation that is not itself subordinate to questions of general policy. It is no part of social life to engage in these economic speculations, although politicians must have some grasp of them. But whatever grasp they may seek or acquire, it will be useful to them only if they are possessed of a political doctrine – a set of beliefs capable of generating coherent policy and securing the understanding and agreement of those on whom the policy is imposed. Hence, before questions of economic management can be properly discussed, it is necessary to review the political factors that will be at stake in their solution. We must therefore examine the way in which questions of distribution will enter the basic principles of conservative thought.

Distribution, in Britain, has been the great socialist cause. But we must notice that the desire to arrive at an 'equitable distribution' is not the desire to abolish private property, but the desire for an adjustment in what liberal (or 'classical') economists have thought to be the natural order. British socialists have in general upheld the institution of private property, partly in response to the intuition that I have elaborated, the intuition of a deep connection between property and family life. With the 'radical' critique – the view that private property is simply an evil, to be abolished as soon as possible from the world – I shall be concerned only later.

Perhaps it may be wondered why we should now consider socialism even in its parochial form, the form which aims at redistribution. For, having defended private property can we not leave it to take its course, establishing itself in society according to the natural laws of the market? The answer is, of course, that we cannot. Not only would it be absurd to dismiss out of hand the demand for redistribution (as though the many who have argued for it were people of no understanding). It would also be wrong, having given essentially conservative reasons for the maintenance of private property, to adopt a merely liberal stance towards its distribution.[47] We can see from the account given that the right to property must be deeply entwined with national and social history, and cannot at any moment be reduced to a mere résumé of human agreements. Property is an institution, requiring realization and protection in the institutions of the state, and a person's right to it is not some overriding law of natural justice, but a right conditional on allegiance to the society which made ownership possible. Hence there is no injustice involved in a law of forfeiture, and if we can show that the order and equilibrium of society requires the appropriation of individual property, then reasons of state will require that the right to private property be defeasible in the public interest. No one doubts that reasons of state may be abused, either in Neronian fashion, or in the more subtle way of bureaucratic power. And even here, in that twilight where the equilibrium between individual right and public necessity is established, there are principles of justice which no government should ignore. But it is no longer possible to imagine, amid the vast contingencies of modern society, that the need for private property should be allowed to dictate a 'natural' right, and that the law of the market (whatever it is, indeed) should therefore be enacted by every ruling power. Whatever natural justice dictates, it will be but a part of the law of property, and insufficient to determine the nexus of legal rights.

Nothing better illustrates this than the richly historical law of land in England, a law which, codified many times, and finally in the great land laws of 1925, represents a thousand years of careful dealing between state and citizen, and expresses a subtle sense of the ways in which a title to land may be lost, gained or granted. It has been recognized throughout history that the law of the market is inadequate to represent the smallest part of what is here at stake, and that any estate may be encumbered with adverse rights that have arisen neither out of contract nor out of any other form of human choice.[48] Moreover, one must bear in mind that, even when property is 'private' and changes hands by private treaty, it may be held subject to interests which prevent it from being exchanged at its 'market' price. The legal owner of trust property, for example, is encumbered by the rights of the beneficiaries, who become the equitable owners of the content of the trust. This introduces immeasurable complexities into property rights; property can now remain owned but immovable, bound by terms which prohibit active dealing. The case of a trust for purposes (as in the endowment of a college or hospital), where no list of beneficiaries can be made, shows private property at the extreme point of attenuation, on the verge of becoming wholly public. For here, while what is held is 'private property', the right to dispose of it lies with no group of individuals (unless it be the trustees, who have no true rights, but only obligations). Such arrangements, while they do not provide our paradigms of private ownership, at least show how private property already contains within itself the possibility of its own restriction. Property rights are precisely the kinds of thing that can be indefinitely qualified in the interests of some 'higher' institution, and why not in the interest of the highest of institutions, which is the state?

But it is only a minority who would now see the market economy as the true end of private property and 'state control' as an unmitigated evil directed against the citizen's natural right. It has never been true, and it is now indeed evidently false, that the choice in these matters lies between 'individualism and socialism', as one liberal[49] declared in the House of Commons in 1923 (the subject for debate being the surprisingly abstract issue of 'The Failure of the Capitalist System'). But we must still face the question of the legitimacy of state activity in the realm of private property, and the precise 'mode of production' (if there be one) that conservatives might be committed to uphold.

Taxation

Let us begin by considering taxation, since, in one form or another, its necessity cannot be denied without at the same time denying the need for government. In England taxation has always loomed large among political issues and, being one of the matters which divided the Stuarts from Parliament, contributed much to our greatest constitutional crisis. When full security in the fiscal relations between state and citizen was established in the last century, it was with the introduction of a permanent income tax by the Peel administration in 1842.[50] As we shall see, it is no accident that a Tory government should have been responsible for this measure, and no accident that arguments from justice should have been used in support of it. Given the necessity of taxation, its legitimacy as an institution need not be doubted. Justice intrudes, however, because we must ask the questions 'How?', 'How much?', and 'When?'

Gibbon, describing the grandiose injustices of the Roman emperors, wrote frequently of 'oppressive' taxes; and I doubt that many of his readers have been unconvinced by the epithet. Solzhenitsyn and others have described in similar terms the Bolshevik and Stalinist systems of taxation, ruthlessly applied in the attempt to destroy every vestige of private profit. And again, turning from the abstractions of political theory to the concrete examples which such writers have so vividly presented to us, few can fail to be moved to indignation by what they read. It seems then that the sense of justice provides us even here with a criterion of legitimacy. But it is not a criterion that is readily understood. One important liberal thinker has concluded – by an argument strikingly reminiscent of Marx's thesis that an employer who makes a profit must do so by the extortion of unpaid work – that taxation is nothing but forced labour, and therefore inherently unjust.[51]

If we are to concede such an argument, then we abolish the conservative enterprise, and cease to acknowledge the web of obligations by which citizens are bound to each other and to the state.

The first problem is to know what the state is doing in extorting taxes. The answer seems to be simple: it is providing itself with funds to meet the needs of the state, and therefore the political needs of the citizen. Natural justice therefore suggests that each should be taxed according to his means. However, in almost every country we find significant departures from that ideal, departures which indicate that taxation is used, not only to finance the offices of state, but also to redistribute wealth, even when that wealth has been legitimately acquired. The wealthy are required to part with a greater proportion (and not just a greater amount) of their income. This is not because the poor are granted relief (for that is usually an independent feature[52]) but because the wealthy are being prevented from keeping what they earn.

There are two arguments for progressive taxation that might carry weight, but neither is likely to recommend itself to a conservative. The first is purely political and goes back at least to Tom Paine (*The Rights of Man*, pt II, ch. 5). Progressive taxation has a long-term tendency to equalize the possession of property, not by giving to the poor, but (what has always proved easier) by taking from the rich. Such an argument must appeal to a socialist, especially to one who believes with Shaw that socialism is merely 'the economic side of the democratic idea',[53] but it has no persuasive power beyond the reach of that particular ideology. Progressive taxation is an act which jeopardizes the ties between the state and its more successful subjects, and can be regarded as a social necessity only if the nation so swells with the resentment of the underprivileged that the rich must be punished to appease them. Conservatives are unlikely to accept that view, since they will instinctively incline to the belief that resentment is appeased, not by equality, but by the 'validating' of inequality, in the forms and allegiances which pertain to the maintenance of civic life. To adapt a thought of Aristotle's, it is not the large inequalities that people resent, but the small ones. People do not suffer from the prosperity of others against whom they are not in the habit of measuring themselves. But the change in their position relative to their immediate fellows is deeply and keenly felt. Thus we should not be surprised if the 'erosion of differentials', or the 'loss of parity' gives rise to a resentment far greater than the 'inequitable' distribution which preceded and survives them.

The other argument is economic. It might seem that the fiscal benefits of progressive taxation must be small, since it disinclines the more talented from work, and so lowers the total product available for taxation. However, this need not be so. It is an evident fact that, beyond a certain point, people will not be disposed to spend what they earn – unless they are of the wasteful disposition that usually accompanies, not the earning, but the inheriting of wealth. In other words, if the surplus is not confiscated by the state, it will accumulate, and not be returned to the market. It will translate itself into a castle, a pile of gold, a collection of pictures, a library, or some other such idle thing. Sometimes the individual may indirectly return the surplus to the market, in the form of a capital investment which creates employment. But there is no guarantee that he will do so. Suppose we accept the Keynesian hypothesis,[54] that the growth of the economy requires the active stimulation of demand. We might then believe that the appropriation of this idle surplus could be used to feed the economy, either through public spending, or through redistribution, so that the poorer classes may transform it into consumable goods. We might also think that economic growth (or the lack of economic decline) is a political necessity. In which case, progressive taxation becomes a guarantee of national livelihood.

Even if one were to accept that argument (and in the next chapter I shall give reasons for rejecting one of the principles upon which it rests), the most it could justify is a very limited form of progressive taxation. To put it roughly, the economic solution to the problem of falling demand will be given by the point of intersection between the curve that measures the growth of demand through redistribution and the curve that measures the fall in the taxable surplus caused by the disincentive to earn. The optimal point of taxation would be that where the marginal disincentive to earn balances the marginal benefit of confiscation. Wherever that point may be (and it would be a matter of great complexity to calculate it), it will certainly be lower than the actual maximum that all governments, including Conservative governments, have tended to impose.

Income tax is not only a budgetary necessity; it is also the form of tax most readily comprehensible to the victim. Having the nature of a repeated blow to a part that is already numb, it is the form of confiscation that is most lightly felt. Moreover, it is felt by the whole society; and not by any subordinate or dominant class: it therefore imposes severe restraints on government expenditure, and leads to a natural balancing of social forces. If the lower class suffers the fiscal effects of some policy at the same time, and to the same degree, as the upper and middle class, then all will be united in their attitude towards it. In no sense need taxation become the cause of social unrest, as it was in the France of Louis XVI, when the nobility were exempt from it, or as it was in Britain under successive Labour governments in the Sixties and Seventies, when the middle class was subject to punitive measures which in the nature of things it could neither accept nor understand.

These punitive measures are explained by the survival in political consciousness of Victorian class resentment. Somewhere in the heart of every socialist, the image of Mayhew's London lies indelibly engraved, and despite everything that has happened to dispel such things from the hearts of more ignorant people, no present reality has power in comparison with the ghosts of that vanished age. No society can survive if its rulers contemplate with fixed attention evils that can no longer be remedied, and conjure in themselves resentments that can never be appeased. But this feeling has been dominant in Britain until very recently. It has resulted, for example, in the use of taxation to attack hereditary wealth, both through the imposition of heavy death duties, and through the (now inescapable) capital transfer tax. This tax, since it undermines not only the transfer of wealth between generations, but also the exercise of private gift, constitutes a direct attack against the institution of private property. In being such an attack it wars not only with property, but also with family and friendship. Private gifts are penalized, as is the natural desire to establish and endow a household. In this one may feel the premonition of evil to come, when nothing tangible passes from generation to generation except by stealth. Suddenly the continuity of things is broken, and the past and the future begin to conceal themselves behind the present pursuit of immediately expendable gain.

It seems, then, that the conservative attitude in fiscal matters will be opposed to the attempt to bend taxation permanently and directly to some external aim of redistribution. This does not mean that conservative politicians will subscribe to the view that the only legitimate use of tax is to secure the revenues of the state: they too will be prepared, when necessary, to use it as an instrument of social control. But they will do so only rarely, and in the interests of continuity rather than social revolution.

Public ownership

A sinister picture was painted by the early socialists of the effects of competition, of the greedy struggle of man against man for an ever larger share of the market. Now, in so far as the competitive spirit is a constitutive part of our rational nature, connected with the very sentiments of pride and self-esteem through which we imbue our world with value, it is pointless to bewail its more tawdry manifestations. Conservatives are unlikely to feel confident that an economic arrangement could be devised which would both preserve the motives and the self-esteem of labour, and also dispense with the competition which results from them. In dealing with deep and obdurate facts of human nature, one can only refrain from judging harshly. Nevertheless, one does not have to be a Saint-Simonist to see that matters are far from simple. The unbridled law of the market breeds monopoly – or if not monopoly, business oligarchy[55] – which not only stifles competition, but which may also set up an independent corporation or cartel in rivalry to the state. It has been argued that the cure for this is public ownership, or 'state control'. However, state 'control' only protects the state if it vests the power of monopoly in the state. In communist Russia, where these questions were well understood, that effect was achieved, since the workers in a state monopoly were carefully marshalled by trade union officials who were themselves the servants of the ruling Party. In the West, however, the state has usually made itself not less, but more vulnerable, through public ownership. It has allowed trade unions both to support the principle of monopoly (by excluding workers who do not belong to them) and at the same time to retain the 'right to strike' whereby to bring any enterprise to a standstill. Thus the power that the state wrests from the monopolistic owner (who can be expected to be interested in maintaining the growth and activity of his industry) is vested not in the state, but in 'organized labour', which can blackmail the state into subsidizing any industry that it causes to fail. Organized labour is both hard to appease and easy to antagonize, and being often in a position of power without authority, has tended to see itself in self-protective terms, pitted against the state as against a master from whom to win favours. In the case of essential services the result may be disastrous. When those services are (as they must be) brought under the administration of the state, there ought also to be legal sanctions, curtailing the activity of the workers who are employed in them. No state can readily tolerate the persistence of a 'right to strike' among its immediate servants (policemen, firemen, the army, the civil services, members of parliament, postmen, the judiciary – the list is extended with every nationalization that is not a mere *acte gratuite*).

Many issues surround this one of public ownership, and a conservative view is difficult to state. But the foregoing considerations suggest a distinction which is of some importance, that between a nationalized industry and a public service, between a competitive enterprise taken into public control, and an activity essential to the maintenance of public life. Liberal economists describe such activities as 'public goods', on the assumption that they will not be provided by a market in which individual profit is the sole motive. Advocates of private enterprise could certainly make use of this distinction in clarifying their approach to the complexities of a modern state. Consider the Post Office. The postal service was until recently indispensable to the life of the community; without it, neither private relations nor ordinary business could be conducted in the customary manner. On the assumption that such a service would not be provided privately, or provided only selectively and only in parts of the country, the maintenance of a postal service became one of the responsibilities of government. Evidently, with the advent of electronic communications, the Post Office is losing its public role, and may soon have to compete as one provider among others, of a service that is no longer a public good. Where an enterprise is such a public good, however, the powers of the state may, without violence to the normal rights of property, be invoked to support, protect and extend it. Even in America this is recognized. It is through the incorporation of independent enterprises that the 'frontiers of the state' extend, often to the point of strain.

In recent years, however, there has been a move in the opposite direction, towards the 'privatization' even of those services regarded as essential. In some cases this creates a private monopoly; in others it leads to asset-stripping and profiteering of a destructive kind. But conservatives have nevertheless seen privatization as essential, in order to rescue economically necessary activities from bureaucrats who have no inherent interest in their efficiency. It seems to me that the true conservative position is to recognize that efficiency is not everything, and that, where a service like the railways serves other and perhaps more valuable social goals the state may very well retain an interest in controlling it. Indeed it *should* do so, wherever the costs to the service, which would make it unprofitable for a private entrepreneur, are balanced by social gains that fall within the responsibilities of government. It may be impossible to run the railways at a profit, while providing efficient public transport that removes the need for new roads and more private cars. This is not a reason for the state to sell off the railways, but on the contrary a reason for the state to retain them.

In the case of mere industry, however, conservatives are rightly reluctant to countenance state intervention, not, as some think, out of any overweening sympathy for the successful, but out of fear of being troubled by the weak. It is no part of friendship to cultivate dependence. Likewise it is no part of state activity to bring about the financial dependence of its citizens. But the state does this whenever, in nationalizing an industry, it removes the natural guidance of self-interest, creating instead a pocket of redundancy in which thousands may be kept in futile employment who could be more profitably employed elsewhere. Here, it may be, conservatives should prefer what has been called the 'hard discipline of the market',[56] if only because it effects more quickly what will happen in any case.

It would be lengthy and difficult to rehearse the relevant arguments. But a matter of principle needs to be affirmed. As Hobbes argued, though in other words, it is the absolute duty of the state to have power over its subjects. The state's relation to the citizen is not, and cannot be, contractual. It is therefore not the relation of employer to employee. The state has the authority, the responsibility, and the despotism of parenthood. If it loses those attributes, then it must perish, and society along with it. The state must therefore withdraw from every economic arrangement which puts it at the absolute mercy of individual citizens. This counsel has been many times ignored, and never more blatantly than in modern times. Through the vast and rampant civil service, through local government, through nationalized industry, through all the advisory bodies, 'quangos' and meddlesome councils that surround it, the government disperses its power among self-interested parasites. If it cannot coerce them, then it is at the mercy of any force (a union, for example) which can.

Capitalism

If the state is to withdraw from direct participation in economic arrangements (offering its support to the needy out of charity and not from some contractual right), then it must tacitly uphold that mode of production which has been called capitalist. For the third method of interference in the flow of private property – the method of expropriation – has about it too much of the air of penalty to be used except in times of war, or against the overbearing insolence of criminals. It cannot be held forth as a simple remedy against the over-accumulation of private wealth. And if wealth can accumulate – even to a modest degree – and if redistribution is only partial, then nothing will prevent it from accumulating in the hands of those who most actively desire and pursue it. From them, therefore, it must be borrowed by those who wish to begin any enterprise of their own, and at once the economic structure of capitalism is forced on us, as a consequence of that lending power. For there is the beginning of wage labour, when one person has nothing to bargain with except the gifts of natural power. The only way to avoid this would be to impose a system approximating to feudalism (or at least to feudalism as described by Marx), where wealth is largely inherited and barred from exchange, where people are born into a web of obligations that circumscribe its use and their own activities, and where the free sale of labour is thwarted. But while the imposition of this kind of feudalism was practised with some success in Maoist China (so that people were regarded as born into their station and free to move from it neither in place nor in attainment, all production being handed over to an immediate overlord who took full responsibility for the labourers under his charge), the arrangement has proved impermanent. Besides, such measures fortunately lie outside the purview of contemporary British politics.

The reference to feudalism enables us, however, to clarify the problem – and it is undeniably a problem for conservative economics. From its beginnings the Conservative Party has been characterized by a relatively firm and enterprising fiscal policy, being responsible, not only for constant restrictions on free trade, but also for the introduction of regular income tax, and for legislation which governed the sale and conditions of labour. In the light of history, its post-war conversion to Keynesian economic theory might be seen as a natural intellectual development, a further move away from the view (variously propounded or assumed by Smith, Ricardo and the Mills) that economic affairs are self-regulating (so that little good and much harm may result from the attempt to interfere with them), towards the more plausible view that the posture of the state is all-important, and that, without the state's surveillance, destitution and unemployment could result at any time. And it is perhaps no accident that, when the Conservative Party under Margaret Thatcher abandoned this conception of the state's economic role, and took up the banner of liberal economics, it was, in time, deserted by the electorate, so that the old alliance of interests which it had for a century represented suddenly fell apart. The odd thing, however, is that the policy which caused the Conservative Party's collapse – free market economics, under the aegis of global corporations – is the policy most fervently adopted by the New Labour Party of Tony Blair, and will no doubt be the downfall of that Party too.

The Conservative Party has come under the influence of successive economic theories. But we must again remind ourselves that no economic theory makes proper sense until conjoined to some adequate political doctrine (a doctrine which defines the nature and rights of the social arrangement to be served). The appeal to economics is like the appeal to the doctor, based not in self-confidence, but in hope or fear. It is as much to political doctrine, as to any economic theory, that the Conservatives' restrictions on capitalist enterprise have been due. And such restrictions are by no means peculiar to our times. On the contrary, free trade has always been a cause to fight for, not a norm to be assumed.

The Marxist challenge

It is a distinctive contribution of Marxism, and one to which all historians and politicians are indebted, to suggest that social and historical facts can be illuminated in terms of the economic structure from which they derive. Marx contrasted two structures, capitalism and feudalism. The former requires freedom of exchange, wage labour, accumulated capital, and leads by inexorable steps to the creation of a property owning and a propertyless class. The latter requires serfdom, *corvée*, and an attachment to place and person that hampers free exchange.

Now it is difficult to imagine the presence of real wealth without the tendency to exchange and movement. In those societies that have been *called* feudal (on account of the specific obligations which they encapsulated) the prevalence of money suggests a real reference to exchange as the basis even of the power of a monarch. (In 'feudal' England, for example, villeins could buy, sell, pledge and hire everything from livestock to land; their feudal bond often amounted to little more than an attachment to place and manor, engendered as much by custom as by force.[57]) Now some Marxists believe that there is a genuine and absolute distinction in reality between feudal and capitalist modes of production, and that the transition from one to the other is the single great economic fact, explaining matters as disparate as the Peasants' Revolt, the rise of Protestantism, and the formation of towns. There is an element of fantasy in these explanations, and a consequent emptiness in the attendant description of the real alternative to capitalism. Nevertheless, we can extract from them an important underlying idea. 'Feudalism' and 'capitalism' are the names, not of historical realities, but of 'ideal types', to use Weber's idiom. Societies may approximate to either form, but in reality will always contain some idiosyncratic mixture of both. There may have been (in some sad community, lost in the Dark Ages of our civilization) a genuine feudal arrangement; there may have been (perhaps in late nineteenth-century Chicago or in Victorian Manchester) a genuine capitalist town. But just as history points to an absence of the first, so must it confirm a similar absence of the second. Modern Europe shows how deviant are its economic arrangements from those of the free capitalist enterprise described by Marx. And America, with its great anonymous monopolies and cartels, further demonstrates that even in the absence of state intervention, the *homo economicus* of classical theory has little capacity to survive.[58] No longer do we encounter the small enterprising 'bourgeois', pursuing private gain in the open forum of the market, accumulating profit with which to strike a bargain for labour. Naturally, by their inner life and logic, the corporations pursue their profit, in a market which they can only partly 'fix'. But they contract with all their members: with managers, shop-stewards, salesmen, machinists, advisers and clerks, all of whom become wage labourers, in an organization the profits of which accumulate anonymously, and the purpose of which may be no more stable from day to day than is the purpose of the whale. Moreover, the contract is made under mutual duress: a manager soon becomes indispensable, and can 'fix' his terms. Even the lowest employee – whose wage would otherwise have been determined by his meniality – becomes possessed of similar power, operating, not as an individual, but as part of the union which secures for the manual workers as a class the bargaining power which they could never acquire alone. The concepts of Marxism correspond, then, only to theoretical and idealized arrangements, and while this may render them useful in the study of history, it gives us little ground for accepting the political economics with which they are commonly associated. For one thing, it becomes absurd to divide reality into the exploiters who employ and the exploited who are employed by them (and who therefore sacrifice their hours of 'unpaid' labour). Just about everyone is employed. It follows that the class normally identified as the bourgeoisie is as much given to contract away its labour power as the class which is supposedly oppressed by it. Both produce a surplus (for that is merely another way of saying that their common enterprise is profitable), and they both suffer what Marxists consider to be the injustice of its 'confiscation'.[59] All the distinctions here are obliterated by a philosophy which in any case consigns the idea of 'justice' to the realm of 'ideology', so as to represent (and misrepresent) contractual relations in terms of the exercise of power.

The feudal principle

I have touched on the Marxist theory for a specific reason, which is this: that since it presents idealized models of economic arrangements, it enables us to describe in clearer terms the conservative attitude to the restriction of property. It is not feudalism that conservatives will advocate, but merely its 'main principle – that the tenure of property should be the fulfilment of duty'.[60] That remark of Disraeli's, expressive of the idealistic vision of *Sybil* and *Coningsby*, is of course as false to the reality of 'feudal' Europe as is the Marxist analysis of its economy. But just as there can be idealized models in economic theory, so too can there be such models in politics, which extract from the imperfect arrangements of history some ideal of political obligation.

But now let us face, for a moment, the broad historical perspective. No society has successfully assimilated industrial production, or the discontents which stem from it. Nevertheless, industrialization, mobility, the divide between labour and management, the reckless pursuit of growth – all these have spread with such rapidity across the globe that it would be foolish to suppose their existence to be accidental. The conservative task has been, not to oppose whatever force has wrought these things, but to maintain through all its onslaughts the reality of social order, and the continuity of political life. Even Marxists may have to admit that 'until the end of the eighteenth century the common people of France and England adhered to a deeply felt "moral economy" in which the very notion of ... a dissociation between economic values on the one hand and social and moral obligations on the other was an outrage to their culture'.[61] They too may have to admit that it was in the last century, and under the impact of forces which had no necessary connection with capitalism or indeed with any other system of control that there arose an 'antipolitical economy whose harsh profit-and-loss purgatives voided the body politic of old notions of duty, mutuality and paternal care'.[62] By then, capitalism had been active in Europe for four centuries – as long a span as any historical explanation could assimilate. It seems, therefore, that the loss of this 'moral economy' is a more complex thing than the typical historical perspective can venture to explain.

Now I have represented property as a corollary to conservative thinking, rather than its principal preoccupation. It is quite reasonable to assert that for conservatism social and political unity take precedence over the free accumulation of property. English socialists claim credit for the 'heroic struggle' against the evils of industrial production. They prefer to forget that the Factory Acts, the legalization of trade unions, even the welfare state, were either Conservative inventions, or made possible by conservative forces that had long been striving to bring such things into being.

The broad historical perspective, we shall increasingly find, is not broad enough. It remains fixed on the century which made it possible, and stares so intently at the industrial process as to conjure vast and hallucinatory images of its significance and power. The explanations that it generates seem inexorable only because they derive from the period when 'inexorability' was the notion of the day. But it overlooks the enduring political activity that has steered us through these 'inexorable' changes and seen the old 'moral economy' restored. Of course, there have been changes, and vast ones. Moreover, they have been attended with a strange unhappiness. If the historical perspective has anything to tell us, it is that we cannot let the matter rest. Something deeper needs to be said, about the emergence from the debris of industrialism of the peculiarly 'modern' person.

Conclusion

I have argued that civil society requires an institution of rights in things. It follows that any political view which regards the state as the protector of society must also demand the continuance of property. Moreover, a view which recognizes a title in custom and usage will find nothing wrong with the inheritance and accumulation of wealth. Furthermore, it will seek to protect both inheritance and accumulation, in so far as they stem from the family, and in so far as they lie endorsed in the condition of society. This means that it is income, and not wealth, that conservatives will wish to tax. But they will be forced by the very concern for the civil bond which generates their belief in property to consider the question of its distribution. They will wish to instil into the accumulation of property those obligations without which part of society benefits, while another suffers, from its single-minded pursuit. As I have suggested, a qualified endorsement of modern capitalism seems to be the consequence of these opinions, even when that endorsement accompanies no aversion to general poverty, and no commitment to 'growth'.

But if, as some say, the capitalist mode of production (even in its modern, highly attenuated form) is the sole or principal cause of the evils which beset us, is conservatism still possible as an item of belief? In answer to that question we must show that the condition of modern man, whatever anxiety may attend it, is not the result of private property but of something else. Here we enter a dark area of politics, where both conservatives and radicals aim blows which miss their targets.

6
Alienated Labour

There is a natural instinct in unthinking people – who, tolerant of the burdens that life lays on them, and unwilling to lodge blame where they see no remedy, seek fulfilment in the world that is – to accept and endorse through their actions the institutions and practices into which they are born. This instinct, which I have attempted to translate into the self-conscious language of political doctrine, is rooted in human nature, and in elaborating its foundations I have also been adumbrating a tentative philosophy of man. This philosophy distinguishes from the activities of animals the peculiar behaviour that we recognize as human: the behaviour of a creature who has not only instincts, drives and needs, but also values; who exists, not only in the present, but in the past and the future; who does not merely suffer reality, but who also makes himself part of it, and impresses on the world the imprint of his will.

The modern consciousness

But the task has now met an obstacle. To defend the unthinking prejudice of the normal active person was easy in an age when prejudices followed at once from the dogmas of received religion, or when social continuity ensured that those who rose to self-consciousness nevertheless departed only in the smallest items of belief from the happier mortals who were fated never to question what they knew. Now, however, we find ourselves confronted with that monstrous entity, the modern man, the person for whom all connection with an order greater than himself has to be won through an effort of his own, and who looks for that order, not necessarily in what is or has been, but more often in what will be or in what might be. His restless longing to be rid of the here and now is stilled by no religious faith, and by no patient belief in the necessary imperfection of mortal things. His transcendental urge translates itself into an all-consuming nostalgia, nostalgia not for the past, but for a future which – like heaven – can be only negatively described.

Nor is his restlessness peculiar to the self-portrait that he has been painting over the past two hundred years. It belongs – at least, he believes it belongs – to the entire human world which served to create him, and in his attempt to understand himself he has been forced to understand the condition of all those beings who lie stranded about him on the shore of history, beings who may not follow his new-fangled idiom but whose state nevertheless demands a description which has not been heard before. To the German Romantics we owe the concepts with which 'modern' humanity can be represented, and those concepts reflect a philosophy which I have tried intuitively to follow. But it is now time to make the central problem explicit. And it is here that we must part company with liberalism and engage only with those opponents who recognize the depth of human things. For what, after all, has been the prevailing weakness of the liberal ideal? Surely, this: that it reposes all politics and all morality in an idea of freedom while providing no philosophy of human nature which will tell us what freedom really is or why it matters. It isolates man from history, from culture, from all those unchosen aspects of himself which are in fact the preconditions of his subsequent autonomy. When liberals try to make concrete the ideal of freedom which they propose, they find themselves always constrained to endorse (whether wittingly or no) the habits and predilections of a particular way of life – the way of life of the emancipated urban intellectual. As for the rest of human nature, the human essence, what Marx and Feuerbach called the 'species being' of man, it seems to survive in the liberal philosophy only in atomistic form, a confused bundle of individual desires and needs. Human fulfilment lies in the satisfaction of as many choices as short time allows. Such a philosophy presents no idea of the self, over and above the desires which constitute it: it therefore has no idea of self-fulfilment other than the free satisfaction of desire. It tries to stretch the notion of choice to include every institution on which people have conferred legitimacy, without conceding that their sense of legitimacy stems precisely from their respect for themselves as beings formed, nurtured and amplified by these things. It is not that people have desired and chosen their customs, traditions and institutions, for without them there would have been no choice to make. Nor is it that they know how to draw back from every inherited arrangement and pronounce it legitimate by some sudden sovereign act of will – any more than they can stand back from themselves and ask 'shall I, or shall I not, be this thing that I am?'.[63] Conservatives, like radicals, recognize that civil order reflects not the desires of man, but the self of man. Neither will hesitate to propose or defend a system which frustrates or diverts even the most innocent of human choices, if they see those choices to conflict with the order that breeds fulfilment. But conservatives are also sceptical. They may have a nostalgia for the past, but they will not parade it as a declared ideal, and they will regard their opponents' far more seductive nostalgia for a non-existent future as a kind of intemperate folly, a last inverted survival of the belief in a Golden Age.

Nevertheless, faced with a world which, whether sick or not, believes itself in its self-conscious part to be so, conservatives must seek to define afresh their position, and their sceptical history has left them only an impoverished language in which this might be done. It is for this reason that they would do well to respect the radical's attempt to redescribe humanity so that the modern consciousness may be seen as a proper part of it. Much as English conservatives, through love of constituted liberties, may feel drawn to the liberal cause, its philosophy is not theirs. It describes not man but man's brief caricature, and most of all is that caricature ridiculous when set beside the realities of modern life. In what follows I shall borrow (largely from the Hegelian side of Marxism) the concepts with which to refine our political vision, so that this modern man can at least be discerned by it. The discussion will perforce be brief, touching on matters that require great analysis. But I hope that it will suffice to indicate a direction which conservatives might follow without detriment to their strength or to their refined lack of purpose.

Alienation

The concept of alienation was borrowed by Marx from Hegelian philosophy in order to describe the condition of man under capitalism – not just the condition of the labourer (as was Marx's first thought), but the condition of everyone. Only with the abolition of private property, he argued, could this alienation be overcome, and man restored to himself, to his essence, which is his 'species being'.[64] This abolition would come about as a necessary result of historical processes which Marx saw already at work in society, processes which involved the transfer of power from class to class, ending in the final emancipation of the proletariat and the deliverance of all men from the mutual bondage in which both exploiter and exploited had been held. At that point the truth of history would be revealed and private property would disappear, having no longer any part to play in the dealings between people.

In support of that idealistic vision, a kind of political theology has arisen, and one which requires a certain degree of faith from those who would attach themselves to it. Nevertheless, it is no accident that the descriptions that Marxism offers have, until recently, commanded such widespread assent. Naturally, many social troubles have attended the demise of the 'classical' period of our culture. Industrialization, the loss of religious conviction, the mobility and subsequent affluence of all classes, including the working class, the rise of the media, the debasement of language, the almost universal detachment from place and station – whatever the cause of these things, they form collectively the primary social fact of modern times, which is the triumph of material over spiritual goods. But alongside this fact, representing itself simultaneously as cause and effect, stands the same unsettled ghost – the spirit of alienation, the collective sense that there may be no social order to which we severally belong. This ghost is not the worst of our modern horrors; but it reminds us that not every society is governable, and that there are political problems which cannot be solved by economic policy.

Recognizing, therefore, that there may be truth in the description of our 'alienated' condition, and recognizing too the possibility of a deep connection between this condition and the 'fetishism of commodities' which Marx saw as a necessary part of capitalist production, conservatives will wish to present their own account of alienation, and to rebut the charge that private property is the cause of it. Not that conservatives can propose a remedy. Not all human ills have a cure, and in this case there is none that has been proposed which retains much credibility after a century of material progress and spiritual decline. Marx, far from proposing a cure, relied on a prediction, to which he gave little substance besides a rhetorical eulogy of the abstract 'emancipated' state of man, and a vigorous dismissal of all those concrete ideals which others might confuse with it.[65] In the third volume of *Capital* he (or his editor, Engels) declares that the premise of this emancipation is a shortening of the working day, a premise that has been fulfilled in the increasing idleness and (some would say) the increasing alienation of Western societies. And if private property is actually a necessary part of any positive conception of human freedom, the pursuit of Marx's 'emancipated' state will involve embracing a contradiction. Nevertheless, conservatives must continue to look for a remedy, since the possibility of a conservative politics depends on it. An alienated society is by its nature not a society that can be governed in a conservative way.

Ends, means and labour

Alienation is manifest first in an attitude to work (or 'labour'). Work must not be thought of as just any kind of activity that terminates in production: machines do not work, nor do horses (not, that is, in the sense that I intend). Work is a form of rational conduct, which has, or can have, both ends and means, and which is engaged in as a matter of intention – even when the worker has no 'choice' of job. It was Marx's contention that work is the primary activity of people, since it is only through production that the edifice of society, and the leisure which accompanies society, can be built. People are alienated in their work, and from their work, however, when they are able to see it only as a means, and not as an end. The distinction between end and means is hardly clear enough to allow this description to stand unqualified. Let us ignore for the present the Marxian diagnosis, and try to give a direct characterization.

In writing this book, I am working. Moreover my work is a means to an end – in fact to several ends. (I might hope to earn money through its publication.) However, it is also an end in itself, in that I seek to write this book for the sake of it. The activity of writing is something that I not only desire but also value. It *means* something to me. I have already suggested that the idea of an end or value involves implicit reference to a realm of shared and public concerns. To value an activity is to have some sense of its objective worth, which in turn involves the presumption of a public world (actual or possible) in which that activity has an honourable place. In viewing my activity as an end I therefore see myself as a being in potential relation with my fellows. In doing what I value I find my identity as a social being confirmed. Hence I not only remain at one with my activity, I also remain at one with a real or imagined community of fellows.

Such a case may be contrasted with that of a slave, forced against his will to perform some repetitive task in which he can take no interest, and the profit of which lies always with another. Such a person does not desire to do what he does, still less does he value it, unless he is of the stoic frame of mind recommended by Epictetus, in which the mere consciousness of slavery is sufficient to constitute a refined mode of freedom – a frame of mind which we cannot assume to be common. The slave can see his labour as a means, but not as an end. As a result he is not confirmed in it: his own identity is not present in what he does. He sees what he does as *exacted* from him, and himself not as an end but as a means. In being alienated from his activity he becomes alienated from himself, and from the 'species being' which is his essence.

The industrial process

Lying behind those very brief descriptions of two contrasting states of mind is an important idea of personhood, the idea that rational beings are persons because 'their nature already marks them out as ends in themselves – that is, as something which may not be used merely as a means' (Kant). It was the distinctive advance of the Hegelian philosophy to suggest that we can treat ourselves as ends only if we treat others as ends, and that in each case our activities must involve some concrete notion of the value of what we do.[66] We can therefore possess the autonomy that Kant valued above all other things only if we live in unalienated union with our fellows. Our very being as individuals presupposes immersion in society. In so far as modern people stand in danger of losing their freedom, it is not only on account of the despotisms which threaten to engulf them, but also (and this is more important) on account of their alienation from the social context which would once again imbue their activities with a public meaning. (For it is the state of alienation which, in inviting despotism, makes despotism possible.)

If we present the concept of alienation in some such way, we can see, both that it is indeed a condition of modern consciousness, and also that it does not necessarily have its roots in private property, as Marx supposed. Nevertheless, left-wing writers have tenaciously adhered to the view that it is precisely private property, and the capitalistic modes of production which stem from it, that have reduced the labourer and the clerk to the position of slaves. Yet the loss of identity between man and his world seems distinctive, not of capitalist modes of ownership, nor of the institution of private property, but rather of the industrial process, the artificial division of labour,[67] and the large-scale absorption of public life into the ethos of work, so that fulfilment and value seem not public but private affairs, to be pursued only at home. People no longer fully enact their identity with their fellows, but work alongside them without feeling the value of what they do. Certainly the institution of private property was not always associated with this feeling; nor for example were the capitalistic modes of production introduced by the great banking families in medieval and Renaissance Florence. (Or if Dante lived the life of alienated man, then let us not complain that we must do so too.)

It is true that, for Marx, 'industrial capital is the realized objective form of private property'[68] – in other words, that without private property the industrial process as we know it would disappear. Such an assertion stands in need of proof. And the proof must not be trivial. It would be trivial, for example, to assert that, since private property is a precondition of the industrial process, it is therefore a source of the evils which attend it. (For what remains of that assertion when it is shown that private property is also a precondition of society?) No such criticism can be serious until accompanied by a full description of the alternative.

The slander of private property

Some (Marx included) have tried to turn on its head the argument that I gave for private property, in order to establish a direct connection between private property and alienation, by-passing considerations about the nature of production. They have argued that, in seeing the end of work as property, people terminate their activity in an object, and therefore come to see value only in objects and not in the human activity which they represent. In order to find their own value, therefore, they begin to represent themselves to themselves as objects, as things that may be bought and sold, as means among means. Man becomes his own property, and is dehumanized, both in the pursuit of property and in its possession. The point has been expressed by Fromm[69] in the idea that property has become an 'idol', and in being enslaved to an idol man is himself reduced to an object, frozen into thinghood. (The origin of this is a peculiar theory of Feuerbach's concerning the nature of religion.)

The argument is both more popular and more suspect than the one that I in part endorsed. Those great idolators who once inhabited the Aegean would certainly not have recognized themselves in Fromm's portrait, any more than the author of the *Divine Comedy* could be recognized in Feuerbach's description of religious man. For the Greeks, the worship of gods in rivers, trees and artifacts was part of a process whereby nature became human, and man something more dignified than any merely 'natural' thing. Why is there in the *Iliad* resolution, purpose, activity and character beyond almost anything else in the literature of the world? Surely, it is because the Greek hero had wholly imbued his world with rational will, and made of it a perfect image of himself. And private property played an essential part in the image that he fashioned.

Possession and consumption

The slander of private property becomes more clear if we return to our original description, and draw a distinction between possession and consumption and, correspondingly, between durable property and exchangeable goods (or commodities). There is a difference between a person who pursues something out of appetite, in order to satisfy the appetite in the consumption of the thing, and a person who pursues a thing from some conception of its intrinsic value, not in order to exchange or consume it, but in order to possess it. The object of an appetite does not have the character of an 'end', in the special sense in which ends are the province of rational will. It is, rather, a means to the satisfaction of desire, and is consumed and abolished in the act of gratification.

Consider the distinction (once obvious, but increasingly mis-understood) between lust and love. Here there is usually no question of legal ownership. But there is a contrast of attitudes which may find its equivalent in property relations. Lust may be satisfied by many things, and takes its nature from the fact that its objects are equivalent means to the satisfaction of a single desire. Love is satisfied by the individual object, and exists only in so far as that object is seen as an end in itself and therefore irreplaceable. Love aims at a form of 'possession'. Consequently, the object of lust has a market value, whereas the object of love does not. (Hence the elevation of the market into the sole measure of value must involve the forswearing of love – cf. the opening scene of *Das Rheingold*.)

The example shows the difference between animal appetite and the human attempt to 'possess' something, in the sense of making it part of, and an extension of, oneself. In the case of a person this attempt may seek fulfilment in the institution of marriage; in the case of an object, in the institution of property. Hence the highest form of ownership is that of an object desired for the sake of its beauty. This desire excludes the consumption of its object, and does not regard the object as one among equivalents. Working back from such examples towards the conception of human life and value that is implied in them, one will recognize that there are many aspects of the relation of ownership which cannot be seen in terms of consumption, and which are characterized by the thought of an object as in some way intrinsically desirable (though it will also be to some extent exchangeable, even if only under the pressure of necessity). In particular, one should mention again all those aspects which come under the notion of 'household'. These are pursued, not through the urgency of animal appetite, but through the desire to construct a thing of lasting value, in which human relations, property values and aesthetic meanings are usually all inextricably mingled. Things of the household may not be considered to be fully durable, but they are ends and not means, to be possessed and not consumed. They tend to be regarded as in part irreplaceable, as a house is irreplaceable by the insurance moneys that 'represent' it. (The degree of permanence is less important than the nature of the relation to oneself. A car, a herd of cattle, anything which someone has cherished at least in part for what it is, and on which he has imprinted his identity as a social being, comes to validate for him the relation of ownership. Although it is the fate of cattle to be slaughtered and consumed, one would have to be very stupid not to understand the grief of a farmer whose prize herd, stricken by disease, is condemned to destruction by authorities who nevertheless restore its market value.) Some part of what I am getting at can be understood through the art of interior painting. In the Dutch interior we see, simultaneously, an exploration of the self in its freedom, and a representation of the ultimate value of things. The portrait will contain some arrangement of reflecting objects, which, conceived under the aspect of ownership, represent the inner life of a room and its occupant. In still life, we see further the attempt to overcome through art the attitude of consumption, to represent as an end in itself what is normally seen only as means. The dead rabbit is the rabbit 'reduced into possession', to use the legal phrase. The apples and the silver dish stand in a real but temporary relation to each other, and that relation is a reflection of the soul of man as the spirit of domestic freedom conceives it.

The fetishism of commodities

The reader may doubt the need for such a fanciful digression; however, we are discussing not elementary facts of economics, but subtle features of phenomenology, features which art makes directly accessible to us in the way that volumes of political theory may not. As I wrote in the last chapter, the attitude of consumption differs from that of possession, and the ascendancy of consumption belongs, not to the essence of property, but to its pathology. We can now see why that is so. For if a person's efforts are entirely directed towards the accumulation of objects whose only interest is that they are consumable, then none of his productive activity presents him with a coherent picture of the ends of conduct, independently of his mere subsistence as an animal being. Property – now reduced to the status of 'commodity', i.e. to its fluid, expendable form – no longer has a distinctively human character. In a world of consumption people become prey to the 'fetishism of commodities', persuasively described in *Capital*,[70] in which the constant pursuit of the expendable and the replaceable fills the soul with illusions, and short-circuits the pursuit of fulfilment. The commodity is a means to its own consumption, and consumption is not an end in itself, since nothing pertaining to the self is changed by it. Under the rule of commodities, people come to live in a world of means without meaning. (The ascendancy of the technocrat is already a sign of this species of 'fetishism'; and seeing one's life under the aspect of means, with all one's desires transformed into appetites for this or that consumable, then one can 'live' the political organism too only as a means, and not as an end. It would seem that not capitalism, but rather a form of technocratic and bureaucratic socialism, would be the natural form of commodity politics. Precisely this is what we see emerging in the European Union.)

The distinction between possession and consumption is a matter of degree. And consumption is not an evil but a necessity. Nevertheless we must draw distinctions between the various activities which have property as their aim. And then we see that the mere pursuit of consumption, without the development of a nexus of property rights, constitutes part of the pathology of personhood. Some thinkers have denied the distinction that implies this. Followers of Veblen would say that the only difference here is one of 'conspicuousness'. A person accumulates property only in order to make its consumption more spectacular. But why then should there have been private patrons of art, or the development of that material and visual intricacy known as civilized living? The English gentleman is known and respected precisely for his ability to make consumption as quiet and inconspicuous as good taste requires.

In those reflections we might see why conservatives should be dissatisfied with economic theories which advocate – as the sole remedy against recession – the active stimulation of demand. For what is this active stimulation, if not the transformation of property into its most fluid, most expendable, and most meaningless form? It must inevitably involve the generation or extortion of superfluous appetites, at the expense of social and personal fulfilment. The question poses itself: why should we labour, if all we acquire is *that*? Would it not be better to wind down the economy so that needs alone are satisfied, and all the rest is leisure?

The distinctions that I have tried to make cannot be reflected in economic theory, construed as an exploration of the basic laws of accumulation and exchange. Our animal nature imposes an exchange-value on everything, simply by forcing exchange under the impact of necessity. When someone is starving or in danger of his life, then (unless he has the heroic nature which *homo economicus* is forbidden by science to have) the artifact of self collapses. In such circumstances the exchangeability of everything becomes suddenly apparent. There is a degree in all this, and those two facts between them settle a market value even on objects which normally have no price.

Ownership and control

If we examine the complaints made from both left and right against the world created by the market, then two in particular stand out. The first is the complaint against the mechanization of production, and the associated artificial division of labour; the second is the complaint against consumerism or 'the fetishism of commodities' Mechanization and consumerism togther reduce the world to a place of means without ends, a place where rational fulfilment gives way to consumer calculation. In such a world, the critics say, we are forced to see ourselves as objects, driven by appetites that we do not understand; we live detached from our social life, rarely achieving direct and natural union with our fellow human beings. Politics then stands in danger of being overwhelmed by economics, the philosophy of utilitarianism governs the workings of the administrative intelligence, and people are given over, as Arnold once put it, to modes of thought that are 'mechanized and external'.[71]

But, even if the complaints are well-founded, no change in the control of the means of production will suffice to alter things: if a labourer is compelled to view his activity as means, then this is so whether or not the final product lies in the hands of the individual, the collective, or the state. For it is the nature of his activity, and not the form of control, which imposes this picture upon him. Likewise, it is not private production which turns objects into ephemeral commodities. It is the entire culture of mechanized production, which makes not true objects but only replicas and representations; and replicas, because they are of necessity replaceable by some other example of their kind, can be used and thrown away; they are symbols of the transience of appetite, and of the endlessness of consumption. The direction of human activity towards these things itself creates the appetite for them; moreover, the habit of seeking the repeatable and the replaceable invades all other areas of human experience – even those areas like love and sex which religion and culture have hitherto rescued from the market. When even erotic ties are seen as commodities, a great change comes over the world. People become alienated not only in their activities but also in their relations. The love object becomes the sex object; men and women fall out of relation with each other, and the result is not only a collapse of marriage and the family, but the rise of militant feminism as the vehicle of woman's revenge.

If people are alienated it is indeed because they do not fully belong to the world in which they find themselves. The world of commodities is a world of ephemera, whereas our rational need is to see ourselves as part of something permanent, enjoying durable relations with others, and living in mutual harmony and esteem. In all our true urges towards property, that need is our guide. However, the description that I have given has been necessarily stark. I have described an extreme, not because I believe that it locates the present reality, but because it presents us with the contrasts in terms of which to envisage the actual complexity of the modern world. Only a minority of workers participate directly in mechanized forms of labour; the rule of the commodity is only partly established; the breakdown in sexual relations and the commodification of sex have advanced only so far in the normal conscience. In general – and nowhere more than under modern capitalism – the relation of people to their work is varied, complex and imbued with intimations of, even if not the reality of, genuine satisfaction. Nevertheless, although the reality lies somewhere between the extremes of alienation and the natural, social being, who finds his work and leisure as equally harmonious offshoots of himself, the reality is one that must be faced by any political outlook. As I have argued, there is no cure in the transfer of ownership. On the contrary, if, as Marx says, the real grief of labour is that 'its product ... stands opposed to it as an alien being, as a power independent of the producer', how much more will this be so if the nature of labour remains mechanical, while its end product becomes a mere abstraction, seen to belong to no one in particular, being the concrete embodiment of no intelligible interest? In such a condition, the degradation of property becomes absolute and irremediable, and, as in Huxley's *Brave New World*, the world of objects benignly consumes the world of people. The history of socialism tells the same story; and it is what Marx ought to have meant (but didn't) when he wrote that, under communism, 'the government of men gives way to the administration of things'. For under such a system men *become* things.

In the attempt to make sense of the condition of people under modern economic arrangements I have strayed from the path of politics into difficult regions of human psychology, and what I have said is inevitably contentious and one-sided. But before proceeding it is necessary to return to the political realm and to reassert the one important fact that the philosophy of 'fetishism' overlooks. This philosophy envisages property not as an institution, but as a form of mindless attachment to things. The institutional reality of property lies, however, in the nexus of property rights. This nexus is a human artifact; but it is an indispensable artifact, one which arises inevitably out of our desire to belong to our world and to find fulfilment in it. It is part of private property to possess a right of way across another's garden, a right to seclude yourself in a private place, a right to wear a suit of clothes, to eat at a certain table, to dispose of the clippings of your hair and toe-nails as need or fancy should dictate. There could be no society without such rights, since it is part of social nature to claim them. (To suppose otherwise is to suppose people to have *social* relations with their kind, while remaining in a mere state of *nature* towards objects.)

The state of leisure

I have tried to describe one of the sicknesses of modern humanity, and to separate the description from the diagnosis. It would be unprofitable to proceed without facing the question of policy. Is this state of things irremediable? And if it is not, is there anything that a conservative might do, by way of advancing towards its resolution? Some might regard alienation as merely one of the inevitable but tolerable imperfections that characterize every social arrangement. But that is hardly plausible. Alienation is not a condition of society, but the absence of society. It may lie beyond the purview of liberal politics, but, for the true conservative, its existence poses a direct political problem.

The condition of alienation involves the perception of self as object, propelled towards a satisfaction that is merely animal and individual, in which others are seen as means. But, while certain conditions of labour may generate this outlook, leisure, properly conducted, does not. Whatever image a person may derive from his leisure will have a tendency to imprint itself on his work, not necessarily by 'making drudgery divine', but by reminding him of the end towards which his activity is directed. The reality of civil life is therefore intimately bound up with the quality of leisure, and it is in the theory of leisure that conservatives will look for the cure of the modern disease. A builder, for example, who lives by an ideal of dignity and honest accountability, will attempt to imprint that character on his work. He will 'do the job properly', for that is the kind of person he is. Another workman may see his activity only as the prelude to some act of personal consumption. He will work without pleasure and without pride. The difference between the two has nothing to do with ownership. The material reward is the same – a set of counters in the game of exchange. But there is a difference in the two men's image of what they are doing, and of themselves as agents in the doing of it. That difference reflects two separate experiences of social life, and this social life exists not merely in work, but more particularly in leisure.

The narrow historical perspective

Throughout this chapter I have employed conceptions which a true Marxist would regard as unimportant. I have been discussing the social appearance of things, believing that politics must engage with this appearance. And how things appear is how they appear to *me, here, now*. Thus, if tradition is integral to conservative politics, it is because it represents, not history as such, but history made present and perceivable (see the argument of Chapter 2). The historical perspective to which I have several times alluded may be unconcerned with such things. It rises above the world of activity and searches for a comprehensive pattern, divorced from present politics. The sentiments that I have expressed belong to 'bourgeois humanism' and inevitably reflect the station to which history and upbringing have assigned me. They are destined to disappear, together with every doctrine, policy and project that I could presently imagine. No one can fail to be impressed by such a prediction. It is hardly surprising if this narrowing perspective dominates the thought of our times, constantly recalling us from the business of politics to the spectacle of history.

   I have already given reasons for rejecting the great prediction in which the Marxist theory culminates – the prediction of man in his 'emancipated' condition, without private property, without greed or exploitation, without ideology or religion, in a state of complete and lasting brotherhood based on nothing but the supposed desire for it. But if we abandon the great prediction, what of Marxism remains? Only this striking, convincing, and yet futile hypothesis: that the nature and movement of society may be partly explained (in so far as anything so complex can be explained) in terms of the productive forces which constitute its active principle, and the economic structures (the forms of control) through which those forces find expression. Such an hypothesis has no evident bearing on political activity. Its lesson for the conservative is no more obvious than its lesson for any other political being. If it refers to inexorable processes which political activity cannot change then it is of no greater significance in politics than is the theory of anatomy in friendship. If it refers to processes that we can govern and control, then it is useless until we know the direction in which we wish to bend them.

The narrow historical perspective shows that, knowing too much, people may become uncertain of everything. Faced by the complexity of history, they see their activity as absorbed in the impersonal forces which propel them. Nothing is more tempting, in such circumstances, than the 'reductive' view, the view of people reduced to their own self-interest. And if not the self-interest of individuals, then the self-interest of a 'class'. It is a necessary but trivial truth, that the class which benefits from some historical process is the class whose interest is served by it. It is a necessary but trivial truth, that the exercise of power lies always with the powerful. It only remains to describe the process of change in terms of the self-interest of the powerful, and everything falls into place. The theory is almost vacuous, but for that very reason there is no fact which it cannot appear to explain. But for people who take this reductive view, the present is clouded in mystery. To justify their activity is to show that it presages or permits the ascendancy of some other, future, state. To take their will from their surroundings is simply to surrender to the powers that be. If they see themselves as agents, it is because they have projected themselves forward into another world. They do not belong to *this* world; they are at odds with everything that has nourished them. To sustain their self-image, therefore, they begin to glamorize their posture of detachment, to arrive (by negation) at the imaginary 'purity' of the social outcast.

Concluding remarks

Alienation does not stem from private property, nor even from capitalist production, but, in all probability, from complex and inescapable features of material prosperity. There is no clear socialist attitude towards it which does not base itself in a discredited prediction. But conservatives will feel able to confront alienation, once they have seen that it is a matter of degree. There will always be issues of policy, both small and large, in which the advance of alienation can be arrested or reversed.

However, there is a vociferous opposition to the attempt. The historical perspective, for all its protestations to the contrary, wills the destruction of society. It rises to self-consciousness only by glamorizing its detachment, attempting to destroy the capacity either to respect or even to perceive the social order that surrounds it. 'Demystification' makes a mystery of human things; it must therefore be part of conservative doctrine to describe the world, not in neutral, but in ideological terms.

7

The Autonomous Institution

It is part of conservatism to resist the loss of ideology. The 'value-free' world is not a human world: it contains no intimation of society. But how should ideology be generated, and what form should it take? This is not a question of policy, but a question of doctrine, a question of the fundamental suppositions at work in determining the particular political choice.

It is of the first importance to develop the conservative viewpoint in the proper order, working always towards the full conception of citizenship, and never tacitly assuming it as a premise (as it is assumed, for example, in the liberal aim of freedom, or in the idea of a 'Natural Right'). Thus while it is true that conservatism involves the maintenance of a hierarchy, and the attempt to represent the unpleasant fact of inequality as a form of natural order and mutuality, it is impossible (and not just impolitic) to begin from this. There is an order of argument and conception that leads naturally to conservative conclusions, and which begins in what is smallest, in the activities where people first relinquish their savagery for the comforts of civilized life.

The need for roots

Our task is to locate the practices and institutions in which we are at rest, and in which we view ourselves not as means but as ends. Such practices must themselves contain the ends of conduct, and hence must generate the ideology through which those ends can be valued and pursued.

It is perhaps not a happy description of this task as a search for 'roots', for although that word captures the ideas of tradition and allegiance which conservatism requires, it also suggests a kind of nostalgia which it cannot afford. Naturally, nostalgia for the past is more reasonable than nostalgia for the future; nevertheless it is, like every form of sentimentality, a way of 'standing back', a refusal to engage in the practice of rational life. It consigns its subject to inaction, and its condition is that of Dante's Limbo: without hope, living in desire. While the love of country and tradition is to some extent confirmed in the nostalgia with which English people view their eccentricities, their countryside, their architecture, and the ghostly presences of England, this nostalgia depends upon the possibility of something more concrete – of a deliberate activity of citizenship of which it provides only a sepia-toned reflection.[72] Here we see the distinction between true conservatism and mere 'conservation'. There is no sound politics of antiquarianism. It does not matter whether the 'antique drum' sounds from the pastures of rural England, or from the warm backyards of the slums. You can follow it, but you cannot lead it.

Our search, then, is for the immediate forms of social participation, those forms which intelligibly present to the citizens the fact of their public life, and so generate their values. As I suggested, it is to leisure that we must look for these forms. They contain the intimation of value, and hence must be 'autonomous'. Yet their autonomy may require protection and sanction through law. In order to explain those thoughts I shall consider examples, beginning with the simplest, which is that of sport.

Competitive sport

Competitive sport represents an activity in and through which millions of people constantly express their allegiance to team, town, region and country, and their sense of the 'proximity' of these things. The aim of a team is of course to win. But winning is defined by the rules of the game, and cannot be achieved except within the institution that defines it. Thus the aim of football is both internal and highly complex, not only defining but also entirely permeating the activity which leads up to it. No footballer can possibly see his activity 'as a means only' or himself as 'alienated' in that activity from his self-identity or from his 'species being'. Here is a tangible and rational end, which permeates and redeems the means to its realization. Moreover because it has that character, the player can be an object of immediate imaginative involvement. Social feelings of an elaborate kind can be projected on to his activity. His strength, courage, loyalty and perseverance warm the hearts of his following as though they were their own. The spectators are confirmed as social beings in the act of watching, as the team in the act of playing.

I have referred to 'autonomous institutions', and autonomy can mean many things. It can mean financial independence; or it can mean self-government. In the sense that I intend, however, an institution is autonomous if its purposes are peculiar to it. Whatever aims the institution has are aims which can be achieved through that institution alone. (One cannot win at football by playing cricket.) Of course there might be an external purpose too. A football team may earn money. But it is autonomous so long as its real meaning lies within itself. Members of a team sometimes earn money; but the interest of football for those who are immersed in it lies in the game and its outcome.

An autonomous institution is not just any arrangement with an internal purpose. It is also an institution. It is an arrangement which can outlive its individual members, and which offers to them a transcendent bond of membership. It is in such arrangements that activity most readily generates and confirms an ideology. The case of spectator sport demonstrates this. The player who actively pursues the goal, and the spectator who pursues it only vicariously, both rehearse a sense of shared identity. The pursuit symbolizes the social values which are inspired by it – loyalty, courage, competition, endurance. Here, then, is a simple and spontaneous institution, which, in pursuing its internal purposes, generates a consciousness of social ends.

The family

The point becomes more obvious if we turn to the second example, which is that of the family. It hardly needs saying, in the light of all that has gone before, that the support and protection of this institution must be central to the conservative outlook, and that changes in the law which are calculated to loosen or abolish the obligations of family life, or which in other ways facilitate the channelling of libidinal impulse away from that particuar form of union, will be accepted by conservatives only under the pressure of necessity. It also hardly needs saying that the family is weakening, and that unstable 'partnerships' are becoming the norm. Hence the primary experience of home, and the loyalties to place and people that stem from this experience, are much weaker than conservatives would like them to be. Indeed, if there is a fundamental difficulty for conservative politics in our times, it lies here: that the family is being blown apart, and nothing meaningful is coming in place of it.

The family is the origin of self-respect, being the first institution through which the social world is perceived. It is also autonomous: a form of life which has no aim besides itself. What is achieved through family union could not be achieved in some other way. The family is therefore instilled with concrete values, providing each of its participants with an unending source of rational objectives, which cannot be specified in advance but which arise from the realities of family life. The child who saves her pocket money in order to make a gift to her mother acts under the first impulse of rational conduct, acting towards an end the reality of which is more vivid to her than anything she might abstractly understand. Thus she makes her mark in the family, learns the 'ways of freedom', discovering herself and another through the act of love. To say that such a child is learning the habit of alienation (because it is money that mediates and fulfils her aim) would be to utter some kind of morbid joke.

I have previously taken the family as the clearest example of an institution based in a transcendent bond. It is a clear example because it is an extreme one. Almost nothing about the family union rests in contract or consent, and none of the values which spring from it can be understood except in terms of the peculiar lastingness with which it is endowed. While a football team has an identity which can outlast the contributions of particular members, it is not for its lastingness that it is valued. (Although it would be of less worth were it to be constantly formed and re-formed without some trappings of continuity.) In the case of the family, however, the experience of continuity is immediate and dominant. Parents play with their children and so re-enact childhood. They also educate them, preoccupied by the future character and happiness of their offspring. This motive reaches forward beyond death, and also backward, to a sense of former dependency and a remembrance of the parents who protected it. In the commerce between parent and child, past and future are made present, and therein lies the immediate and perceivable reality of the transcendent bond which unites them.

It matters enormously to parents that their children should be something, and not just anything. It is natural to seek preferment and security for them, and to be pleased when they acquire it. It is also natural to wish to pass on to them every attribute that might survive one's own departure. The principle of legacy – whereby a household outlasts its members – is therefore a consequence of family love. So too is the principle of hereditary privilege. This is not confined to a particular class. It is as much a desire of the labourer to work for the advantage of his child (rather than anyone else's), as it is a desire of the landed aristocrat. Massive legal interference in legacy and hereditary right constitutes a direct affront to the securest of social feelings. It is therefore impossible for those affected by it to be persuaded of its legitimacy. In this matter conservative politics directly supports and stems from a fundamental social experience. It seeks to conserve social continuity, so that people may envisage generations which stretch before and after them. Without that vision much of the motive for procreation is lost, and children become an accident, an anxiety, a reminder of one's isolation – and, in due course, the responsibility not of the parents but of the state who deprived the parents of power. Parents at rest with their child have a dominant desire, which is this: what we are and what we value we here pass on. The complexity and consolation of this thought has never been better captured than in the passage of *Ulysses*, sometimes known as 'Ithaca', in which Bloom projects towards Stephen the image of himself as father. Reflect on these things, and you will see that, however vociferously people may declare their attachment to other ideologies, in their most solemn innervations they are naturally conservative.

Autonomy and law

The two institutions that I have so far mentioned are basic examples of the institutions of leisure. They are inevitable manifestations of civil life, and no one can doubt either their essential autonomy, or the value that is bound to it. Moreover, they each generate ideology, and so ratify the impulses which find expression in them. In the first case the ideological content is precise: it is the assertion of team spirit, competition, courage, endurance, all connected with particular loyalties to place and people. In the second case the ideological content is more general, embracing everything of value, everything that might be 'passed on'.

But now, what attitude can the law take towards these institutions, and towards their claim for autonomy? The question is an interesting one, and provides a clear demonstration of principles for which I argued in Chapter 4.

The institutions of sport require little protection, since their spontaneity makes them immune from internal decay. Nevertheless, they have a special kind of existence in law. This existence is extremely difficult to define, precisely because of the need both to grant legal status and to conserve autonomy. The natural form of such spontaneous institutions is that of the 'unincorporated association' – an entity which, since it is not a legal 'person', poses complicated problems for the law.

Where there is an external purpose, then it is usual to 'incorporate', in order to safeguard assets and liabilities should the purpose fail. But because associations arise spontaneously, simply to do the peculiar and often indefinable things that they do, it is impossible to lay down by fiat that they should incorporate as soon as formed. The law is forced nevertheless to recognize them. It therefore grants protection and assigns liability to institutions which possess no legal personality. The great jurisprudential problem of the unincorporated association stems precisely from the fact that the only legal relation that can exist among its members is a contractual one, whereas the reality of the institution transcends that of any contractual arrangement.[73] A vivid example, then, of the law accommodating itself to civil society. It is also an ancient one, responsible for some of the finest intellectual constructs of Roman law, such as that of the *universitas*, adapted in medieval times to its present use.

The family illustrates the point more poignantly. Every legal system includes a branch known as 'family law', which is specifically concerned with the obligations generated by this peculiar form of membership. The bond of marriage is not contractual. Marriage is chosen, but its obligations are largely indeterminate, being generated by the institution itself, and discovered by the participants as they become involved in it. (It would be absurd for a man, faced by his wife's mortal illness, to say 'I did not bargain for this', and so think himself justified in leaving her.) Family law has changed in response not to individual claims, but to variations in the social arrangement. The law offers its protection to that arrangement conceived as a whole, not to this or that individual grievance that may arise from it. (Consider why it is, for example, that the law has sought to make divorce, not easy, but difficult.) Once again we notice the collusion between social values and legal norms. And since there is no external purpose to marriage, there is no definite point at which the law will say that the obligations of marriage have ceased. The obligations endure until the parties can persuade the law to absolve them.

Education

The two examples that I have taken illustrate certain fundamental conceptions to which conservatives must refer in their quest for ideology. But these two simple and natural institutions do not exist alone in any developed society. There are as many autonomous institutions as there are forms of social flourishing, and not all of them will have political significance. I shall consider, as my principal example, the institutions of education, through which politicians have rightly perceived that a major battle for the soul of society must be fought, some moved by a sense that education has certain inherent 'standards', without which it imparts nothing to the value of human life, others moved by the knowledge that it also confers 'privileges' which they demand to be more widely distributed. Through the smoke of this quarrel we discern the vital distinction, between education as means, and education as end. Whether or not there are 'privileges' involved in education is not a matter that is likely to trouble conservatives. It is in the nature of all institutions to create privileges and to determine their distribution. Forced redistribution of a privilege that arises internally will usually abolish the institution. Imagine for example the attempt to spread the privileges of kingship to more than one: to succeed is to abolish both the institution and the privileges. Egalitarians have been divided in the matter of education (in their practice, if not in their rhetoric). Some aim at an 'adjustment', others at the direct subversion of the whole arrangement. I suspect that only the second are thinking reasonably.

Education is a peculiar process, and one that presupposes that its subject is a rational (or potentially rational) being. Whatever the degrees and nature of the discipline administered, children receive education only if their rational nature is engaged in the process. They are learning, reasoning, reflecting, and whatever constraints hold their noses to their books, their minds will be held there only by the exercise of their own understanding. This process is so very different from the kind of 'training' that is administered to a horse, where there is no question of understanding but only of exact performance, that it seems absurd that anyone should have confused the two. But it is a fact that they have, and that the word 'conditioning' has been used to refer to all forms of disciplined education, as though the process and the product differed in no material particular from the training of a horse. The purpose here is to 'demystify' or 'demythologize'. It is the purpose of refusing all validity to the lived surface of human things and to the concepts (such as that of the 'authority' of an institution) which are contained in it, allowing only an alien picture of the 'depths' of established power. And it is of course not authority but power which trains the horse, and which treats the present horse only as a means to his future and more useful incarnation. Education too involves the exercise of power – power vested in a school or teacher. But school is conceived as an arena of legitimate and not merely of established power. Of course, there is a problem as to the true origins of a teacher's authority in the modern state. One of the undesirable consequences of making education (or rather the attendance at school) compulsory at law is that it becomes impossible to construe the teacher's authority as acquired by parental delegation, so that the two institutions of home and school do not so readily call upon the same fund of natural deference. The teacher's authority is seen as arising independently, and if it can rely on no agreed fiction for its validity other than the inherent right of the state to command obedience, then the institution of school is in danger of losing its autonomy, and becoming prone (as in France and Italy) to whatever disaffection may be directed towards the state.

Nevertheless the absorption of school into the machinery of the state is not complete, and the idea of educational autonomy is still vivid in public life. This is because the aims of education are again internal. In education children learn to pursue things that must be pursued for their own sakes. The value of these things is not (as a rule) to be seen in any end to which they lead, but rather in their capacity to embody social meaning. (Consider the study of history, of language and literature, even of natural science and mathematics as these first capture a child's attention.) In a bureaucratic society it is natural that people should attempt to see education as a means (for example, a means to social advancement, or to 'economic growth', or to reducing unemployment). To take that view is to abolish educational values in favour of other, usually more material interests. But the value of education lies precisely in the immediacy of the aims involved in it. The reasons for learning a subject that is truly educational lie in the subject itself. Education, and the accretions of tradition which surround it, provide their own direct picture of a human aim.

Naturally, not all people would wish to spend their leisure in education; nor would they gain from doing so. Apart from the family, we find a division among autonomous institutions, some adapted to the fulfilment of one person, some to the fulfilment of another. And the very idea of 'autonomy' suggests that this must be so. Values can be diverse and yet not conflicting, and, so long as there is a suitable establishment, to broker the activities of people in every autonomous field, these can exist in relative independence without risk to the social order. I shall return to that point in the next chapter, but will first concentrate upon a complex issue in the theory of education, in order to reveal just what is meant by educational autonomy, and just why it is politically desirable.

Relevance

The issue is that of 'relevance', and the confusion which it has introduced into the study of the humanities in higher education. It is one of the merits of university education in Britain that it has been built around certain recognized academic disciplines, with 'combined degrees' taking a subordinate place, governed by the intellectual standards of their constituent subjects (and this has been made possible largely by the standards of education achieved at school, which sometimes enables a university teacher to assume a knowledge of English grammar, of Latin, of literature, of history, and of calculus). But the humanities stand opposed to certain factitious disciplines, usually put together out of pieces that have no obvious connection, in order to continue the illusion of an educational process that may in fact have ceased by the age of ten. The guiding principle of these subjects is the principle of 'relevance', according to which education is not an end but a means, even in those non-technical disciplines where such a construction might have previously seemed impossible.

The first gesture towards 'relevance' is the creation of the 'second-order' subject, or 'meta-discipline'. Consider again the art of football. This requires great skill and physical endurance, but little theoretical learning. 'Football' might appear as an American 'course unit', but it is not a possible subject for an academic degree. Which is not to make any deleterious comparison between the amateur footballer and the graduate in sociology, but rather to repeat the point just mentioned, that autonomous institutions are of their nature many and varied, so that the ends of one cannot be transported into the practice of another without detriment to the value of both.

Now someone with a consuming passion for football, and with no ability to play it, might wish to communicate his enthusiasm, preferably in comfortable and leisured circumstances. And others, equally deficient in aptitude and skill, might welcome the opportunity to live for three years at public expense, thinking about nothing but football. A subject is therefore invented, called 'Football Studies'. It contains a variety of papers (or 'modules', as they are now called). For example, there is the sociology of football (involving the study of the structure of crowds and the 'charisma' of players); the philosophy of football (beginning from Aristotle on catharsis and centreing on the role of alienated labour in spectator sports); the psychology of football (containing dry reflections on how the motion of the ball is perceived by the human eye, together with much wetter reflections on 'football and the unconscious'); the ethics of football (including studies of 'social responsibility' and the true origins of hooliganism in capitalist society); the history of football and its relation to class structures; and so on. This subject is welcomed by many sociologists – for it is 'relevant' to the working-class student, and directly applicable to social and political problems facing the world of today. It is more useful, the sociologists suggest, for a student 'faced with the problems of living in post-industrial society', to study for this degree than for a degree in classics or theology. The degree is adopted at once by one of the new universities (where for sociological reasons, classics and theology are already banned). Famous football teams, anxious for publicity, endow chairs and studentships at their local polytechnics. Soon the academic world is saturated with teachers of football studies, and the dole queues are swelling with their graduates.

The artificial degree

The example parallels the history of 'Black Studies', 'Women's Studies', and 'Gay Studies' (now known – 2000 – as 'Queer Theory') in the American colleges. When the first edition of this book appeared in 1979 the account of football studies was dismissed as a ridiculous straw man. Since then, however, 'sports studies' has become a standard subject in the former polytechnics (themselves elevated to universities by John Major, the first genuinely uneducated Prime Minister that our country has known). Such subjects arise by throwing together rival disciplines and by creating artificial links with areas of 'relevance' and 'social concern'. They illustrate the misunderstanding of education that ensues, when education is conceived as a means and not as an end in itself. The first such subject to penetrate higher education in Britain, in fact, was 'Education', conceived as a necessary preliminary to the career of teaching. This fraudulent subject has probably done more to damage our educational system than any other. It led at once to the formation of 'Schools of Education', and the invention of the Graduate Certificate in Education, which conveys neither the understanding of a subject nor the ability to teach it, and which was for a long time required of all who would work in a state school and who lacked the advantage of a non-university training. It also produced a new class of bureaucratic experts, the 'educationists' who dictated the practice of the classroom on the strength of utopian theories that showed little awareness of what ignorance really means. It was thus that 'child-centred learning' became the orthodoxy of the primary school, along with the 'relevance revolution' which insisted that learning be made relevant to the interests of children who had yet to acquire it.

Those ideas were given official status by the Plowden Report, produced for the then Labour Government in 1967, a report accepted with enthusiasm by teachers disenchanted with their newly imposed task as child-minders to the nation. By shifting attention from the teacher to the child, by suggesting that if children do not learn it is not because of a lack of discipline but because of an excess of it, and by advocating an 'individualized' teaching process, in which the relation between teacher and pupil is rewritten as a form of partnership where 'active learning' and 'learning by acquaintance' replace the traditional approach of 'learning by description' – in these and other ways the Report seemed to lift from the shoulders of teachers a burden of responsibility that could no longer be easily borne. And this is true of almost every educational theory developed in our schools of 'education': the theory is believed not because of its truth, still less because rational arguments have been offered in its favour, but because it produces 'experts' without knowledge: people who have the social benefits of education, without the real cost of acquiring it.

Since the first edition of this book appeared, the orthodoxies of the Sixties have been called in question. Meanwhile, however, so much damage has been inflicted on our schools that in many parts of the country it is impossible to obtain an education through the state system, and the old social mobility, which enabled me to rise through grammar school and university into the ranks of professional people, is rapidly disappearing. For this reason, if for no other, conservatives should fight to preserve private schools. For they have provided examples of what education really is, and it is by following such examples that the state schools can lift themselves from the sink of mediocrity.

The example of 'Education' is a vivid reminder of the damage that can be done, when pretend disciplines usurp the place of real ones. It is of course hard to identify the quality which makes a discipline genuinely educational. Some might think that the factitious nature of the second-order degree derives from the factitious unity in its first-order subject. To say that there is one subject of 'Communications Studies', for example – which focuses on speech, gesture, painting, music, television, politics and photography – is like saying that there is one theory of holes, which covers the holes in shirts, in shoes and in the earth; black holes, key-holes and holes in an argument. (Perhaps such a subject might venture to ascertain the truth of Laurence Sterne's assertion that 'more sin and wickedness have entered the world through key-holes than through all other holes put together'.) But the absurdity of 'Hole Studies' is of a different order from the absurdity of 'Football Studies', 'Communications Studies' or 'Media Studies', being more like the absurdity of the latter's continental rival – 'semiology' – which dominated for a while the humanities in Italy and France. It stems from adopting a first-order classification without a theoretical basis, where no other basis is possible. But even when the first-order subject has no theoretical unity, it may still have a practical unity. And in the case of the major humanities – English, classics, history – there need be neither theory nor practice involved in their study, but something more elusive, and, from the educational point of view, more valuable than both.

The true failing of the factitious degree like 'Education' or 'Media Studies' lies in its second-order nature, and its consequent attempt at an unearned 'relevance'. It is precisely this which keeps the discipline at one remove from a serious understanding of its subject. For consider the hypothetical subject of 'Mathematics Studies', a degree option for those who dislike the barren rigours of old-fashioned mathematics, and who wish to see mathematics in its 'wider context', as a discipline potentially relevant to the problems facing post-industrial society. This degree offers courses in the sociology of mathematics (which studies the effect of 'disprivileged background' on mathematical eminence, and of mathematical competence on social standing); the psychology of mathematics (which is again very dry except for the 'module' devoted to the unconscious); the philosophy of mathematics (which, being unable to presuppose any competence in logic, stays with the jargon of 'dialectical' thought); and the history of mathematics; with options in 'Mathematical art', 'Pythagorean cosmology', 'Number symbolism', and 'The universal history of the number 2'. Nobody will suppose that such a subject produces understanding, either of mathematics, or of anything else. It is impossible to gauge what qualities of mind would be adapted to it, or what value or discipline would result from its pursuit. The subject is a pure fantasy, and even educationists might consider it unfair to inflict it on students – at least, not before 'further research'.

What is wrong with such a subject is not that it leads to no career (for that is true of almost every academic subject), nor that it is unscientific (for that is true of English and philosophy, both of which have been represented by thinkers of the highest seriousness as representing the best in academic discipline). What is wrong with the subject is simply that it involves no critical reflection on an identifiable field of study, and, for that reason, embodies no educational value. The true critical appraisal of mathematics is reserved for those with a mathematical understanding. It is not possible to emerge from this degree in 'Mathematics Studies' with the ability to assess or dispute a mathematical proof, or with any other intellectual accomplishment that would show itself in reasoned critical reflection, applicable beyond the range of examples used to teach it. The second-order subject has neither the scientific method required for an established body of results, nor the more elusive discipline of the humanities, the discipline which leads to genuine critical intelligence.

Critical intelligence

It is difficult to define critical intelligence, because it is difficult to make clear, in terms external to the specific forms of education, just what the value of education is. But let us consider another example, that of history. History is not a true science: it has few theoretical concepts and no experimental methods. The facts which it studies are studied not under the aspect of scientific law, but under that of everyday memory and perception. Nevertheless, the study of history involves the direct application of intelligence to those facts, rather than the self-conscious reflection upon its own 'methodology'. We speak of a historical understanding, which is something distinct from both factual knowledge and philosophical reflection, involving an ability to reason about history, to understand historical processes, and to bring an intellectual training to the assessment of familiar and unfamiliar facts. Sometimes historians explain, sometimes they merely describe; in every case they are bringing into relation matters which illuminate one another, and showing some perception of their human essence. Voltaire, Hume and Mommsen were great historians, simply on account of their articulate understanding of human things; and while accuracy is a precondition of historical analysis, it is of no independent significance. No one can regard the licence of Thucydides as a flaw in his historical understanding. On the contrary, his brilliant procedure of 'dramatization' succeeded in representing an entire human episode as intelligible, in a way that no 'science' of historical facts is likely to rival. It is through such examples that the idea of 'critical intelligence' may be understood.

What I have implied about history is true also of classics, philosophy and English, at least as these are usually conceived. But nothing similar is true of the second-order discipline. It should be obvious, therefore, that the 'relevant' degree is either associated with a serious first-order discipline (which will then naturally take precedence over it, as mathematics takes precedence over 'mathematics studies'); or else wholly independent. And in the latter case it can involve no discipline at all. For it will then be without any coherent body of facts to study, and without any critical method to apply to them.

I say that all this should be obvious, but apparently it is not so. Not only do children have to suffer daily from the fraud of 'Education' (the ascendancy of which has ensured that those who most love and understand a given subject are those least likely now to teach it in a state school). There is also a sign that governments will listen to those for whom education is a means to an end, and at best a branch of technology. They might therefore come to consider that second-order subjects are a source of genuine understanding and useful expertise. For example, a prominent member of Lord Bullock's Committee on Industrial Democracy was Professor of Industrial Relations (a course not unlike the 'Football Studies' envisaged earlier) at the University of Warwick.[74] This perhaps bears on the single most ominous feature of the report, which was its uncritical adoption of the view (echoing the Plowden Report) that 'self-expression' is essentially 'creative', and that 'education' has made unprecedented advances since children were encouraged not to 'accept authority' but to 'make up their minds' on the subjects presented to them. Indeed, at every point in the Report where it is possible to insert an idea (and these are few enough, both premises and conclusion having been preordained by the then ruling party) we find similar fragments of sociological liturgy.

What is wrong with this liturgy is not that it embodies palpable falsehoods or unwelcome prejudices. What is wrong is that it is the expression of a mind working at one remove from its subject. Sociological liturgy is simply the easy rigmarole of the 'second-order mind', which substitutes ready-made concepts for critical understanding. Such a mind has no ability to test its ideas against reality, or to understand reality through its stock of ideas. The ideas are essentially factitious, often deriving from subjects which have neither method nor theory; and the facts, being of that complex kind which must be understood in terms not of scientific theory but of critical intelligence, are essentially elusive, being masked by nothing so much as the blind statistics which are the common recourse of a mind devoid of concepts. To the second-order mind social realities are not merely incomprehensible, but also imperceivable. Here indeed we have the true 'mind' of alienated man, of man for whom the pursuit of means has swallowed and obliterated the understanding of ends.

The autonomy of education

I have dwelt on the example at some length, because it illustrates the most important points of principle that I wish to generalize.

First, it shows the manner in which education, as traditionally conceived, contains its end internally, so that the aims of education are inseparable from the means by which we arrive at them. It is in this sense, and no other, that the institutions of education are autonomous. Their autonomy is not necessarily (although it may be in fact) affected by the financial dependence of educational institutions upon state funding. Everything here depends upon the attitude of the state, just as it once depended upon the attitude of the Church. Naturally, if government lies in the hands of people who are active in the pursuit of 'social goals', and who do not recognize the validity of any independent reason, then every autonomous institution stands in danger. But this is an accident of policy. And the accident is not peculiar to the goal of 'social justice': it follows equally from the single-minded pursuit of economic growth, or international power, or racial purity (although not of tradition, since that is a goal internal to the institution).

Second, the example shows that, precisely because its aims are internal, education may be a point where the values of people are formed, elicited and sustained. Education is essentially a 'common pursuit', formed by traditions, and directed towards recognized ends. To engage in it is to envisage a form of community, and to desire it is to desire that community. It is in this kind of pursuit that the grip of alienation is loosened, and fellowship is born. Naturally it is very difficult to describe that fellowship: but it is shown in the ability of educational institutions to survive, just as it is shown in the institutions of entertainment and sport. There is something about the ends of education which prepare us for this social interaction – something about their closeness to human life which is perceived in the pursuit of them, but lost in the description.

Values and institutions

A third point should be noted, which is that the values implicit in the pursuit of education (or in the participation in any such autonomous arrangement) cannot necessarily be reduced to a code of conduct, a system of rules, or an ideal of the 'good for man'. They consist, rather, in an intimation of a human world, and of access to that world through understanding. Hence the idea of education coexists with that of culture.

In the language provided by a culture all ideals and morality may be more finely and more accurately expressed. Nor is this peculiar to education. Every arrangement that allows people to value an activity for its own sake will also provide them with a paradigm through which to understand the ends of life. The working-man's club, the businessman's marina, the institutes and societies of urban and rural life – however remote these may seem from some snobbish ideal of fellowship – are in fact the stuff of human society. Through them men and women are able to define themselves, and to discover the language in which to express their common essence. Such institutions contain a 'presentiment', and in terms of that presentiment other aims may be located, and sometimes described. An autonomous institution provides language, custom, tradition, fellowship: a member may transport that mental framework to the rest of life, and so make sense of himself as a political being. Indeed one may say that the autonomous institution is the alternative to the ceremony of initiation which anthropologists have presented as the gateway into the tribe.

Such reflections enable us to see that an institution which has an internal aim may also have an external value. Consider friendship. The internal aim of friendship is the well-being of someone loved, but its benefit is greater than that. What friends desire is only a part of what they achieve. They achieve, for example, a reciprocal affection, and their own security. But they do not aim at what they achieve, for that would be to treat the other as a means, and so to deny the spirit of friendship. Likewise people will achieve education only if they desire it for its own sake. But what they achieve will be far more than that. They will acquire the ability to communicate, to persuade, to attract and dominate. In any social arrangement, such abilities must be advantages; but education can never be pursued merely as a means to them, even if they are its natural consequence.

Because the nature of education is determined by its internal aim, these advantages can be removed from it only by the destruction of that aim. And it is precisely against this aim that the ethos of 'relevance' is directed. Similarly, when conservatives uphold the ideal of 'standards' in education they too are appealing to an aim which can be made sense of only by consulting, as I have, the institutions of learning, and not by reference to any advantages that those institutions may incidentally confer. And in fact the autonomy of the institution *must* require that emphasis on standards; an institution does not have a defining purpose unless it purposes to do the thing well. And that means that it may have to be selective, not just in respect of those it engages to administrate it, but also in respect of those it chooses to admit. No more than a football team can a university admit just anyone; and if we see this demand of education extended backwards along the line from maturity to birth, we shall have to concede that there always will be a point – the point where the pursuit of educational values becomes earnest – at which some form of selection takes place.

Moreover, while of course this does nothing to defend one manner of selection against another, it does immediately grant privileges to those who come to the institutions of education better prepared – for example, to those whose parents encourage them to read and write, to those better endowed with natural intelligence, to those with the resources to employ private tuition. Even if we abstract from every actual educational arrangement, including those which have sacrificed the aim of education to that of social equality, we are forced to recognize an inevitability here: a collusion between the institution of the family and the later institutions which prepare a child for the adult world. Unless we are to snatch our babies from their mothers and rear them in battery farms, this 'inequality of opportunity' could not be eradicated. And even then, its full eradication might depend upon depriving children of some part of their natural understanding, say by subjecting their skulls to repeated hammer blows, or by removing parts of their brains.

Autonomy and advantage

Now the social advantages conferred by autonomous institutions are not all of the same kind. Some institutions provide only the fellowship of their members; others (such as education) provide indefinite possibilities of relating to people who do not necessarily belong to them. And this is natural: some people do not want their universe to be indefinitely expandable – expandable, say, beyond the yachting club or the public house. Others do. Thus while every institution may return privileges that are not involved in its aim, these privileges cannot be of equal value. Some enable people to form ties of a new kind, others only ties of the same kind. In the former case – which is the case of education – the achievement of the aim brings also the gift of social mobility. (Even if this is not obvious *a priori*, it will, I think, prove to be a historical truth.)

The persistence of autonomous institutions already points in the direction of a stratified society. The advantages conferred by education are to some extent transmissible across generations and, even if not so transmissible, are inevitably bound to divide those who can obtain them from those who cannot. The example shows, incidentally, the absurdity of the aim of 'equality of opportunity'. Such a thing is neither possible nor desirable. For what opportunity does an unintelligent child have to partake of the advantages conferred by an institution which demands intelligence? His case is no different from that of a plain girl competing with a pretty girl for a position as model. The attempt to provide equality of opportunity, unless it is to involve massive compulsory surgery of an unthinkable kind, is simply a confused stumble in the dark.

At once, however, we see an enormous political issue arising. It is not possible to provide universal education. Nor, indeed, is it desirable. For the appetite for learning points people only in a certain direction; it siphons them away from those places where they might have been contented. There are many occupations, from the operation of a signal-box to the management of a bank, which require great natural intelligence, and yet which may not appeal to someone who has been flattered by the gift of education. It is important for a society that it contain as many 'walks of life' as the satisfaction of its members may require, and that it accord to each of those stations its own dignity and recompense. And it must somehow safeguard itself from the loss of virtue in trade, profession and industry, by sustaining institutions which are not educational, and which do not merely siphon away gifted people to the point where they no longer wish to do what in fact they might otherwise have done willingly and well. It is difficult to express this point without sounding either patronizing or totalitarian. For it may seem that one is committed to the view that people should be 'confined' or 'allotted' to their station. But it is not necessary to believe that the authority of the state need be invoked to forbid or encourage the adoption of any particular way of life by any particular citizen – provided, of course, that the way of life forms part of the civil order.

The stratified society

It is difficult to imagine a contented society in which every signal-box was manned by a graduate in sociology, every shop-floor directed by a philosopher, and every field tilled by a barrister-at-law. It is necessary that the state should contain institutions which make contact with these occupations, where leisure may be exercised and recompensed without the adoption of some specifically educational purpose. But what attitude can the state take to such a vast and complex problem?

Now in fact it has taken an attitude over recent years, and it is an attitude which has proved destructive of social values. The dictatorship of the Treasury has ensured that children with no aptitude for education should stay at school long after their lack of desire for it has become clear to them. The institutions of education, in other words, have been used largely as a means to reducing unemployment. There are two reasons for this. First, educational institutions have strong and definite internal purposes, which enable them to survive considerable abuse. Second, they have become dependent upon government support, and therefore answerable to government policy. And here we see that, when it matters, autonomy can be subverted at once if there is financial dependence on the state.

This attitude of the state has made the problem of leisure acute. Not only have educational institutions been subjected to pressure at variance with their internal purposes. More important, the rival institutions through which idleness might be transformed into leisure have been neglected. Without these rival institutions children are forced, either to engage in the pursuit of education, or else to remain uselessly at school until suddenly ejected, on the brink of adulthood, into a world that expects that they should both work and provide their own amusement. It needs only the absence of work for the absence of amusement to become chronic and unbearable.

The problem here should not be underestimated. Autonomous institutions can be created, endowed, and protected through charter. They have legal status, and inherent authority. Nevertheless, they are not institutions of government. They are part of civil society, and depend on society for their strength. The state may commandeer them, and they may survive if it does not also force them towards an external goal. But it always runs the risk of confining institutions within a predetermined frame. In lending its power to one institution, it withdraws authority from those that rival it. The rivals wither, while the favourite stands in danger of being absorbed into the bureaucratic state.

What then happens to the people who do not desire, or cannot acquire, the benefit of education? It is surely a mark of deep disrespect to force them, despite that, to spend their early years in the vain pursuit of it. There must be rival institutions, and they must have comparable authority. And if social stratification results, then this must be accepted. For it will result in any case, as our discussion shows. Even when all people are forced through the mill of education, some emerge formed, and others emerge formless.

What rival institutions can we imagine? The custom of apprenticeship – which, while being a part of work, also demonstrates the continuity between work and leisure – has been eclipsed by the forces of industrial production. Much the same has happened to the exercise of craft, and to the clubs and organizations which surrounded and legitimized the activities of popular recreation. But there is a degree in all this. Consider American rural society. It is neither barbarous, nor civilized, nor decadent. It is of no great interest to the outside world, but seems, despite that, to get on happily with itself. And we find in this society a proliferation of clubs and organizations, even old habits of craftsmanship that have disappeared from Europe. This is partly due to the lack of governmental presence. The American state is not given to regimenting its citizens into forms that are alien to them, and while the resulting chaos of childish eccentricities may have little appeal to an outsider, it is clear that it is not without considerable consoling power for those who engage in creating it. The result of this burgeoning of autonomous institutions is an extreme, though formless, social stratification.

The loosening of the bond between state and education might therefore prove beneficial to the British. Other institutions might arise to console them, and so find their charter and protection in the law. Consider the following example. A boy is fascinated by electricity. He sets it up as a hobby, designing circuits and playing with lights. It becomes interesting for its own sake. We do not have to believe, with Schiller, that it is in play that the spirit of man first finds itself;[75] we can at least agree that play has a peculiar and immediate value.

The child also learns through his diversion the rudiments of a trade. When in later life he becomes an electrician, his leisure will turn quite painlessly to work. Naturally, too complete an absorption in his hobby is unlikely to make him fascinating company. But he will find social consolation in associating with others of a like mind, learning through them and from them, moulding his character according to the common spirit which they come to share. The result of that process is a guild of electricians. This institution has peculiar value to its participants; it proceeds to embellish itself with the customs and ceremonies of social life, and becomes the focus of both work and leisure.

The example is not so far from contemporary reality. It shows two things. First, that, left to themselves, the institutions of leisure diversify as society requires. Second, that some institutions, such as the one I have imagined, will be ideologically impoverished. They will not confer the social mobility or the social power that is conferred by education. This may matter if stratification is dangerous. But as we shall see, it does not matter, because it is not.

It is not easy to translate such reflections into policy, except by preventing the spread of fraudulent institutions which pretend to be educational while being no such thing, and by encouraging, wherever possible, the activities which compete with them. But this difficulty in stepping from doctrine to policy is precisely the difficulty of overcoming the alienation of civil society. It is not surprising if it exists, since the problem is not amenable to a panacea. Alienation is overcome piecemeal, or not at all.

Concluding remarks

In this chapter I have surveyed certain of the institutions which provide the ends of social life. I have argued that such institutions must be autonomous, focused on internal aims. I have also tried to show how the attempt to subject them to external aims is dangerous and impolitic. The role of the state here is that of guardian and foster-parent. It cannot invade the institutions of leisure without perverting them to its own uses, and losing sight, in the process, of what those uses are.

As we have seen, important conservative instincts are upheld in the aims of leisure. The desire for continuity, the bond of allegiance, the pursuit of excellence, even the stratification of society itself, all seem to be natural and even inevitable outcomes of institutional autonomy. But now we face a problem. If envy and resentment are not to be the result of this, then we shall want to know why and how. This leads us to the culmination of the conservative viewpoint: the ideal of a legitimate establishment.

8
Establishment

Some of the problems of the last chapter will begin to seem less intractable as we consider the idea of establishment, an idea which has caused some difficulty to conservatives, partly because their flirtation with liberalism has led them to conceive the matter from the wrong end, from the standpoint of the individual. We have now advanced beyond that standpoint, and must try to formulate our vision in more political terms.

Power and authority

Establishment comprises both power and authority. It is a plausible assumption (defended in Chapter 2), that power and authority mutually require each other. Power without authority is 'unhappy' power. It is 'at large' in the world, distributing violence without earning respect. The transformation of power into authority confers recognition, and so removes the element of arbitrary force. Power and authority seek each other. Their search is the process of politics, while establishment is the condition which their meeting creates.

This process can be perceived, and its political importance ascertained, even in the life of the individual. Consider erotic love. Love stakes an enormous claim, and demands satisfaction. Its initial gestures point towards something which may be as much feared as wanted – for the power of love may be greater than the power of the individual who experiences it. What is surprising, however, is that, even in a society like ours, in which romantic love is taken more seriously than the legal forms which endorse it, those forms are nevertheless considered necessary.

Wife and husband face each other with the authority of a legal tie. Thus an elemental social force becomes constituted in authoritative terms. The resulting law has to attend, not to the initial gesture of consent, but to the felt reality of the bond which results from it. There is and always will be love outside marriage. But it is love, and not some other power, which requires the forms of marriage. In these forms the violence of love is ended, while its strength remains. The authority of an established institution protects and makes intelligible the power which seeks for it. The daily demand for love becomes a painless ritual, but in no way relinquishes its essential power; while the confused, sad feeling of one who loves and is betrayed becomes intelligible as a violated right.

The example points to a political meaning. Establishment requires three things: power, authority, and the process that unites them. Moreover the virtue of establishment consists partly in the mollification of power, and in the creation of the rights through which power becomes intelligible.

Local government

Some conservatives, wondering how the establishment of power can be justified, have sought not for the establishment but for the fragmentation of power, through some process of devolution which has not national but local government as its aim. It is important to understand the mistake in this – and along with it the fraudulent nature of 'local government' as it has been practised in Britain – if we are to provide an accurate account of what establishment really means.

Local government was the reality from which America formed itself. However, less and less do the states retain their individual authority. As the apparatus of constitution grows, so can it form and reform the civil society not merely in New York and Washington, but also in Oregon and Alabama. Such autonomy as the states retain begins to be seen as delegated from central government, by whose decrees the states are ultimately bound. It is only comparatively recently, and under the pressure of international politics, that the image of the state of America has emerged from the confused idea of Union. And what has made that image possible is the progressive rendering up of local privilege to centrally constituted power. Conservatives have a tendency to regret this, since the federal power, and the Supreme Court which is its inquisition, are in the hands of liberals, and relentlessly impose the liberal world-view on the conservative societies of rural America. But I doubt that the reaffirmation of 'states' rights' would change this situation. Precisely because of its detachment from local loyalties, and its claim to speak for a universal human nature, liberalism is an intolerant creed; it is also the creed of modern elites, the by-product of free competition for social and economic success. The difficulty for American conservatives is that they are destined to be educated, railed at and governed by people whose primary concern is that they should be, in Rousseau's notorious words, 'forced to be free'.

Local loyalties in Britain are so deeply buried in history as to have no more than a legendary force. The advocate of 'devolution' cannot really consider that he is returning to the people something which they once surrendered. (Not even when there was a definite Act of Union, whose ultimate cause was the accession of a Scottish King.) Local government cannot be conceived as a natural or prior right of the citizen, but only as a delegation of power. It is for this reason that, while in America much of the strength of the country derives from its separately constituted states, in England, the extent of local government indicates not a strength but a weakness in the political organism. It cannot be in this way that we should derive or justify our idea of what is established.

If there were to be genuine local government in Britain, then the national constitution might lead us to expect that it be an exercise of delegated power. This is in fact what we find. Yet it is true to say that there would be room for something else, and something healthier, within the framework of the British constitution. This healthier arrangement would construe local government simply as an administrative organism, financed by local people, in order to supply and maintain those services which agreement and tradition had placed in its hands. These services are to be maintained both for the benefit of the community which pays for them, and in accordance with certain established principles of order and charity. There might even be, as at present, a procedure of representation, so that those who surrender their money to local administration can see that it is neither squandered nor misapplied. Perhaps the proposal could be further embellished through the supposition of local events, contests and ceremonies for which the council takes responsibility, so conferring on the community all the trappings of civil life, in the manner of the little parliament of Mastersingers so brilliantly represented by Wagner. Members of the council would be chosen in whatever way (and not necessarily democratically) from those with an interest in the identity and continuity of the local community. Their framing of by-laws would be nothing more than a ratification of custom, defeasible in some higher court. The result would be the town, as it came into being in the Middle

Ages, autonomous not in law but only in usage, created from the leisure of its members, a representation of the values of civil life. Such an arrangement wields no power beyond the power of association, and defers to the state as the sovereign power. Its authority is the authority of custom, an authority which should not be despised but which stands (as Hans Sachs admitted) in need of some other protection.

Such would be the ideal of local government pursued, not as a delegation of power, but as an institution of citizenship. Imagine now a community which establishes itself in that way, setting up a common fund from which to provide schools, police and services, with a power to house and relieve those who are destitute. Those who administer the fund are able to levy taxes according to need, and to exert limited powers of compulsion. Already we are moving away from the idea of administration towards that of constituted power. Imagine now, therefore, a local council which attempts to acquire by compulsory purchase street upon street of occupied houses, in order to replace them with new and expensive dwellings for people who are neither recognized members of the community nor seriously destitute. And suppose that it proposes this scheme as its main item of expenditure, seeking to increase the local tax in order to realize it. Given the status that I have imagined for local administration, such a body would be in breach of trust, and members of the community would be absolved from their obligation to pay their local taxes.

The situation I have just described is easily imaginable, and indeed sometimes occurs, under the actual procedures of local government. How is this possible? First, legal enactment has made it a criminal offence to withhold the council tax, and with that act of state local government becomes the recipient of enormous delegated power. It can no longer be governed by any variant (however sophisticated) of the law of trusts, but only by the more lenient and more cumbersome law of administration – a law empty of those equitable principles that control not only the form but also the content of administrative decisions. Moreover, the administrative machine does not – as in my example – aim simply to return its resources in symbolic or transmuted form to the community that provided them; it has external aims, aims of 'social justice', for example, or of government policy, which require it to call on resources that are provided not only by local people but also by central government. There is no fund of local custom that could legitimate such a machine, since it has become subject to the purposes of the state, a kind of vast and desultory civil service. Because of this massive delegation of central power, the local council has itself become a part of national politics: it is formed according to the party structure of parliament, and is used as a practice ground for aspiring politicians. It is thus that a business cartel can – as in Newcastle in the Sixties – draw upon the power and authority of a national party in order to overcome all the local feelings which might otherwise oppose it. The result naturally makes a nonsense of planning law, just as it makes the idea of a 'local' school into a constitutional fiction.

Clearly, to proceed further in the direction of delegated power is to cause an increasing fragmentation of the state, and an increasing vulnerability to corruption. As the example shows, establishment in England does not arise at the local level, but is transferred from above, by the filtering down of sovereign power. And often, what is transferred is power without responsibility. The citizen's attention and interest is always diverted towards the source of power – towards the national government and the parties which compete for its operation. Hence the 'local' representatives need never regard themselves as answerable to the local community, but rather to the national party in whose name they hold office. If there were to be genuine local government in Britain, the first requirement would be to forbid the national political parties to take part in it.

Delegation and ratification

I have advocated the existence of autonomous institutions that are not subordinate to government aims. The question to consider is not how they can become instruments of delegated government, but rather how they can be ratified by established power. This is a vital question, since it seems to me that it is only in some process of ratification that the tensions created by the multiplicity of subject institutions, and by the class divisions which they generate, will be resolved.

As the example shows, the delegation of power is not in itself the delegation of authority. The distribution of the powers of the state to bodies which should be directly answerable to the citizen diminishes the authority of the state, without augmenting that of the subject institutions. Authority becomes naked power, but diminished power, with no serious allegiance except that which stems from coercion. Every delegation which separates power from the dignity of government therefore weakens both the power and the authority of the state. It is for this reason, and not out of economic conviction, that conservatives resist the nationalization of private industry, the expansion of the civil service, the endless and fruitless activities of 'commissions of inquiry', and the massed army of bureaucrats and quangos by which government has now found itself encumbered.

Power and authority need each other. To delegate power alone is to weaken the centre of authority. Conversely, if power and authority reside together, new powers can be made subservient to the power of the state. Thus they acquire a nimbus of the authority which it is with the state alone to provide. I shall call this process ratification, meaning the gathering up of quasi-autonomous powers as subjects of a single sovereign authority. Now it is clear that ratification must occur. If there is a power at large in the state, then it must not be allowed to generate its own authority, as the Mafia does. It must either be destroyed by the state, or else hold its authority *from* the state.

In exploring the concept of ratification, I shall consider various examples. I shall begin from one of the institutions of state, in which power and authority are inevitably conjoined. Having drawn certain conclusions as to the necessary ingredients of ratification, I shall consider two further cases. The first of these – the Church – is a power losing authority; the second – the trade-union movement – a power attempting to gain it. Through studying these powers, both of which lie on the edge of establishment, we shall form a picture of what lies, and what ought to lie, at the centre.

State institutions

Much of what I said concerning autonomous institutions could be applied, in modified form, to institutions with primary aims that are not internal, in particular, to the subordinate institutions of the state. I shall briefly reflect on one such institution, in order to show that the external aim may be both remote from the actual motives of the participants, and yet intimately bound up with the institution's authority. The institution I shall choose is the military, specifically the army. This is an institution not of civil society but of the state. It also stands directly, not only for the authority of state, but also for its power.

The primary aim of the army is to pursue by violent means all those purposes of the state that can be pursued in no other way, such as defence against foes, suppression of rebellion, and the conquest of desirable assets. (Let us ignore the question whether all those aims are now feasible or politic: the issue of 'defence' is not one of fundamental doctrine, but one of seeing who one's enemies are.) Now the primary aims of the army may often be in abeyance – there are times of peace and civil order in which the army has nothing to do. Nevertheless, it sustains its social life throughout those times, and this life cannot be understood in terms of the external aims which are allotted to it. The army has customs, modes of participation, social and private practices, which compose the character of the soldier's life. Involved in those practices are many internal aims and values, aims of honour, comradeship and regimental duty. And these values, while they clearly serve the end of military discipline, have an effect in the life of a soldier which transcends the requirements of his occupation. A soldier takes back to the civil world the picture of himself that he acquired in the army, and this picture, while it reflects the external aim of the military, is also imbued with a particular self-justifying ethos. This ethos lends itself to the respect for established power.

Person, office and ceremony

Certain features of the arrangement are clearly of more than ordinary importance in bringing about this respect. The first and most significant is the separation of individual from office. This exists at its clearest in the army, but is an essential feature of every true establishment, and part of the appeal of establishment to all those who take no immediate part in it. This separation provides a sense of who a person is, what his power and position entail, and the nature and extent of his accountability, independently of any personal qualities. The soldier owes respect to his officer not because of that officer's personality, but because of his office. In grasping the distinction he acquires the conception of a common order to which both he and his officer belong. Naturally, personality and office affect each other, so that an unworthy person may lower the dignity of an office, as a worthy office may raise the dignity of its occupant. But it is the recognition of the distinction between the two that accords to the office and its duties a kind of objective necessity in the eyes of those under its jurisdiction. Any genuine establishment must consist of such offices, successively filled by individuals whose personality is to some extent absorbed by them. Otherwise, it will wear the aspect only of arbitrary power.

The army displays another interesting feature. This is the pervasiveness of ritual and ceremony. While the respect for office is integral to discipline and hence to the external military aim, ritual and ceremony show the army not in pursuit of its ruling purpose but simply at ease. Yet, as everyone knows and observes, military parades and displays are of immense symbolic power, glorifying participants and spectators alike, and becoming a focus of common loyalties. All recently founded states – from the South American republics, through the Soviet empire, to the petty despotisms of Africa – have exploited to the full this natural charm of military ceremony, where power, through its transformation into symbol, acquires the aspect of authority. One of the weaknesses in Western democracies is that a certain coyness about these things overcomes the urge to participate in them. On the one hand lingering memories of the Great War and its indescribable stupidities lead to a reluctance to express even the smallest respect for the pomp of military display, while on the other hand the desire for it becomes sublimated into a kind of helpless nostalgia, nurtured on Elgar and Lutyens rather than on any real political allegiance. To overcome these over-delicate sensibilities it has proved necessary to shift all ceremonies of state in the direction of a civil meaning.

It is interesting to note how, in civil matters, loss of ceremony coincides with a loss of the distinction between individual and office, so that modern presidents and statesmen, in their efforts to claim for themselves, as personal attributes, what are in reality the dignities of their office, try to dispense in so far as they can with state ceremonies, becoming 'informal' only in order to seem the more extraordinary. Thus recent American presidents have cultivated a kind of easy-going informality, which has not only vulgarized the gestures of government, but also made the presidents themselves into objects of purely personal feeling. It is not the President but Mr Nixon, or Mr Clinton, or Mr Carter, who becomes the focus of attention. And so it is hardly surprising if Mr Clinton or Mr Carter is held personally liable for actions made necessary by their office, or if they are personally blamed, resented, voted for, and discarded, purely on account of some apprehension (however misguided or parochial) of their quality as individual people. It is important to see how dangerous it is for a state to cultivate this identity between the official and his office. For how can a president order the bombing of a city, if the blame is individually his? The aggressive acts of a state are, for the individual, morally impossible. Rather I should die than undertake to kill so many. But acting as President, the responsibility is mine only if I act illegitimately. And it is reasons of state which require that a city be bombed. Which is not to say that 'reasons of state' should always be listened to. There are just and unjust acts, even in war, whether or not the war itself is just.[76]

In reflecting on these matters, one may come to the conclusion that, among state institutions, that of constitutional monarchy is one of the wisest. In the figure of the monarch there is condensed all the ceremony of office, and all the majesty of the state. The personality of the monarch, being detached from direct involvement in government, is freed from the oppression of responsibility. And yet, through the intellectual construct of the 'Crown', the monarch also represents the entire authority of the state. If honours and authority stem from the Crown, then they are seen to flow objectively, not from personal whim, but from the life of the state. The process of ratification which arises from that will bear both ceremonial dignity, and the authority of the sovereign's office.

Ideology and myth

But now we can see how the institutions of state have their own way of generating ideology. Consider again the example of the army. The internal organization of army life generates a common code of conduct, the call of 'honour'. And while there is inevitably a certain rigidity about this code – for it must remain in harmony with the ruling military purpose – it is one which implicitly recognizes and endorses the distinctions between people.

Now this internal code of army life is paralleled in every purposeful institution. It corresponds to the professional 'ethic', to the 'solidarity' of the factory floor – indeed, to precedents, duties and answerabilities which proceed from any social organization, irrespective of whether they further or hinder its principal aim. Naturally these codes can be considered usually to be of service to the ruling purpose, but this is not necessarily the case. In business, for example, the professional ethic of fair dealing can put a company at an impossible disadvantage in international trade. This internal 'code' or 'ethic' is in its turn bound up with and reinforced by the features referred to: by offices, roles and ceremonies (nowhere more manifest than in the organized activities of the trade unions, which once tried to re-create, in some small measure, the glory of the guilds).

It is in considering again the true meaning of ceremony that we come across the most powerful and most intransigent feature of establishment, the feature of myth. All ceremony requires a symbolic depth – a sense that it reaches below the surface of things, and touches upon realities that cannot be translated into words. It thereby expresses something more than the chance union of these particular participants. It seems to point them to something 'transcendent', which they may only partly understand. The emotions which attach themselves to state ceremonies constantly outrun the objects which occasion them. Participants and spectators find themselves taken up into something greater, of which the reality of military or political power is no more than a pale reflection. Thus there emerges the myth of the 'glory' of the nation, the myth of its absolute unqualified right to allegiance. This myth belongs to every national culture, determining the form of its religion, art and literature, and being reinforced with every manifestation of civil or military power. It is out of such myths that war is made, and equally peace.

In referring to 'myth' I by no means wish to disparage these beliefs. On the contrary, they constitute the great artifact whereby institutions enter the life of the state and absorb the life of the citizen. In a sense the Marxists are right in saying that bourgeois man robs the world of history by creating myths which represent as natural and inevitable what is in fact historical and subject to change. But they are deeply wrong in supposing that it is only bourgeois man who does this, and that there is some other form of man for whom the necessity would not arise. For it is clear that my rudimentary sketch of military institutions (a sketch which points to their significance in the life of any state) ought to apply to all state institutions, in whatever form of economic order (even when the state is founded, like the Soviet Union, on the eccentric myth of its own 'withering away').

Religion

But this brings us to the ruling idea of establishment as it has thrived, made itself tolerable, and incorporated the various forms of life of the peoples of Europe: the idea of a Christian society. In *The Case for Conservatism*, Lord Hailsham was straightforward enough to place the connection between English conservatism and Christian practice at the heart of his political creed, arguing that 'there can be no genuine conservatism which is not founded upon a religious view of the basis of civil obligation, and there can be no true religion where the basis of civil obligation is treated as purely secular'.[77] In support of this, Hailsham quoted remarks by Burke and Disraeli, neither of whom ingenuously believed in the religion to which they both subscribed. They believed, if at all, in the self-conscious manner of the romantic, out of longing for an innocence which is lost in the process of reflecting on it. Naturally there are serious and complex attitudes involved in such belief. T. S. Eliot's Anglicanism, for example, was highly self-conscious but not hypocritical. But it is implausible to suggest that Burke, Disraeli or Eliot were types of the normal religious person.

Moreover, while there is a connection between conservative and religious feeling, it is now difficult to argue for their identity. Not only does that serve to exclude from the conservative viewpoint precisely those people who most seek to regain it – those for whom the passing of God from the world is felt as a reality – it has also left the creed of conservatism helpless in the face of the Church's growing disposition (in its vocal parts at least) to reject it.

Nevertheless, before discussing the issue of Church and State, we must look a little more closely at the motive of religion, if only because some might think that religion is one thing and politics another, and therefore that policy can be pursued without regard to the beliefs of the ordinary citizen. Of course, political activity may be independent of the existence of God, and independent of the will of God; but it is not independent of the belief in God. It is the possession of that belief which enables people to direct their most powerful dissatisfactions away from the ruinous hope of changing things, to a more peaceable hope of being one day redeemed from the need to do so. It follows that the state of religious belief will be reflected in the state of civil society, and will seek its expression in law. To think that politicians can proceed while ignoring the actual religious beliefs of those they propose to govern, is to view politics as a detached machinery of administration. Such a view is either unworkable (cf. Iran), or tyrannical (cf. Russia), and in any case hardly conservative.

The reflections of the last paragraph might lead one to suppose that religion is an essentially conservative force. It is certainly true that both Burke and Disraeli believed it to be so, and while their professions of faith were not necessarily a consequence of that belief (any more than are Lord Hailsham's), it is surely right to suggest the presence of a deep and complex intellectual connection underlying their commitment. The nature of this connection can be perceived at once, as soon as we consider again the character of the social bond. This bond, I have argued, is transcendent: it contains obligations and allegiances which cannot be seen as the result of contractual choice. It is a small step from belief in a transcendent bond to belief in the transcendent Being who upholds it. The vision of another and vaster world, from the laws of which all actual obligations spring, lends incomparable support to bonds that were never contracted. Seeing such bonds as the expression of Providence, people will be the more disposed to accept them. They will accept as a divine command what they might reject as a personal undertaking. It is some such message, the cynic might say, that is contained in the quoted remark of Hailsham's.

Nevertheless, the acceptance of transcendent bonds does not require belief in transcendent beings. The Japanese, who are famous (indeed, notorious) for their willingness to accept the former, are equally remarkable for their reluctance to believe in the latter. And the Romans, to whom we are indebted for the concept of piety, were casual and even non-committal in matters of religion (a feature which they shared with the more dexterous representatives of the Papacy). It would seem then that the conservative vision of society can survive in the absence of clear religious belief, despite the fact that it will always benefit from its presence. However, there is nothing more dangerous to the state than the transfer of frustrated religious feeling to petty secular causes. In so far as religious feeling exists, it is therefore better that it be channelled towards its proper object. And if its existence sustains the social order, then that is another reason to propagate and also to influence it.

Church and state

But we cannot discuss these issues until we have considered the nature of religious institutions. Whatever part religious feelings play in providing the background sentiments of establishment, it is with the offices of religion that politicians must deal. So – in a Christian or post-Christian society – they will first have to concern themselves with the Church. The power of the Church, while it ultimately depends upon the power of religious feeling, has the backing of historical precedent, hereditary privilege and popular trust. Whatever the legal position of the Church, it continues to provide the major institutions which reinforce the attachment of citizens to the forms of civil life, and which turn their attention away from themselves as individuals and towards themselves as social beings. It provides ceremonial embellishment to every kind of leisure, apportions the days of work and the days of rest, seeks to dignify the occupations of the laity, and to support and fulfil every endeavour in which the application outstrips the aim. Be its fundamental doctrines true or false, it is nevertheless the most considerable of all institutions whose authority is not identical with the authority of the state. It is therefore fully established in European life, so much so that all the institutions to which I have referred have recourse to it as the one binding principle which joins them together. Consider the family, education, even the military.

But it is in the relations of Church and state that we find one of the most difficult problems for conservative doctrine, and one of the most elusive features of establishment. It goes without saying that much of European politics was until recently determined by the state of these relations. Every attempt to break away from Rome has led to the incorporation of a rival Christian church into the political establishment.

The influence of the Church of Rome shows, however, that there can be 'establishment' without military power, and that there can be the values associated with establishment even when an institution is not specifically ratified by a sovereign power.

We must recognize, therefore, that the fact of establishment, as I am attempting to describe it, is not merely a legal or constitutional idea. Establishment at the state level may not be required, when establishment at the level of civil society is sufficiently entrenched. The Catholic Church, because of its amazing constitution, has bestowed on itself the quality of establishment throughout Italy, Ireland, Spain, France, and even (what is now of great political significance) Poland. In comparison with the influence and power of Rome, the legally established Church of England seems more feeble even than that of Russia under the communists, when most of the Orthodox bishops were agents of the KGB. Likewise the organized trade-union movement in England acquired under post-war Labour administrations some of the features of establishment, even though it is not (and as I shall argue cannot be) legally established under the existing constitution. Establishment, while it means something more than power, may require something less than direct incorporation into the apparatus of the state. The authority which it requires may arise directly from its ability to generate consoling myths, provided these myths prepare people for the acceptance of a given civil order.

According to the ancient system of precedence, our Lords Temporal and Lords Spiritual stand in similar proximity to the Sovereign. But the power of the second amounts to very little when it ceases to convey the authority vested in their calling. Whether it be a passing fashion, or whether it be the sign of a deeper uncertainty, it is undeniable that the leadership of the Church – and not only of the Anglican Church – has begun to reject the old order of European society. Some see in this nothing more than the effort of the Church to remain established at all costs, however much the prevailing political forces may change. And certainly, from its beginning, the Church has had that attitude, as can be seen from Tertullian's assertion on its behalf, less than two centuries after the death of Christ: 'We are for ever making intercession for the emperors. We pray that they might enjoy long life, secure rule, a safe home, brave armies, a faithful senate, and honest people, a quiet world, and everything for which a man and a Caesar may pray ...'

However, it is most implausible that the Church should retain political power while losing its spiritual authority. The instinct to which it appeals is, in fact, a conservative instinct, manifest principally at the momentous occasion of death, when people feel their fragility, their need of protection and the proximity of transcendent things. The true meaning of the Church in civil life leads away from the political issues which have bemused its leaders, for whom 'third-world-ism' has replaced the spirit of mission. The consequent weakness in an institution which, while necessarily political, has lost the true principle of its politics, and therefore the allegiance of its congregation, is a source of almost universal discomfort, so that already the religious sense seeks fulfilment elsewhere than in any kind of orthodoxy. Mere legal establishment is no substitute for political centrality: the place of the Church is either at the heart of things, or nowhere. Whichever it is to be, the Church will have significance only if it attends to the consoling myths which have drawn people to it. Were the Church to become merely the helpless repository of secular causes – a kind of sanctimonious addendum to Gay Power – then the objective dimension of its authority would disappear.

Consider, for example, what becomes of death and burial when the Church retreats from its inherited prescriptions. The old rituals and dogmas of the Church served to create the sense of continuity in death; they spread around the dead person a kind of embrace as though receiving a soul into its natural home. When there is no custom, no common dogma, no solemn enactment, then death and burial become mysterious. Thrown back into the trauma of ultimate personal choice, people do not know how to proceed. Uncomprehended necromancy is summoned, alien religions are experimented with; even the world of art is called upon to make sense of this unknowable thing (as in the vast triumph of human confusion at Forest Lawn). The oneness between the living and the dead is destroyed, and the dead themselves, having lost individuality in a world where only individuals have meaning, are cast overboard, so to speak, to float in rubbishy waves back across the sea of history, encumbered by the flotsam of a thousand irrelevant creeds.

With the eclipse of religious feeling comes the loss of the consciousness of destiny. People need the concept of fortune: they need to believe that matters which deeply concern them may nevertheless be removed from remedy or blame. The belief in Providence relieves the harshness of this outlook. Distinctions of beauty, health, intelligence and capacity are natural; they are also essential to our ideals of human perfection. Not to see them under the aspect of fortune is to lose one's grip on human things, to become fascinated by a fantasy of interference, to take steps towards that brave new world in which the pervasive meddling in what is 'given' destroys both nature and value together. Not seeing birth as a part of fortune, a person might sue his parents for their lack of genetic control, or lay blame for his deformity upon the doctor who refused to abort him. We should not think that these cases are fantastical. At this very moment they lie before American courts of law.

Such is the confusion that the idea of fortune served to control that, lacking it, people find it hard to accept, and hard even to entertain, one of the fundamental thoughts upon which civilization depends, the thought that there is a profound, mysterious and beneficial difference between women and men. The thought that I exist as an individual independently of my sex, is one with the thought that my sex might have been chosen. So that, being only accidentally male, I experience my sexuality as alien. It is not of my essence. It has become an attribute, which I might change as I change my clothes. Much passes from the world when sexuality is seen in this way. In particular, the clarity in the relations between man and woman disappears – being an accident, sexuality ceases to determine their relationship. It becomes a confused performance, of no more emotional significance than a shaking of hands. That is what Henry James foretold as the 'decline in the sentiment of sex'.

The 'demystification' of our religious outlook has brought with it the complete mystification of fundamental things: roughly speaking, of birth, copulation and death. At the same time the theory that there are not, cannot be, or ought not to be, important or immovable differences between sexes, races, and even individuals, is upheld with a bigotry that has all the fervour of religion, yet with none of religion's consoling power. The absurdities of secular ideology – 'political correctness' as it is now called – are such that one can hardly believe it to be the expression of an improved education or a growing enlightenment. Its claim to clarity of thought masks the fact that it engenders unclarity of feeling. People 'hesitate to feel': every chance to expend personality in emotion is made meaningless, momentary or grotesque. It seems then that the withdrawal of religious doctrine does, after all, bring about a withering in transcendent social bonds. Religion – and in particular Christianity – was too much a part of the common way of seeing things. The destruction of its dogmas, its liturgy, its rituals, and its ceremonial presence, has left a vacuum.

The very unsatisfactoriness of the secular picture of the human condition leads one to suspect that it will not in fact last. There will be religious revivals; hence the need for an established religion, and, if possible, for an established Church. In times of disestablishment religion fragments into fierce and muddled gestures – as among Levellers, Ranters, Muggletonians and Seekers during the Interregnum. It is with no surprise that one should observe the spread of Manichean sects and witchcraft in America. Moreover, one cannot regard as 'apolitical' beliefs which explode with such violence on impact with the air. A firm established Church, with a tradition of non-conformism that relies on the same sacred texts and practices, is able to gratify the search for religion both immediately and intelligently. Perhaps popular feeling is still seeking for such a Church.[78] If that is so, then the loss of authority in ecclesiastical offices must be attributed not to the offices but to their present incumbents.

The trade unions

I shall return to the question of ecclesiastical politics – for clearly, those last remarks raise questions which are not merely questions of policy. I have assumed that the religious sentiments of our nation are not extinguished but merely eclipsed and that this eclipse is largely the result of liberal-minded 'enlightenment'. And the vast social power of religion seeks endorsement from the state – if not explicitly, as in the United Kingdom, then implicitly, as in the dominions of Rome. How this is done becomes clear when we consider another institution that is, as it were, on the edge of establishment, the institution of the Trades Union Congress.

It would be a quibble to argue that, because it is only *de facto* that the Lords Temporal are partly drawn from the trade-union ranks and because the privileges of the trade unions at law (for example, the privileges in contract and tort granted by the Liberal Trade Disputes Act of 1906, and re-enacted in the Conservative Trades Union and Labour Relations Act) are only privileges, and not part of the overt constitution of the state, therefore the labour movement and all that it represents is not part of the establishment of British politics. The process whereby the trade unions have moved towards a position of establishment is a recent one, and as much the outcome of unintended accidents as of real political choice. But this move has served to anchor in the national consciousness a new body of myth, and an indelible impression of the reality both of class distinctions and of the social mobility which has always mitigated them.

But is the establishment of the labour movement complete, even at the civil level? Nobody seems to have a clear or coherent answer. Conservatives used to try to prevent the completion of the process, being frightened at the irresponsibility of trade-union power, and at the threat to democracy involved in the close and exclusive relation that exists between this powerful autonomous body and a parliamentary party to which it 'pledged' sole support. But that very 'pledge' had about it an air of myth, and the myth is one that derives directly from a value that informs the civil order – the value of 'solidarity', integral to the feeling of class. It would be hard to oppose it directly; much easier to incorporate the trade unions into the apparatus of the state. Besides, if, as I have suggested, the constitution of Britain has in fact only a small part that is governed by democratic representation, and if the conservative's main interest is in the continuance of that larger part in which the institutions of civil life are enshrined, then it seems difficult to reject the undemocratic ethos of the Trades Union Congress, unless one believes it to be genuinely subversive.

Here lies a main source of confusion. If a power cannot be ratified (say, because its purposes are at variance with those of government) then it is subversive. Now extraordinary qualities of leadership would be required to fight the trade-union movement with the weapons of the state; for it could be done only if the loyalty of the working class were first detached from that movement. If there are signs, therefore, that the trade-union movement really is subversive – that it seeks power without responsibility, and so resists ratification in the institutions of government – it would be necessary to create and encourage rival organizations which attract the loyalty of the present union membership. In particular it would be necessary to foster and encourage 'unofficial' strikes, 'unofficial' unions, and 'unofficial' returns to work, since these are a usurpation of trade-union power, and a snub to its self-constituted authority. Such was Margaret Thatcher's successful tactic, in confronting the National Union of Mineworkers under Arthur Scargill. Moreover, one could envisage sound conservative principles that would wish for the proliferation of 'unofficial' actions. Labour disputes would again become contractual. That is to say, they would consist in a confrontation not between 'classes' but between a particular employer and his staff – a confrontation that may not spread beyond the workplace, and would be resolved either in the destitution of the parties, or in a revised contract of work. Such 'industrial action' would serve to remove labour relations from the centre of politics, and to confine them to the business of civil life. The contractual nature of the labour relation would then be fully upheld, as would its security. Within no time the trade-union movement – as an independent power – would wither and die. In effect we now see this happening, as a result of recent Tory legislation which makes it impossible for workers to be called out on strike without a local ballot; and the result has been both a weakening of the TUC, and a decline in the class-sentiment that inspired it – to such extent, indeed, that relations between the TUC and the New Labour

Party, whose power base is among the middle classes, are almost as strained as relations used to be between the TUC and the Tories.

New corruption

It might seem that the trade-union movement would be loath to become part of the establishment. For while there is some truth in the view that 'in decisive questions people feel their class membership more profoundly than their membership of society',[79] does that not make it impossible for the trade unions to become affiliated to any kind of ruling class? Did not their claim to authority rest on the view that the class they represented was the class not of rulers but of ruled? If the aim was simply to abolish the distinction, then it was an aim that could not succeed. Besides, such an aim is incompatible with the myths that provided the trade unions with their erstwhile image of authority.

The trade unions were therefore faced with a choice. And the nature of this choice is most clearly seen when it is recognized that it is in the interests of the state to grant, if it can, legal establishment to all *de facto* established powers. Power then becomes directly answerable to the interests of the state, and its autonomy is restricted in all those issues where it may be an obstacle to policy. Compare the easy relations between Church and state in England since the accession of William of Orange, with the uneasy relations between Rome and the rulers and rebels of France, resolved only in the magnificent gesture of Napoleon at his coronation. And compare the disorder created by trade-union power in England with its tranquil exercise in communist Russia. This answerability can have far-reaching effects. It was the House of Commons that in 1929 fought the proposals for the reform of the Book of Common Prayer. And when the Worship and Doctrine Measure of 1974 was unsuccessfully opposed in Parliament it was to the great detriment of the power and authority of the Church. (It was this measure that has allowed the creeping disestablishment of the Church, so that 'alternative services' can be laid before the congregations as though it were freedom rather than certainty that they wished for.) It is still an office of government to ratify the choice of bishops. While the Church – resenting these intrusions – has tried to move further from the centre of power, it is also clear that there can still be a successful ecclesiastical politics that would force it either to lose itself in mediocrity and faction or to return to its social centrality. That is why the current popular feeling against the fragmentation of ecclesiastical authority can still find its political expression. In general it is through the process of ratification that the state makes institutions into subjects. And thereby it remains aloof from the interests that compose it.

It follows that there is a certain self-destructiveness in a trade-union movement that is fully established. Such a movement claims to possess the authority of a class; it cannot aim to destroy the feelings of class without destroying its own authority. If it is wise, it therefore hovers always on the fringes of direct establishment, since it loses more than it gains by pressing itself into the centre of power. Most of all, in losing its class identity, it loses its close relation to the working class. It was therefore in the interests of the state that union leaders were able to accept and rejoice in peerages. It is in the interest of state that they were granted powers and privileges that completely outran the power that arises autonomously. Under Old Labour governments, trade-union officials became recipients of extensive political patronage. (In 1977, according to one estimate,[80] 39 members of the TUC General Council held no fewer than 180 state offices between them – most of them salaried.) This 'New Corruption' was of vast extent – vaster by far than the patronage exerted by the Whigs or by the Stuart monarchy. But it would have been misguided for a conservative to oppose it. For the sudden emergence of a power into the offices of government spells the eventual diminution of that power, and its incorporation into the state. Initially it was costly. But in the long run it has surely been beneficial. The influence of the trade unions over their membership became less a matter of will than of office. And the oligarchical nature of trade-union power enabled the state to deal directly with a small number of stubborn but often bribable officials. It is true that what was thereby established was not the labour movement itself (which began to seek 'unofficial', and consequently less damaging expression), but a collection of interests that have used the labour movement as a means to power. Having obtained power, they then retired with the profits.

Class

The examples that I have chosen show that ratification is basic to conservative government, in that it provides the process whereby the power of the state links itself to and becomes one with the power of society. But as we have seen, there have been efforts to sunder the two, as well as attempts to win ratification by powers unsuited to it. In all this we have encountered the principal social reality of Britain: its clear, but flexible, social stratification.

To speculate further on the origin and structure of social classes is no part of my purpose: it suffices that they exist and that everything that I have described so far as integral to conservative doctrine seems to point to their existence as a necessity. The conservative must believe that class distinctions can be represented either as a necessary evil or as a social good. And the question will turn upon the extent to which their power reflects, or can be made to reflect, a genuine acceptance on the part of those who do not partake of the privileges – whatever they might be – which divide upper from lower in the social scale. The conservative is likely to think that this acceptance can be induced, and even that there might be no enduring sense of legitimacy without it.

In one of his deepest reflections on the relation between public and private life, Shakespeare wrote thus:

> Take but degree away, untune that string,
> And, hark, what discord follows! each thing meets
> In mere oppugnancy: the bounded waters
> Should lift their bosoms higher than the shores,
> And make a sop of all this solid globe:
> Strength should be lord of imbecility,
> And the rude son should strike his father dead:
> Force should be right; or, rather, right and wrong –
> Between whose endless jar justice resides –
> Should lose their names, and so should justice too.
> Then everything includes itself in power,
> Power into will, will into appetite.
> *Troilus and Cressida, 1, iii*

We speak now not of degree but of class: the social arrangements of the modern world do not contain the complexities of precedence which Shakespeare saw as morally indispensable. Nevertheless, what he wrote contains an insight. The disintegration of authority means the collapse of justice. Power is once again at large in the world, reducing itself from rational will to appetite: social fragmentation then begins. The purpose of establishment is to prevent fragmentation. Hence we must ascend from power back to authority. How can that be done, unless people are prepared to recognize – in this or that individual, in this or that office – a vested authority by which they are constrained? And is it not plausible to suggest that, if this habit of deference arises, however qualified and however disparately directed, it is better that it should find the world already adequately provided with objective signs of authority, in the form of office, position, and established right? And how, if that is so, can one either prevent or bewail the formation of social classes, in which the unequal distribution of power becomes ratified by an unequal distribution of authority? One must surely therefore be tempted by the view of Shakespeare's Ulysses, that the artifact of authority is one with the artifact of class.

Does that give cause for complaint? Certainly the mere fact that one person has what another does not have is not itself the cause of envy, nor does it cast credit on the one who has or remove it from the one who has not, nor does it in any way directly undermine their sense of belonging to a common civil society. If it were true that class distinctions were merely economic – reflections of the relation to the means of production and of the extent to which that relation can translate itself into private wealth – then it would perhaps be true that in a wholly materialistic society (a society with no myths other than those engendered by money), class distinctions could at once translate themselves into open war. But the United Kingdom has enjoyed a kind of permanent (if at times uneasy) truce. The occasional outbreaks of war have tended to take a religious form. If we are to accept the economic definition of class, then we should have to say that the present conflict in Northern Ireland is internal to a single class: an idea that looks very odd when set beside socialist theories of 'class struggle'. And it is equally odd to use those theories in describing the English Civil War. For there is no single economic category to which the contending factions in that war can be assigned. Historical explanation becomes immediately clear and plausible when we study not economic control, but ideology – in particular, when we study the religious and cultural rivalries that so suddenly burgeoned in that age. If we are to speak of 'class war', it is a war that is fought, if at all, on the level of myth, and achieves there a variable, but for the most part peaceable, compromise. Economic distinctions then cease to be important in determining class feelings, and no change in the economic order is likely to eradicate them.

If that is true, then it is surely easier to understand social class in terms of an ideological picture than in terms of relative wealth or economic control. The middle class, for example, which devotes its resources to education, to the purchase of durable goods, to the general stance and improvement of the 'self' is, as a result of these costly interests, seldom conceived as an object of envy by a class that does not share them. Only a minority of the 'middle' class is in a position actually to dispose of wealth greater than that available to the average working man. And that minority in its turn is unlikely to be seen by the upper class – whose command of social intercourse in no way corresponds to any real command of material resources – as qualified for admission to its circle. Here all the complexities, and almost all the realities, have to be seen in other than economic terms.[81] Hence the myths which enable people to see a given social position as natural can develop independently of the transfer of wealth. It is this sense of the 'natural' quality of social divisions that is created by the autonomous institutions examined in the last chapter. Education, for example, 'naturalizes' property, by making it the instrument of social success. (In periods of the highest culture, therefore, wealth tends to take on a symbolic form, the form of luxury, splendour and *gloire*.) If there has been a problem of class, it has been because the working class, during the years of its formation, lacked the institutions through which to 'naturalize' its predicament. If this was so (and many people have argued the point), then it was not because the working man inevitably resented his station, but rather because he lacked the home-grown institutions that gave inwardness and consolation to his way of life.

The growth of popular sports and entertainment in our time, and the creation of a popular culture based in TV, football and mechanized music, have to some extent enabled people to live without those home-grown institutions. They have also effectively abolished the working class as a moral idea, provided everyone with a classless picture of human society, and in doing so produced a new kind of social stratification – one which reflects the 'division of leisure' rather than the 'division of labour'. Traditional societies divide into upper, middle and working class. In modern societies that division is overlaid by another, which also contains three classes. The new classes are, in ascending order, the morons, the yuppies and the stars. The first watch TV, the second make the programmes, and the third appear on them. And because those who appear on the screen cultivate the manners of the people who are watching them, implying that they are only there by accident, and that tomorrow it may very well be the viewer's turn, all possibility of resentment is avoided. At the same time, the emotional and intellectual torpor induced by TV neutralizes the social mobility that would otherwise enable the morons to change their lot. So obvious is this, that it is dangerous to say it. Class distinctions have not disappeared from modern life; they have merely become unmentionable.

One might agree with the socialist historian who claimed that 'class is defined by men as they live their own history, and, in the end, this is its only definition'.[82] But then one moves away from the view that classes arise from the varying relations to the means of production, and away from the view that classes must necessarily be at war. Classes are shaped and made tolerable by their own self-image. There seems, then, to be no reason why we should think of class distinctions as evil or unjust. They stem from the basic principles of social order; hence it will be an important part of conservative politics to uphold the picture through which they acquire their validity.

The welfare state

In the past the relations between classes were often mediated not by the state but by the Church, which was the principal agent of charity, the provider of education to those who could not otherwise afford it, and the generator of a career structure through which talent and industry were rewarded by social and political power. The idea of a universal education is not a modern invention; nor indeed can we be sure that the standard of education of the lowest classes of society has noticeably improved (except locally) since the decretals of Pope Gregory IX. (By the end of the fourteenth century all legal restrictions forbidding the education of villeins had been abolished, having been more or less ignored through two hundred preceding years. And by 1400 the Paris *scholasticus* was able to command each parish to provide for scholars both rich and poor the education of the *trivium* – an education requiring greater mental exertion than anything demanded by a modern primary school.) This general supervision of the exercise of charity naturally sustained the institutions of private property and legitimized inequalities of wealth. The recipient of charity was the recipient not of a personal gift but of an objective privilege associated with his actual impotence. The Church legitimized the self-seeking of the rich, as it consoled the misery of the poor, by constantly ministering to the spiritual needs of each only on condition that the one should alleviate, while the other should accept, the lot of poverty.

Wise people, seeing the gradual retreat of the Church from the offices of civil life, sought always to supplement or replace its ministrations through organized poor relief, and through public facilities of education and medical care. Over such issues conservatives and radicals have often fought together. But it was not until the last century that the full force was experienced of the political obligation to provide (either through compulsory insurance, or through direct provision) a complete system of welfare for those who could not otherwise afford it. Thus Bismarck, in creating the Prussian state, incorporated into its constitution a standing principle of social welfare. It was thereby possible for the professional classes both to pursue the tasks which make them indispensable, and to gather adequate material reward for doing so (a reward adequate to maintain the self-image without which the professions would wither away). At the same time the poorer sections of the community were supported in the needs which they could not satisfy alone, and so sustained in the sale of their labour. The result was the welfare state, as a distinctive form of capitalist society.

The welfare state has become a social and political necessity. Nevertheless it requires the support of a highly qualified professional class, which will seek its rewards either at home or (since mobility is its most evident feature) wherever else it may be provided. It is therefore important to sustain all the trappings of 'private' advantage, despite the universal dispensation of medicine, education, shelter and bread. Doctors, lawyers and teachers – who, because they provide the services, are the principal beneficiaries of the welfare state – need to be sustained in the self-image of their professions. This self-image arises only if there are autonomous institutions – inns of court, medical societies, private schools – devoted to the internal purposes of law, medicine and scholarship. Hence the success of the welfare state will always depend upon the existence of flourishing and partly autonomous institutions. The state may profit from those institutions, but it cannot wholly absorb them, without risking the hostility or the demoralization of the professional class. If it profits from these institutions it is because they have a life of their own, and it cannot be part of the pursuit of welfare to destroy that life.

In every institution of the establishment the interests and identity of the separate classes have to be consulted and reconciled. That is merely the business of government, and the unavoidable corollary of power. It is clear, then, what the conservative view of the welfare state must be. English conservatives will not – like their American counterparts[83] – regard it as an abomination, neither will they seek to extend it beyond the point which ordinary humanity requires. They will be reluctant to see the state make weaklings or dependants of its citizens, and yet at the same time they will not cancel what has become a hereditary right. The important thing has been to maintain, through all this compulsory charity, the professional self-respect which makes true charity possible.

The issue is again one of ratification. Poverty and indigence are powers at large in the state. Not to relieve them is to foster resentment. It is to encourage a permanent and universal sense of the moral instability of the social order. Yet to relieve want is one thing, to make all people equal in respect of it another. And to inflict on the professional classes a compulsory form of charity without regard to the moral specificity of the charitable motive, is to destroy the ability of that class, either to profit from its industry, or to make itself acceptable to those who do not belong to it. To bring all these forces together in an established system of right and duty is a matter of the utmost political delicacy. And the first step towards that end must involve the separation of the idea of public welfare from the egalitarian crusades with which it has become entangled. The purpose of the welfare state is not to abolish the distinction between rich and poor, but to encourage people to accept it.

The danger, however, is that, by relieving indigence, one also rewards it. A new form of exploitation arises – exploitation from below – in which a class which has never fended for itself, is reproduced by means of welfare, becoming a permanent cost to the state. And the cost is not only economic. Indiscriminate welfare produces crime, family breakdown, illegitimacy and drug abuse.[84] The response of American conservatives has been to recommend 'work-fare' rather than 'welfare' programmes, offering relief only to those who are prepared to re-enter the community as productive citizens. This return to the ethos of the work-house has much to recommend it. But it·does not solve the real problem: which is that of illegitimacy, and the social breakdown which follows when illegitimacy is normalized. The cure for this is not to reward the actions which lead to an unmanageable underclass, but to punish them. And it is in this matter that all the thinking still needs to be done.

Concluding remarks

I have tried to show, through a series of examples, how the powers that flow through civil life can seek and achieve establishment in a constituted state. Establishment is the great internal aim of politics: the aim of government. It is through this that the forces of society become subject to the power of the state, by finding authority through the authority of the state. The conservative belief is that the order of the state must be objective, comprehensive, and felt to be legitimate, so that the contrasting conditions of society can achieve their ideological fulfilment by being subject to a common sovereign power. Without this completion in establishment civil society remains always on the brink of fragmentation.

But to maintain establishment it is necessary to uphold the offices of state as distinct and honorific. It is equally important to combat the attempt of power to constitute itself independently. Hence there is an important motive for trying to represent the authority of certain peripheral institutions as stemming from government. But when these institutions generate an internal sense of opposition (which is to say, when they represent themselves as being not governed, but oppressed), then the process of establishment, however desirable, becomes fraught with difficulties. It is these cases that require the greatest political acumen, and which generate the major political problems of our age.

It remains now to say something more general about the relation between individual and state, and about the distinction – briefly touched on in this chapter – between public and private life.

9
The Public World

The last two chapters have surveyed those areas of domestic politics where social cohesion is lost and formed. It is in these areas, on behalf of 'freedom', 'equality', or whatever enthusiasm should command the time, that the fissure between state and society is opened. My description has been inward, concerned with the motives of cohesion and their ratification in the *status quo*. But society has both a public and a private life. It declares itself through gestures of authority, which embrace citizen and alien alike. The state is the completion, and also the champion, of society. It is only through the formation of a state that a society can come into direct, secure and explicit relation with its neighbours.

The nation state

The state is no modern invention. Every society contains the seeds of a constitution, in the form of custom, tradition, precedent and law. But it may have to fight to preserve these, and from every successful fight a degree of 'nationhood' emerges. For most of us the state means, not just government, but also territory, language, administration, established institutions, all growing from the interaction of unconscious custom and reflective choice. The nation state is the state at the extreme of self-consciousness. It has its territory, its people, its language, sometimes even its church. And it holds these things up to the world not as gifts of nature but as rights of possession for which it is prepared to commit its citizens to die.

From the spirit of the nation state much good has sprung, and also much harm. Without this spirit the very idea of a 'balance of power'

174

would be impossible, and peace correspondingly more precarious. But this balance of power depends upon a sinister invention – that of the conscript army. Nations now fight wholly, absolutely and to the death. Every man, woman and child takes part in the struggle, and it is assumed that such is war. Renaissance Italy produced the highest culture, resplendent institutions, a constant surge of political life – all from a state of war. But war was semi-private, conducted by mercenaries who changed sides when plunder or payment tempted them No mercenaries would have planned the battle of the Somme, the siege of Stalingrad or the bombing of Dresden and Hiroshima. Now such things are the normal course of war.

For good or ill, the nation state is the condition of Europe, and the most settled way of representing to the people the complex notion of political allegiance. Given this fact, it is only an unfortunate society that cannot lay claim to nationhood. Nevertheless, such is the fierceness of our attachment to that which we regard as our own, that societies may endure through conquest, occupation and reform. Consider the fate of Poland, overcome again and again by rival powers, yet resolute in the defence of its identity, aided and abetted by the Church of Rome. Consider too Alsace, and the many unfortunate states which, barely released from the benign authority of the Austro-Hungarian Empire, were almost at once incorporated into the barbarous empire of the Soviets.

If I have tried to argue against the reforming spirit in British politics, it is partly because it constitutes a threat, not only to the state, but also to society. The spirit of reform has been too much concerned with private 'rights', and not enough concerned with the public order and private duties that make them possible. Since public order is now the order of a nation state, foreign policy and national identity are its immovable preconditions. It is perhaps true that nationhood has become necessary only in recent times. When a royal dowry could contain a whole domain, together with its laws and customs (so that Flanders could pass by a kind of domestic agreement from Spain to France), then it can hardly be thought that this fact of ownership had any great effect upon the continuity of social life. But now we must struggle for that continuity, and lack the consoling ideas (such as the idea of 'Christendom') through which to view the sovereign as given to the society just as much as the society is surrendered to the sovereign power. The nation state has therefore become a necessity. At the same time, its citizens need to be protected from the state's encroachments, and it has even been said that the ruling conservative motive in this world of nations is to 'roll back the frontiers of the state'.

If there is any meaning to this slogan it is this: that in order to maintain and assert its power, the state must concern itself first with those matters which could not be ordered by private initiative. It must maintain law and order, the defence of the realm, and the framework within which individuals can pursue their ambitions in ways that contribute to social harmony. No doubt this implies that the state must also withdraw from direct participation in enterprise and manufacture, where its role is to regulate, but not to initiate. However, we have seen a staggering growth in regulation in recent years. It is almost as though the universal conversion of political parties to private enterprise and the market has happened only because the state has found itself able to control our lives more effectively through regulation than through ownership.

Over-regulation results in part from the decline in the sense of nationhood. The nation state is a state in which law springs from within, expressing the mutuality and the common allegiance of the people. In such a state there is a clear perception of the limits to law, and a jealous attachment to freedom. The European Union grew from a hostility among the post-war elites to the idea of nationhood. Nations, they believed, cause wars, whereas unions settle them. (The American civil war seems not to have come to their attention.) Hence arose a system of trans-national regulation, which called on no national loyalty as its endorsement, and which was imposed as law without having the moral force of law. The resulting bureaucracy has set itself the task of dissolving national loyalties, by dividing the continent into regions rather than nations. In this way local loyalties will be severed from legal sovereignty, and laws will be imposed on communities from outside. It should be evident that there is no prospect for conservative politics in such a situation. The task of conservatism is not to 'roll back the frontiers of the state', but to re-establish the frontiers of the nation state, and to reanimate the natural hostility that we feel, towards laws that are imposed on us by people with whom we do not in our heart of hearts belong.

The statesman

The public world must be a reality, possessed of the power, dignity and centrality that will make it so. Politics creates the image of public life, and of the statesman as leader of the people. The conception of leadership is not an easy one. Far easier, indeed, for a statesman to pose as an ordinary and unassuming person, with an arduous employment from which he would rather retire. Thus he earns sympathy, appeases enmity, lives in so far as he can without the burden of office. But he does not serve the people. There is a deep and ineradicable demand that decisions should both issue from the statesman, and at the same time represent the interests of subject powers. A statesman must be a 'figure of state' – someone whose identity bears the impress of the state, and who seems to act and speak for interests that are simultaneously the state's and his own. His decisions must be intelligible to the citizen as decisions which affect the general welfare, but which without the statesman's will and adroitness could have been neither conceived nor made. It goes without saying that much of the dignity of statesmanship is lost in the current deference towards the 'expert opinion', the 'advisory body', the 'commission of inquiry', the complex of established civil servants whose expert knowledge can never amount to wisdom, and who are themselves in need of the guidance which no mere body of facts or statistics could provide.

There are various ways through which a statesman might become the public voice of the nation. Domestically this can be achieved through the ceremony of office. In a republic ceremony attaches directly to the president, providing an immediate sense of the reality of presidential power. In a monarchy, however, it attaches to the monarch: it represents, not the power and significance of a particular office, but the dignity of the state. It is difficult to doubt the wisdom of this. Since losing monarchy France and Italy have undergone constant upheaval, because in those countries opposition must necessarily appear to be disloyal. The dignities of the state are successively borrowed by temporary presidents, who represent, not the state, but some dominant faction within it. A rival faction, in setting itself against the one in power, must therefore first confront the state as the incumbent president's mantle.

In Britain the dignities of the state have not in general belonged to any politician but to the sovereign. Opposition is therefore contained within the institutions of government. It is no longer a joke to speak of 'Her Majesty's Opposition': that is the reality. Until recently, the only special dignity which the Prime Minister enjoyed was the dignity of office, all other dignities being bestowed, not equally or impartially, but at least widely, over the factions which have power enough to want and strive for them. This is now changing as a result of the populist stunts of Tony Blair and his spin-doctors, the purpose of which is to present the Prime Minister as an elected monarch, with absolute powers bestowed by popular vote. For the duration of the New Labour regime, therefore, offices will be expropriated by their tenants, and objective authority displaced by personal charisma. Only in some future Parliament will the country be again led by a true servant of the Crown.

Foreign policy

More important, however, in creating the public world of politics, is the dealing between states. The statesman is seen as protecting the country's privileges, furthering its advantages, exercising the force, cunning or bargaining power which are *ours*, and which represent our inviolable claim to exist as a free and independent people. An unfortunate effect of the reformist attitude is that it turns political activity away from international affairs towards domestic issues, which become exaggerated out of all proportion to their real significance. But it is in international affairs that the reality of government is most clear. Foreign policy, under the rule of reform, becomes cagey, non-committal and vague. Unable to measure up to the powers that surround us, we cease from the habit of bargaining with them and make public exhibition of our 'conscience' over past glory and colonial power.

The result has been a strange mixture of impetuosity and dither. In place of the 'concert of Europe', the League of Nations, and a hesitant treaty of defence, we enthusiastically subject ourselves to a law that is not our own. In place of colonial power we hand out vast sums to countries which are either hostile or indifferent to our interests, and whose people will never benefit from the gesture.[85] Either we are an international power or we are not. And if we are not we must secure our place by treaty. We prefer to forget the ideas of war, defence and civil order. To turn Western Europe from an alliance of nations to an anonymous bureaucracy; to allow civil war to continue undeclared within our frontiers; to acquiesce in the devolution of power to parliaments which have no true sovereignty – these constitute a retreat from the public reality of nationhood. It is hardly surprising if the British people have come to doubt their national identity.

But for a democracy international politics is difficult and ungainly. A dictatorship moves with unchanging will and makes long strategic gestures. Bismarck had insight and genius. But without dictatorship he could not have created the German nation state. The incumbents of the Kremlin were anonymous, inscrutable and perhaps not particularly intelligent. But they too, through maintaining a single stubborn policy over years, made steady advances towards the empire that they desired, notwithstanding the social fragmentation and economic catastrophe which they thereby engineered for the Russian people. An elected government – unless ruled with style – makes gestures for the present moment alone.

To adopt some single-minded domestic purpose – the purpose of equality, say, or of free enterprise – is a familiar gesture in the face of international threat. But no purpose makes sense without the continuance of civil order. The true statesman must make decisions not out of some overriding policy or ideal, but out of the day-to-day necessities of politics, and from a desire to present in the public forum a symbol of national continuity. De Gaulle's greatness consists in the fact that, by two or three gestures of command in foreign affairs, he was suddenly able to transform the confusion of civil life in post-war France into a concerted harmony, to command renewed respect towards the institutions of the state, and to establish stable government where there had previously been chaos. Conservative statesmen, since they are not misled by dominant ideals or internationalist philosophies, are able to perceive the necessity for such gestures, and to make them when the moment requires.

The private world

In this book I have argued for a view of legitimacy that places public before private, society before individual, duty before right. Nevertheless, the satisfactions of social life, and the motive to engage in it, lie only with the individual. And individuals have become sophisticated beings, anxious for a sphere of privacy in which to seclude the eccentricities that fulfil them. Their fulfilment, they think, is impossible without the 'right of privacy' which Englishmen regard as indefeasible.

But what does this right amount to when unprotected by the state? Nothing. What is fulfilment without the values of a social order? Nothing. And what is eccentricity without the norm against which to measure it? Nothing. This Anglo-Saxon privacy which we esteem is in fact nothing more than the public order, seen from within. It is not the vacuous freedom of liberalism, but a substantial and enduring thing, whose content becomes clear only with its limits. It is the principles determining those limits that I have attempted to lay down.

Silence and practice

It may be wondered how this statement of position can be reconciled with the sceptical temper from which it was born. How can one willingly close one's mind, in so many ways at once? The direct answer is of course that one cannot. Nevertheless, there may be no persuasive alternative, it seems to me, to the attitude that I have sketched. At least, the usual alternatives are so radically under-described as to carry no conviction, and no authority that will outweigh that which is already incipient in the civil order. It is not by some act of faith that one closes one's eyes before the spectre of endless political experiment. The only necessity here is to live, and to respect the reality that makes life possible.

However, there is a problem. No one can retreat from the pursuit of truth once he has acquired the habit of self-conscious analysis. Yet the pursuit of truth leads one to doubt the myths that reinforce society. Some have set up as their ideal a society in which myths are no longer necessary. Like Marx, they have sought for a freedom from 'ideology', for a world in which there is no obfuscation of choice by the concepts peculiar to an established order. Marx's inability to provide the concrete description of this enlightened state may cause no surprise. For what remains of freedom when there is no self-conception, and how can there be self-conception in a world that is seen only in abstract terms? Without ideology the world is no more than the totality of facts, to be seen (if at all) only with the clinical vision of a dispassionate scientist. But fortunately we lack that vision, and lack the knowledge that would enable us to live it through.

Nature abhors a vacuum. Into the value-free world a host of airy ideologies has flown, and none less substantial than the secular myths that I examined in the last chapter. And in politics too these myths have appeared, bringing with them the idiotic language of 'progress'. Politicians can now speak as though the affairs of state move 'forward', or 'backwards'. The conservative is said to 'arrest progress', the liberal to 'advance' it. A conservative is 'reactionary'. 'Revolution' means not the turning of the wheel, but the 'overthrow' of 'regressive' forces. In all this compulsive newspeak, which has decorated the 'millennium' speeches of Tony Blair, we find the same frivolous myth. Things 'go forward', since that is their nature. The only truth here is that time moves forward, namely from past to future. But no politics can represent itself as announcing so trivial a truth. The movement of time is therefore mixed by free association with the movement of knowledge. Things progress, in the way that knowledge grows. Hence they get better each day, unless some conservative meddles with the process.

Such is the nonsense that abounds in the speeches of Tony Blair. But it is not only politicians who utter it. Even respectable historians can describe conservatives as 'staving off', for a period of years, an inevitable 'forward' movement, while others 'advance' the liberal or socialist cause.[86] Franco was not successful in Spain: he merely held up the liberal enlightenment. Metternich did not create or sustain an enduring order: he simply 'crushed', for a time, the spirit of history. And so on. A socialist state that lasts ten years is a prelude to eternity; a conservative state that lasts thirty years is only a gesture of survival. But once we see how foolish are the myths of 'progress', then we shall cease to see things in such a way. And then we might turn our attention to institutions of the present, and in particular to those institutions which sustain the ideology whereby people live and find their happiness.

But conservatives who have risen above the fragments of their inheritance and reflected on the desolation that has been wrought in it, cannot return to an innocence which their own thinking has destroyed. They are not in the position of Sartre's existential anti-hero, forced to take responsibility for a choice which they lack the concepts to describe. They know what they want, and know the social order that would correspond to it. But in becoming self-conscious they have set themselves apart from things. The reasons that they observe for sustaining the myths of society are reasons which they cannot propagate; to propagate their reasons is to instil the world with doubt. Having struggled for articulacy, they must recommend silence.

This problem is insoluble. It stands in the way of every political creed. The 'natural right' and 'freedom' of the liberal; the 'classless society' and 'emancipation' of the radical; the 'social justice' and 'equality' of the socialist – all these are myths. They have immediate appeal. But when we examine what they really mean, we see that they too can be defended to the elite which recognizes them, but only in terms which must be concealed from the ordinary voter. In discussing their basis we emerge from the sea of politics on to a strange desert shore of pure opinion, a place of doubt, bluff and subterfuge. The wisest course is to turn back and re-immerse oneself.

Philosophical Appendix:
Liberalism versus Conservatism

'Liberalism' is a term with many overlapping senses. In one use it denotes an attitude towards (and also a theory of) the state and its functions; in another use it denotes a moral outlook, which sometimes rises to the level of theory, but which for the most part remains hidden in the crannies of everyday existence. Its guiding principle is tolerance – although, as its critics do not fail to say, its tolerance towards non-liberals is quickly exhausted. In all its forms, liberalism incorporates an attitude of respect towards the individual existence – an attempt to leave as much moral and political space around every person as is compatible with the demands of social life. As such it has often been thought to imply a kind of egalitarianism. For by its very nature, the respect which liberalism shows to the individual, it shows to each individual equally. Partiality is itself a form of intolerance; by enlarging the space around one person, it diminishes the space enjoyed by his neighbour. In the perfect liberal suburb, the gardens are of equal size, even though decked out with the greatest possible variety of plastic gnomes.

Clearly, such an outlook – which could fairly be described as the official ideology of the Western world – is not without far-reaching assumptions concerning human nature and human fulfilment. In particular, the freedom of the individual is proposed as unquestionably valuable, and as the sole or principal criterion against which the legitimacy of social custom and political institutions is to be tested. As is well-known, the criterion proves complex, and perhaps even contradictory, in its application. The very instinct which leads us to respect the freedom of an individual, leads us also to curtail it, for the sake of the freedom of his neighbour. Moreover, the demand for 'equal treatment' often seems to be so pressing a requirement of the liberal outlook, as to justify the most massive interference in the spontaneous projects of normal capitalist man – the 'possessive individualist' whose ideology this supposedly is. It should not go unremarked that the same emphasis on the free, self-fulfilling individual underlies both Milton Friedman's vision of a spontaneous order of private property, and Karl Marx's spectre of 'full communism', in which the freedom of all is guaranteed by the simultaneous disappearance of private property, and of the institutions of the 'bourgeois' (which is to say, liberal) state. I shall argue that this tension in liberalism – which can be readily observed between the two principles of justice proposed by Rawls – is inevitable, and derives from an imperfect philosophical anthropology; the defects of this anthropology cannot be remedied without abandoning some of the fundamental tenets of the liberal outlook.[87]

What, then, is meant, by the 'freedom of the individual'? I shall distinguish two kinds of liberal answer to this question, which I shall call, respectively, 'desire-based', and 'autonomy-based' liberalism. The first argues that people are free to the extent that they can satisfy their desires. The modality of this 'can' is, of course, a major problem. More importantly, however, such an answer implies nothing about the value of freedom, and to take it as the basis for political theory is to risk the most absurd conclusions. By this criterion the citizens of Huxley's *Brave New World* offer a paradigm of freedom: for they live in a world designed expressly for the gratification of their every wish. A desire-based liberalism could justify the most abject slavery – provided only that the slaves are induced, by whatever method, to desire their own condition. The defect of desire-based liberalism lies in its caricature of human nature – a caricature that may have appealed to Hobbes, but which ought to be accepted by a post-Kantian philosopher only with the greatest reluctance. Clearly, if freedom is to be a self-evident value, something more needs to be said about the kind of agency which requires it. This 'something more' is what I shall summarize with the word 'autonomy'. Autonomy-based liberalism argues that we are not the simple creatures of Hobbes, propelled by desires as by electrical impulses, but the more complex creatures of Kant, whose motives are shaped and reshaped by the ubiquitous operation of practical reason. We have choices and intentions, as well as desires. We act from a sense of value – and in pursuing what we value, we find a reason which both compels and justifies our conduct. Such conduct seems to issue, not from the arbitrary compulsion of a transient desire, but from the self, as the ultimate origin and final beneficiary of rational conduct.

In saying that the liberal wishes each individual, in Dworkin's words, to 'work out and live according to his own conception of the good' (the idea which is in fact common to the liberalism of Rawls and Dworkin), we are saying that it is not desire, but autonomy – the peculiar structure of motivation which characterizes the Kantian rationaĺ agent – that the liberal wishes to fulfil.

Autonomy-based liberalism argues, then, that we are rational agents, or selves, and that this feature defines our predicament. Fulfilment of the individual is fulfilment in and through autonomous conduct. In order to respect the individual we must, therefore, leave room for the exercise of his autonomy. Not to do so is quite simply to deny his existence – for it is to impede the flourishing of the rational centre in which his self, or essence, resides.

It is clear at once that autonomy-based liberalism has no difficulty in explaining the value of freedom, or in finding the reason for elevating individual freedom into the ultimate test of political order. Not to respect freedom indeed, is to threaten the very existence of those individuals for the sake of whom political order exists, and in the eyes of whom it must be made to appear in the fair colours of legitimacy.

We can also see how the concept of a right becomes central to the theory of liberalism. Rights define the sphere of privacy within which the individual resides – the sphere which must be safeguarded if his autonomy is to be preserved. His freedom may be curtailed in every particular, except this: for to curtail his rights is to diminish his existence. This is what is meant by the idea (to use Dworkin's words) that 'rights are trumps': by invoking his rights an individual invokes his autonomy, and places in the balance of deliberation, the absolute value of his own existence.

A vast gloss is required if the theory of autonomy-based liberalism is to be made cogent. For present purposes, I must assume that its broad outlines are intelligible, and that its basic vision of the human agent – as a creature motivated by rational choice – is understood.

I wish now to make, in my own terms, a familiar contrast: that between the first-person and the third-person view of human actions – between the view that I have upon my voluntary activities, and the view which another might also have upon them. Connected with each point of view is a mode of justification: some justifications of my action may be reasons for doing it; some may be simply reasons why it should be done. To take an example: a tribesman may be dancing so as to worship the god of war. To the observing anthropologist (one persuaded by the tenets of functionalism), the dance has quite a different meaning: it exists so as to raise the spirits, and increase the cohesion of the tribe, at a time of danger.

In this example the third-person justification could not be part of the first-person reasoning of the dancer. To think of his dance in that way is at once to be alienated from it, to lose the immediate and imperative quality of the motive. Hence it is to lose the spirit of the dance. The first-person reason ('Because the god demands it') is here opaque to the third-person perspective: by shutting the dancer within his dance, it abolishes the distance between agent and action. In general, it could be said, many of our actions have quite separate justifications from the first- and the third-person points of view, and what may seem rational from one of those perspectives may seem quite incomprehensible from the other.

The much-canvassed opposition between liberalism and utilitarianism has, I believe, its origin in this contrast. The liberal view of human freedom is simply a generalization of the first-person viewpoint: its idea of justification is circumscribed by the idea of a first-person reason. The justification of any constraint must consist in reasons that can be offered to the agent: reasons for *me* to obey it. And the value of freedom lies precisely in the fact that it is presupposed in every first-personal point of view.

Utilitarianism, by contrast, sees the world as it is, and not just as it seems to the agent (although of course, how it seems to the agent is a very important part of how it is). The utilitarian rises above the individual's predicament and sees the meaning of his actions in their long-term success or disaster. Actions that are justified from this perspective may naturally seem irrational or impermissible to the agent. For the utilitarian justification may identify no motive to action – it may even identify a motive to refrain. And a consideration that provides no motive provides no reason for me. It is because the first-person perspective is at least partly impermeable to third-person reasons, that utilitarianism fails as an account of practical reason. And its clash with liberal values derives from the fact that, for the liberal, the first-person perspective is sovereign, and also sufficiently equipped in itself to generate the measure of political order, and the criterion of a just society.

It seems to me that the liberal is profoundly wrong in believing that the first-person perspective can generate such a measure, and such a criterion. He is right however, in believing that the perspective of the autonomous agent is inescapable, and that it is one of the first tasks of political existence to ensure that it may flourish as best it can.

The point may perhaps most clearly emerge, through the contrast between liberalism and another political outlook which, like utilitarianism, is, or ought to be, wedded to the third-person perspective: the outlook of conservatism, as outlined in the preceding pages. Conservatives resemble functionalist anthropologists, in their concern for the long-term effects of social customs and political institutions. They see wisdom in those immediate and consoling prejudices whereby people conduct their lives, and are reluctant to countenance the reform of institutions that seem to promote the happiness of those who submit to them as well as any that might be offered in their place.

Liberalism, however, is essentially revisionary of existing institutions, seeking always to align them with the universal requirements of the first-person perspective – this, I believe, is the true meaning of Rawls' 'hypothetical' contract, designed to identify a point of view outside present arrangements, from which they may be surveyed and, where necessary, amended or condemned. This revisionism pertains not only to liberal political theory, but also to the individualistic emphasis that guides the daily conduct of the liberal-minded person. In all its variants, and at every level, liberalism embodies the question: 'Why should *I* do *that*?' The question is asked of political institutions, of legal codes, of social customs – even of morality. And to the extent that no answer is forthcoming which proves satisfactory to the first-person perspective, to that extent are we licensed to initiate change.

There are, broadly, two kinds of answer which the liberal will tolerate: an answer in terms of a first-person reason for action, and an answer in terms of a human right. In respecting rights, you respect the first-person reasons of others, by conceding to them the autonomy within which those reasons prevail. The inevitable tendency of liberal theory towards an idea of natural rights can be seen to reside in this – that I can give you no reason to restrain your conduct, unless I can show that there is an objectively binding reason for you to respect the rights of others. If there can be no such reason, then no rights are 'natural' – none has greater sway in the deliberation of the autonomous agent than is provided by his own contingent willingness to accept them.

It is on this assumption that the liberal is able to assault the conservative's position. His argument is – and in the first instance must be – 'onus-shifting'. 'Why should I do that?' he asks; and the conservative must show either (a) that the liberal has a first-person reason to do what is in question – in other words, that he can be brought rationally to consent to it, or (b) that he is bound to do it by his obligation to respect the objective rights of others. Without recourse to (b), the onus-shifting argument, which has proved so powerful a weapon in liberalism's war of extermination against natural intolerant humanity, reduces merely to a form of radical scepticism, to a self-centred rejection of servility, and the renunciation of all truly political existence. With the help of (b), however, the liberal is able to erect, from that very first-person perspective which is the premise of his outlook, the picture of an alternative political condition, of laws and institutions that are something more than the arbitrary legacy of custom and prejudice, and of the contingent circumstance of human history. But since I do not believe that the liberal is entitled to (b), I do not believe that he can succeed in shifting the onus of proof in quite the simple way that he supposes.

It is difficult to show this. But I shall consider a representative liberal theory, and hope that my argument will suggest its own generalization. This theory derives originally from Kant, and puts forward a succinct but seemingly inescapable description of the first-person perspective, which is held to be definitive of our condition. I shall argue that the theory embodies a contradiction, that this contradiction is integral to the liberal idea of autonomy, and that it is also responsible for the tensions which emerge in the application of liberal theory. I shall defend a modified conservatism, as the alternative, and more reasonable outlook on the human condition – on the condition from which the first-person perspective grows.

According to the Kantian theory there can be first-person reasons for action only if there are reasons which motivate action. It is because it motivates me that a reason is *my* reason. In choosing to act, I suppose myself to be inspired by reason, and also constrained by it, so that reason alone may set limits to my choice. But the heart of this supposition is the thought of my self, as an initiating cause of action: I act, not simply because acted upon by this or that desire, but because I have chosen. In this very thought, according to the Kantian, lies the constraint of obligation: not just, what shall I do, but what ought I to do, or what would be the good course of action? If a Kantian believes that an autonomous being should be allowed to work out his 'own conception' of the good, it is because this is what his autonomy requires.

The exercise is held to generate real objective constraints. The autonomous being, the Kantian argues, is constrained by the thought of his own autonomy – of himself as motivated by reasons – to accept the guiding principle of practical reason, which is the categorical imperative that circumscribes his ends. This categorical imperative has three compelling variants, forced upon us by our self-conception as rational agents, and each variant seems to capture some separate strand in the outlook that has since become known as 'liberal universalism': we must act only on those considerations which we would also impose upon our fellows; we must treat rational beings not as means only but as ends; we must conduct ourselves so as to realize in our actions that 'Kingdom of Ends' in which free and equal rational beings are alike subjects and sovereigns under the law of reason.

These three ideas can be paraphrased thus: we cannot make exceptions in our own favour; we must acknowledge the universal right to autonomy; and we must endeavour to realize the ideal of equal freedom. In other words, for the Kantian, the desired liberal conclusion emerges from the premise of autonomy: the first-person viewpoint constrains the agent to recognize objective rights, and to recognize also the equal entitlement of all agents who are, like himself, blessed with a first-person perspective. Kant's résumé of this idea – the theoretical cornerstone of liberalism – is, I believe, more persuasive than anything that has since been said in support of it. Hence serious difficulties may be projected for the liberal position, should Kant's exposition be involved in a self-contradiction.

Already we can see emerging some of the practical contradictions of liberalism: the 'as if' of the Kingdom of Ends, which points towards a world of real equality, encounters obstinate resistance from the individual right – from the injunction that others are to be treated as ends. This, I believe, has been shown by Nozick, who incautiously believes that he can sever the second categorical imperative from the countervailing claims of the other two. In fact, it seems to me, a proper study of the three formulations will show us not only that socialism and liberalism issue equally from a single idea – that of the first-person perspective – but also that the conflict between them can never be resolved. The history of 'actually existing socialism' shows this, I believe, as well as it is shown by the history of 'actually existing liberalism'.

The major problem, as I see it, is this: Kant wishes to derive, from the premise that we are, or at least think ourselves to be, motivated by reason, the conclusion that we are also constrained by an objective principle of equal rights. In order to do this, he proceeds by a method of abstraction. He supposes that I advance to the standpoint of reason, by discounting my 'empirical conditions' – by removing from my thought every consideration which ties me to the 'here and now'. Only in this way, he supposes, can I reach that standpoint 'outside nature' in which I respond to the call of reason alone. It is from this standpoint that the universal, equalizing law of reason is apparent. However, as Kant acknowledges, in so abstracting from my 'contingent', or 'historical' condition, I abstract also from the circumstances of my act – and in particular from the desires and interests which initially raised, for me, the question of action. I posit my own existence as a 'transcendental self', and indeed, in so far as there is 'motivation by reason alone', only such a transcendental self could display it.

But now the paradox is obvious. Clearly, a transcendental self, outside nature and outside the 'empirical conditions' of the human agent, has no capacity to act here and now. It responds to reason, but only because the world of action, having been abstracted away, no longer resists the demands of reason. The transcendental self is not an agent of change in the actual world, in which case how can the reasons which affect it, also motivate it to do this, here, now? If I think of myself as a transcendental self, therefore, I think of myself as without a coherent motive. On the other hand, if I retain the thought of myself as an 'empirical self' – one subject to the demands of circumstance and the promptings of desire – then I can no longer reach an appreciation of my predicament by the process of abstracting away from it. This process – which may indeed take me to the point where I recognize the rights of others – deprives me of the very motive which would make it necessary.

In so far as I remain within my predicament, then, I must accept the historical givenness of my aims and projects, and refrain from removing myself to the point where their significance dwindles into nothing.

In short, the Kantian abstraction invites me to think of myself as the subject of an irresoluble dilemma: either I am a transcendental self, obedient to reason, in which case I cannot act; or else I am able to act, in which case my motives are part of my circumstance and history, and remain unresponsive to the voice of reason, which calls always from beyond the horizon of the empirical world. The supposition that I am a concrete, historical agent of change, and at the same time bound to recognize the rights of others, becomes contradictory.

It will be said that, even if such considerations show that a contradiction arises from the Kantian attempt to justify rights from the first-person perspective, they show no more than that. They do not provide any general reason for thinking that autonomy-based liberalism must fail to justify natural rights.

However, it seems to me that the considerations that I have presented are generally applicable. For – while I have, for clarity's sake, presented them in the form of a familiar objection to Kant's ethical theory – they do not depend upon the detail of that theory for their force. They derive, rather, from a conflict contained in the very idea of a valid first-person reason for action. To be objectively valid, such a reason must be divorced from the conditions which distinguish *me*. It must derive its rational force from considerations which abstract from my present predicament. At the same time, it can have no motivational force – and hence can form no part of my first-person reasoning – unless it derives directly from the circumstances which prompt me to act. It must refer to a motive for *me, here, now*. It is the contradiction between those two requirements that I have described, and it is a contradiction that may equally be discerned in the 'Kantian constructivism' of Rawls. In Rawls' case it takes the following form: granted that, when choosing from behind the veil of ignorance, I choose the abstract principles of justice, what then binds me to that choice when the veil is removed? Either I am bound, in which case I cannot emerge into the real world of agency; or else I enter that world, in which case these merely 'hypothetical considerations' cannot bind my action. Once again, the first-person perspective, which casts this shadow of natural justice in the world, remains indifferent to its shadowy demands.

Although Hume never expressed himself in the term that I have chosen, we can see his insistence that 'reason is, and ought only to be, the slave of the passions', and his attack on the idea of practical reason generally, as a rejection of the first-person perspective, on the ground that it is fraught with illusion. For Hume, the correct outlook upon the human world must adopt the third-person point of view, in which people are seen to be immersed in the contingencies of social life, acting from passions which respond to the changing circumstances of existence.

The first-person perspective, which flatters me with a picture of my rationality, misrepresents my condition. The only justification that can be found for the virtuous stance that it recommends to me – the stance of justice, in which I extend toward others an active recognition of their rights – is to be found in the long-term benefit conferred upon humanity, by our desire to deal equally with each other. But this justification is not a first-person reason for action.

Even if we accept my conclusion, however (and I realize that much more needs to be said before we are compelled to do so) this will not require the total rejection of liberalism. Indeed we cannot reject liberalism entirely without also abandoning the first-person perspective – something that it is neither possible nor desirable to do. I believe that Kant is right in thinking that the argument which takes him to the categorical imperative, and to the postulation of a 'transcendental self', is not just a piece of philosophy. It is, rather, the continuation of a thought experiment that haunts the actions of the rational being. Each of us is compelled to think in this way whenever he asks himself not, what *shall* I do?, but, what *ought* I to do? And he cannot cease to ask that question without losing all conception of the good. To safeguard his autonomy, therefore, we must safeguard the perspective from which the question of duty can be asked. The Kantian thought-experiment is, in one form or another, integral to our condition as autonomous beings – as beings who have values and intentions in addition to desires.

The argument suggests, however, that this necessary perspective is also a systematic illusion. It is necessary to sustain the illusion in everyday life. But in an important sense, it cannot sustain itself. Kant sought to validate the first-person perspective internally, so as to derive from it an abstract system of natural law. In doing so (as he repeatedly acknowledges) he came up against an insuperable barrier. It seems that the first-person perspective cannot validate itself. The best it can do, is to remain innocently unaware of this, to continue peaceably as if it were a member of a Kingdom of Ends, and to conceal from itself the mighty, Humean, fact – that its only reason for respecting the rights of others is that this is what it wants. The first person must hide his own benevolence from himself, in order to think of himself as bound. For it is the thought that I am bound by duty, Kant rightly argues, which awakens the idea that I am free.

The liberal, therefore, who rightly respects the first-person perspective as definitive of our condition, must ask himself the question: how can this perspective be sustained? If his onus-shifting argument is too often repeated, it will inevitably defeat itself. At some point, the person who asks 'why should I do that?' of every custom and every law, must force upon himself the more devastating question, 'why should I do anything?' For as long as he can sustain the first-person view of action, he may comfort himself with a kind of answer: the answer in terms of Kantian natural law, which enjoins him to respect the rights of others. But, in these ultimate reaches to which the liberal pushes us, the illusion of such a law is on the point of vanishing. It needs only one further question, one more 'why?', for the edifice to collapse in ruins, and for the liberal to confront the spectre of an intransigent scepticism.

Nor can the problem be solved by moving to the third-person perspective: for to make this move is to leave motivation behind. While there may be very good reasons why I should be motivated by a concern for others' rights – reasons which even relate to my own happiness – they will not generate that motive. For they will not be reasons for *me*.

Nevertheless, the third-person point of view is able to give us some purchase on this problem. There is something inescapable in the Kantian theory of autonomy. It is impossible that I should *be* a transcendental self; but it is necessary that I should suffer the illusion that I am. If I am to be fulfilled at all, I must belong to a world in which this illusion can be sustained, so that my projects are also values for me, and my desires are integrated into a vision of the good. There is, therefore, a third-person justification for the first-person perspective – a justification which, because it recognizes the illusoriness of that perspective, cannot cross the barrier into the first-person point of view. Hence the conservative anthropologist will smile indulgently on the liberal; his only concern will be, lest the liberal's disposition to question every given fact of community, might not leave him entirely disinherited. And it is a real concern. If there is no point at which the liberal can rest with what is given, and find value immanent in the world, without recourse to transcendental illusions, then the liberal will never rest – not, at least, until he has torn down every law and every institution with his exterminating 'why?' He who shifts the onus, will have to shift everything; he will confront, then, a world bereft of social artifacts, principal among which is morality itself.

I can do no more than hint at the vision which this third-person perspective proposes. But that it should be a conservative vision, in the sense outlined in these pages, is, I believe, inescapable. For consider what it is that leads people to see the world in terms of value, and so to develop the transcendental perspective which the liberal requires. People are born into a web of attachments; they are nurtured and protected by forces the operation of which they could neither consent to nor intend. Their very existence is burdened with a debt of love and gratitude, and it is in responding to that burden that they begin to recognize the power of 'ought'. This is not the abstract, universal 'ought' of liberal theory – or at least, not yet – but the concrete, immediate 'ought' of family attachments. It is the 'ought' of piety, which recognizes the unquestionable rightness of local, transitory and historically conditioned social bonds. Such an 'ought' is essentially discriminatory; it recognizes neither equality nor freedom, but only the absolute claim of the locally given.

Until they have felt that claim, rational beings have no motive to find value in the human world. Gradually, however, as they recognize the incommensurability between the demands of love and the imperfect object of love, the shadow world of transcendental illusion begins to grow. Liberalism is the salve with which they attempt to heal a primal disappointment. It is the expiation of an original sin: the sin of dependence.

It seems to me, therefore, that if there are arguments for liberalism, there are stronger arguments for conservatism. For we must conserve the institutions, customs, and local attachments through which the first-person perspective of the liberal is nurtured. At the same time, these attachments, being founded not in abstract justice, but in Wordsworth's 'natural piety', are corroded by the very liberal conscience which they generate. They can no more resist the 'why?' of reason, than parents can resist the withering reproaches of a child.

The Hegelian defence of the family at which I have just hinted requires much more elaboration than I have provided. But, by way of illustrating the paradox of liberalism – that it is doomed to corrode the conditions which nurture it – I should like to give a political illustration: the institution of monarchy.

There is no doubt in my mind that, from the third-person point of view, monarchy is the most reasonable form of government. By embodying the state in a fragile human person, it captures the arbitrariness and the givenness of political allegiance, and so transforms allegiance into affection. The attachment to a monarch is a natural response, and the simplest possible way of discharging the debt of obligation into which every political being is born. And what more reasonable way to govern people, than by their affections?

At the same time, from the first-person perspective, the loyalty to the monarch is mysterious. It is an immediate, unthinking prejudice, which has no reason beside itself. To look for reasons – in the character of the sovereign, for example – is to open the way to irony and doubt. Once the liberal asks his question, therefore, the institution begins to suffer from the shock. At the same time, that he asks this question is inevitable.

When the medieval jurists such as Fortescue advocated the *constitutio libertatis*, it was in order to bind the monarch by his own laws – in other words, in order to subject the absolute attachment to the will of the sovereign, to the equalizing discipline of an abstract right. By a series of compromises, both the attachment and the discipline have survived. And there is no doubt that the result has been beneficial. But whether either could survive, when liberalism finally triumphs, is a matter of doubt. The best we can hope for, I believe, is that liberals will begin to take their own ideology seriously, and so compromise with conservatism. They may call this compromise 'reflective equilibrium', as Rawls does, and thereby imagine that it is reasonable, in just the way that the first-person singular is always reasonable. But of course, it will not be reasonable, and the best that can be hoped is, that by this and similar devices, the liberal rationalist may finally rest content with a prejudice that is not his own.

Notes

1. The awareness that conservatism has no universal purpose, definable for all peoples and for all times, has led to a tradition among English conservatives, according to which their beliefs are essentially unsystematic, distrustful of theory, practical, empirical and day-to-day. (See, for example, Lord Hugh Cecil, *Conservatism*, London 1912, Lord Hailsham, *The Case for Conservatism*, London 1947, and, most recently, William Waldegrave *The Binding of Leviathan*, London 1978.) Such a tradition provides admirable support for conservative policy; but it cannot solve the intellectual problem – which is, why be a conservative in the first place?

2. The call for the political organization of conservative sentiment was vigorously made by Burke, who, although himself a Whig, spoke and wrote before the modern party allegiances had been formed. He is therefore usually considered to be a 'Founding Father' of the Conservative Party. Precisely when that party came into being is a disputed question among historians. In assuming that it was not properly formed before 1832 I rely on Norman Gash, *Politics in the Age of Peel*, London 1952, and Lord Blake, *The Conservative Party from Peel to Churchill*. If I use the word 'Tory' in what follows it is to refer to the Conservative Party, unless the context indicates a reference to the loose association that preceded it. Likewise Conservative with a capital C refers to the party; with a small c to the system of beliefs which that party may or may not embody.

3. See, for example, Sir Karl Popper, *The Open Society and Its Enemies*, Princeton 1950.

4. John Locke, *Two Treaties of Government*, ed. P. Laslett, Cambridge 1960, and Robert Nozick, *Anarchy, State and Utopia*, New York 1971.

5. See Kenneth Minogue, 'On Hyperactivism in Modern British Politics', in Maurice Cowling (ed.), *Conservative Essays*, London 1978.

6. The distinction here corresponds in part to the distinction (much emphasized in nineteenth-century German sociology) between Gesellschaft, and Gemeinschaft (cf. F. Tönnies, *Gemeinschaft und Gesellschaft*, trans. *Community and Society*, New York 1963). The argument of this section can be found more elaborately spelled out in Michael Oakeshott's 'Rationalism in Politics', *Cambridge Journal*, vol. 1, 1947/8, pp. 81–98, 145–57, and *On Human Conduct*, London 1975.

7. Edmund Burke, *Reflections on the Revolution in France*, London, 1960.

8. Hobbes, *Leviathan*, London 1651, ii, p. 21. The thought lies behind Rousseau's *The Social Contract* (trans. G. D. H. Cole, London 1913), and was criticized by Hume in 'Of the Original Contract' (in *Essays, Moral, Political and Literary*, London 1791).

9. This recognition has, of course, been slow and painful, evident not only in the controversies over the 'New Deal', but also in almost every subsequent gesture of policy, whether foreign or domestic.

10. I am indebted to John Casey for impressing upon me that such concepts are indispensable to conservative political thinking.

11. The great champion of this view in recent years has been Robert Nozick (op. cit.).

12. See the reflections in Jacob Burckhardt's *The Civilisation of the Renaissance in Italy*, Leipzig 1877–8, and in Emile Durkheim's *On Suicide*, 2nd edn, Paris 1912.

13. See F. H. Bradley, 'My Station and Its Duties', in *Ethical Studies*, London 1876.

14. Burke, *Reflections* ..., op. cit.

15. The philosophy behind this is nowhere more succinctly or cogently expressed than in G. W. F. Hegel, *The Philosophy of Right*, trans. T. M. Knox, Oxford 1967.

16. See Eric Hobsbawm and Terence Ranger, eds, *The Invention of Tradition*, London 1985.

17. Ludwig von Mises, *Socialism: An Economic and Sociological Analysis*, New York 1951.

18. Michael Oakeshott, *Rationalism in Politics and Other Essays*, London 1963.

19. F. A. Hayek, *Law, Legislation and Liberty*, vol. 1, London 1982.

20. T. S. Eliot, 'Tradition and the Individual Talent', in *Collected Essays*, London 1963.

21. John Casey, 'Tradition and Authority', in *Conservative Essays*, ed. Cowling, op. cit.

22. Burckhardt, op. cit., introduction. The view should really be accredited to de Maistre, *Essai sur le principe générateur des constitutions politiques*, in *Oeuvres complètes*, Lyons 1884, vol. 1. De Maistre, having recognized the bond of constitution as 'transcendent', concluded that it must therefore be the work of God. This passage, from attachment to transcendent bonds to the belief in transcendent beings, is of great political significance. I return to it in Chapter 8.

23. It is interesting to note that the major textbook on the American constitution (by Edward Corwin) is called *The Constitution and What it Means Today*. It has been rewritten thirteen times since 1920. In other words, the study of the American constitution advances, not with the speed of science, but with that of law.

24. H. Marcuse, in *Reason and Revolution*, London and New York 1941.

25. The philosophy has been expounded, in terms that stand in need of revision, in Hegel's *Philosophy of Right* and *Philosophy of History*. Vestiges of it survive in Bosanquet and Oakeshott. The idea is as old as Plato's *Republic*.

26. This logic is difficult to describe. An interesting discussion (conducted largely from the standpoint of the liberal view of constitution) may be found in R. Dworkin, *Taking Rights Seriously*, London 1977.

27. See Ruth Benedict, *Patterns of Culture*, New York 1934.

28. Alexis de Tocqueville, *De la démocratie en Amérique*, bk ii, pt ii.

29. Walter Bagehot, *The English Constitution* (ed. R. H. S. Crossman, London 1963), ch. iii. Bagehot's defence of the House of Lords is a fine polemic, far above the level of recent discussions.

30. *De l'esprit des lois* (1748). The doctrine of the 'separation of powers' is given express enactment in the American Constitution – a fact that has in no way served to make it more intelligible.

31. The liberal view in these matters is given succinctly by Sidgwick, *Elements of Politics*, London 1891, p. 295, where he defends the 'cosmopolitan ideal', according to which the 'business (of government) is to maintain order over the particular territory that historical causes have appropriated to it, but not in any way to determine who is to inhabit the territory, or to restrict the enjoyment of its natural advantages to any particular portion of the human race'. As though 'historical causes' could mark out a territory without at the same time marking out the people that inhabit it! It is hard to imagine what conception of sovereignty, or of legitimacy, can be derived from an axiom so remote from the political feelings of ordinary people.

32. De Maistre, op. cit. See also the comments in Hume's *History of England*, ch. 47, relating to the constitutional crisis caused by James I's quarrel with the common law.

33. See *The Critique of Practical Reason*.

34. Pericles' funeral oration, in Thucydides, *History of the Peloponnesian War*, bk ii, 33–46.

35. J. S. Mill, *On Liberty*, London 1859, and Sir James Fitzjames Stephen's reply, *Liberty, Equality, Fraternity*, London 1873. For the modern discussion, see H. L. A. Hart's succinct restatement of the liberal position in *Law, Liberty and Morals*, London 1963.

36. See the excellent discussion in George Parkin Grant, *English-Speaking Justice*, Sackville, New Brunswick 1974, pt iv.

37. See in particular the cases of *Eves v. Eves* ([1975] 3 ALL ER 768), and *Davis v. Johnson* ([1978] 1 ALL ER 1132).

38. See Oakeshott, *On Human Conduct*, op. cit.

39. Sir Isaiah Berlin, *Four Essays on Liberty*, Oxford 1969, ch. 1.

40. *A Contribution to the Critique of Political Economy* (1859), London 1961, preface. See also *The German Ideology* (1846), in which the view is stated more emphatically.

41. Someone might doubt this, remembering Marx's indebtedness to the theories of Adam Smith and Ricardo, in which 'labour' appears as a concept exclusive to economic theory. But there is another and greater debt: 'Labour is the universal interaction and *Bildung* (self-image) of man' (Hegel, *Schriften zur Politik*, 424).

42. See, for example, P. A. Baran and P. M. Sweezy, *Monopoly Capital*, New York and London 1966, and J. K. Galbraith, *Economics and the Public Purpose*, London, 2nd edn, 1972.

43. In this paragraph I refer back to the considerations of Chapters 1 and 2; the reader of sociology will notice a connection with Dilthey and Weber's concept of '*Verstehen*'.

44. *The Phenomenology of Spirit*, and *The Philosophy of Right*. Some aspects of the view are foreshadowed in Locke, and in Thomist accounts of natural law.

45. Lord Keynes, *The General Theory of Employment, Interest and Money*, London 1936, p. 104.

46. See especially the work of Michel Foucault (in particular *Les Mots et les choses*, Paris,1966, and *L'Archéologie du savoir*, Paris 1970), in which the rewriting of history in mythographic form is taken to splendid and outrageous rhetorical conclusions.

47. The liberal view is succinctly summarized by John Stuart Mill, *The Principles of Political Economy*, London 1848, 3rd edn, 1852, II, 2, i: 'The institution of property, when limited to its essential elements, consists in the recognition, in each person, of a right to the disposal of what he or she have produced by their own exertions, or received either by gift or by felt agreement, without force or fraud, from those who produced it.' (The grammar of this sentence is one rather unfortunate result of Mill's adoption of the feminist cause.)

48. The matter raised here cannot be readily summarized. See the doctrine of prescriptive right, defended honestly but inadequately by Mill (in op. cit. II, 2, ii); see also the discussion of 'competition and custom' in II, 4, ii, illuminating in its attempt to subsume history under liberal principle, and in its honest confession of failure.

49. The liberal in question was Sir Alfred Mond (later Lord Melchett).

50. Temporary income tax had been previously introduced by Pitt, again during Tory office (but before the formation of the modern Conservative Party).

51. Nozick, op. cit., p. 169.

52. See the excellent discussion in Adam Smith, *The Wealth of Nations*, bk v, ch. 2, as glossed by Mill, *Principles of Political Economy*, op. cit., bk v, ch. 2.

53. *Fabian Essays*, p. 33.

54. *General Theory*, op. cit.

55. The theory behind this assertion is in fact unproven and often disputed. While Baran, Sweezy, and Galbraith affirm that something like it must be so (deriving inspiration from the original cynical portrayal of the industrial process in the works of Veblen), there is some evidence that its truth is confined to business in America. Legislation governing monopoly is of such antiquity in Europe that business customs seem to have incorporated many of its tenets and aims. But see Thorstein Veblen, *The Theory of Business Enterprise*, Chicago 1904, ch. 3.

56. F. A. von Hayek, *Industrialism and the Economic Order*, Chicago 1948, ch. 3.

57. See M. M. Postan, *The Medieval Economy and Society*, London 1972, esp. ch. 9.

58. See Baran and Sweezy, op. cit.

59. This point follows either trivially from the labour theory of value, or more deviously from the view that all wage contracts are 'forced', and therefore consign one of the parties to a condition of slavery. The labour theory transforms Adam Smith's view that the true value of a commodity lies in the quantity of labour for which it may be exchanged (*The Wealth of Nations*, London 1776 bk 1, ch. 5), into the view that its value consists rather in the labour necessary to produce it (see *Capital*, vol. 1). It thus assigns values independently of demand, and while this may give the theory useful ideological force, it seems to deprive it of all predictive power. The view that wage contracts are forced depends upon the assertion that the proletarian, while not individually constrained to contract as he does, belongs to a class that is constrained as a whole. Even if that were true, unionization would suffice to remove the unilateral nature of the constraint.

60. Disraeli, preface to the 1870 edition of his novels.

61. E. P. Thompson, 'The Peculiarities of the English', in *The Poverty of Theory*, London 1978, p. 82.

62. *Ibid.*, p. 44.

63. Some modern philosophers have proposed methods of abstraction which they hope will enable us sensibly to ask such a question (or some strategic equivalent of this question). See for example the liberal theory of justice expounded by John Rawls, *A Theory of Justice*, Oxford 1972.
64. See, for example, Marx's *Economic and Philosophical Manuscripts of 1844* (available, trans. T. B. Bottomore, in Erich Fromm, *Marx's Concept of Man*, New York 1961).
65. See, for example, Marx's 'Critique of the Gotha Programme' (1875), in Marx and Engels, *Selected Works*, Moscow 1958.
66. See the discussion of the Master and Slave (Lord and Bondsman), in *The Phenomenology of Spirit*.
67. By the 'artificial' division of labour I do not mean that division that is implied (according to Adam Smith, *The Wealth of Nations*, bk I, chs I–III) in every institution of exchange, but rather the peculiar process of specialization that is engendered by all mechanized modes of production. See E. Durkheim, *De la division du travail social* (2nd edn, Paris 1902). The two kinds of division are independent: either could exist without the other.
68. In Fromm, op. cit., p. 123.
69. *Marx's Concept of Man*, op. cit.
70. *Capital*, London 1970, vol. 1, p. 76f.
71. See Matthew Arnold, *Culture and Anarchy*, London 1876, and also Thorstein Veblen, 'Civilization and the Machine Process', in *The Theory of Business Enterprise*, op. cit.
72. See again, John Casey, 'Tradition and Authority', op. cit.
73. See, for example, *Salmond on Jurisprudence*, 12th edn, by P. J. Fitzgerald, London 1966, p. 325ff.
74. The invention of this subject may be attributed to the University of Cornell, whose school of industrial relations has set the pattern for those elsewhere.
75. F. Schiller, *Letters on the Aesthetic Education of Man*, trans. and ed. M. Wilkinson and C. A. Willoughby, Oxford 1967.
76. I here pass over the vast and intractable problem of the 'just war', over which medieval philosophers and jurists debated at such length. The point is simply that there are acts which would be criminal when perpetrated by an individual, but just when performed by a state.
77. *The Conservative Case*, London 1959 (a revised version of *The Case for Conservatism*, London 1947), p. 19.
78. As was shown in the popular response to the Reverend E. R. Norman's Reith Lectures, of 1978–9. In the twenty years that have elapsed since the first publication of this book, it has become fairly obvious that, while the religious need of the English remains as great as ever, scepticism increasingly rules out the possibility of fulfilling it.
79. Trotsky, in Irving Howe (ed.), *Basic Writings*, London 1964, vol. 1, p. 378. Trotsky goes on to say, following a thought of Hume's, that 'the moral norm becomes the more categorical the less it is "obligatory" on all'. The history of religious and political persecution shows this to be false.
80. See Paul Johnson, *Britain's Own Road to Serfdom*, Conservative Political Centre pamphlet, London 1978.
81. The attraction of the determinist view of history is perennial. An author devoted to providing some modified version of the Marxist hypothesis may

notice the facts that cast doubt upon it and yet pass them over. Thus Perry Anderson, in *Lineages of the Absolute State*, pp. 270–98, is able to notice that the branch of the Polish nobility known as the *szlachta* had for many years an economic position scarcely distinguishable from that of the peasantry, without losing their sense of social distinction. And yet this fact receives no explanation from the theory in support of which it is cited. (Cf. also much of the history of the *samurai* in Japan.)

82. E. P. Thompson, *The Making of the English Working Class*, London 1963, rev. edn, 1968, p. 11.

83. There have, of course, been American conservatives more wedded to the European than to the American idea of legitimacy. See, e.g., the humanistic conservatism of Irving Babbit and Paul Elmer More (especially More's *Aristocracy and Justice*, New York 1915).

84. See Charles Murray, *Losing Ground, American Social Policy 1950–1980*, New York 1984.

85. See the arguments given by P. T. Bauer, in *Dissent on Development*, London 1971.

86. The tendency is natural for Marxists. But it is surprisingly frequent in 'fair-minded' historians too. See, for example, David Thomson, *Europe since Napoleon*, London 1957. Nowhere in Voltaire's *Siècle de Louis XIV*, or in Thucydides, is there the slightest hint of the view that history has a movement. The mark of great historians is that it is not history which lives for them, but rather the people and societies which constitute it.

87. The two principles of justice given by Rawls are to be found in his *A Theory of Justice*, op. cit. Briefly, they are that each individual has an equal right to the most extensive basic liberty, and that social and economic inequalities may exist only if reasonably expected to better the position of the least advantaged. The quotation from Dworkin is from *Taking Rights Seriously*, op. cit.

Index

201